Get the eBook FREE!

(PDF, ePub, Kindle, and liveBook all included)

We believe that once you buy a book from us, you should be able to read it in any format we have available. To get electronic versions of this book at no additional cost to you, purchase and then register this book at the Manning website.

Go to https://www.manning.com/freebook and follow the instructions to complete your pBook registration.

That's it!
Thanks from Manning!

Code Like a Pro
in Rust

BRENDEN MATTHEWS

MANNING

SHELTER ISLAND

For online information and ordering of this and other Manning books, please visit
www.manning.com. The publisher offers discounts on this book when ordered in quantity.
For more information, please contact

> Special Sales Department
> Manning Publications Co.
> 20 Baldwin Road
> PO Box 761
> Shelter Island, NY 11964
> Email: orders@manning.com

Manning Publications Co.
20 Baldwin Road
PO Box 761
Shelter Island, NY 11964

Development editor: Karen Miller
Review editor: Aleksandar Dragosavljević
Production editor: Deirdre Hiam
Copy editor: Christian Berk
Proofreader: Katie Tennant
Technical proofreader: Jonathan Reeves
Typesetter: Gordan Salinovic
Cover designer: Marija Tudor

ISBN 9781617299643
Printed in the United States of America

brief contents

contents

3 Rust tooling   43

preface

I love learning new programming languages.

I've been writing code for a long time, but I still find myself occasionally banging my head against a wall when learning new languages or tools. Rust is a unique language in many respects, and it introduces several concepts that some people may have never seen before, even if they have been programming for many years.

I have spent a great deal of time working with Rust both professionally and as a contributor to community projects, and I have written this book to share what I learned along the way. By taking the time to read this book, you will save yourself a lot of time by avoiding the common pitfalls and problems people encounter when they're new to Rust.

acknowledgments

I'd like to thank my friends Javeed Shaikh and Ben Lin for providing feedback on early drafts of the manuscript as well as Manning Publications for working patiently with me in completing this book.

Specifically, I would like to thank the development editor Karen Miller, the review editor Aleksandar Dragosavljević, the production editor Deirdre Hiam, the copyeditor Christian Berk, and the proofreader Katie Tennant.

I thank all the reviewers—Adam Wendell, Alessandro Campeis, Arun Bhagvan Kommadi, Christian Witts, Clifford Thurber, David Moshal, David Paccoud, Gianluigi Spagnuolo, Horaci Macias, Jaume Lopez, Jean-Paul Malherbe, João Pedro de Lacerda, Jon Riddle, Joseph Pachod, Julien Castelain, Kevin Orr, Madhav Ayyagari, Martin Nowack, Matt Sarmiento, Matthew Winter, Matthias Busch, PK Chetty, Rohit Goswami, Satadru Roy, Satej Kumar Sahu, Sebastian Palma, Seth MacPherson, Simon Tschöke, Sri Kadimisetty, Tim van Deurzen, William Wheeler, and Zach Peters—your suggestions help to make this a better book.

about this book

While writing this book, I've paid special attention to noting when features or interfaces are subject to change. While core language features may not change substantially, practical use of Rust may involve hundreds of separate libraries and projects. By reading this book, you'll be introduced to strategies and techniques that help you navigate this evolving ecosystem.

As you continue to read, I would like to mention that the Rust ecosystem is rapidly evolving. I have written this book with the future of Rust in mind, but I cannot guarantee that the language and libraries won't change substantially after the book has been published.

How is this book different?

This book focuses on the practical usage of Rust, while considering the big-picture themes, limitations of Rust and its tooling, and how developers can become productive with Rust quickly. The text is not an introduction to the Rust language, nor is it a replacement for the official Rust documentation. This book supplements the existing documentation and resources available for Rust and provides the most important lessons you won't find in Rust documentation in one place. While *Code Like a Pro in Rust* does not provide an exhaustive reference for the Rust language, I do indicate where to go for additional information when appropriate.

Who should read this book?

Readers of this book should be familiar with Rust and consider themselves beginner to intermediate Rust programmers. If you have never used Rust, you may find this book difficult to read, as it contains many references to Rust-specific features, for which I will not spend much time discussing the background. If you find yourself confused about Rust syntax or technical details, I recommended starting with *Rust in Action* by Tim McNamara (Manning, 2021) or the official Rust book at https://doc.rust-lang.org/book/.

For those who are intermediate to advanced Rust programmers, some content in this book might be familiar. In your case, I recommend you skip ahead to the chapters most interesting to you.

How this book is organized

The chapters of this book can be read in any order, according to what interests you most. While I would like for every reader to read every chapter from start to finish, I also understand that readers have varied goals and experience levels. Most of the later chapters build on top of content from earlier chapters, so while it isn't a requirement, you'll get the most benefit from reading the chapters in order. Throughout the book, I make references to other chapters or topics as needed, and you may want to make notes to go back and read other sections accordingly.

If you are relatively new to Rust or programming in general, then I recommend reading the whole book from cover to cover, to get the most out of it. For an excellent introduction to the Rust programming language, I recommend you first read the official Rust book (https://doc.rust-lang.org/book/).

Part 1 covers an introduction to Rust and its tooling:

- Chapter 1 provides an overview of Rust and what makes it special.
- Chapter 2 introduces Cargo, Rust's project management tool.
- Chapter 3 provides a tour of key Rust tooling.

Part 2 covers Rust's data structures and memory management:

- Chapter 4 discusses Rust data structures.
- Chapter 5 goes into detail on Rust's memory management model.

Part 3 discusses testing methods for correctness:

- Chapter 6 provides a tour of Rust's unit testing features.
- Chapter 7 dives into integration and fuzz testing.

Part 4 introduces asynchronous Rust programming:

- Chapter 8 provides an overview of Rust's async features.
- Chapter 9 walks through implementing an async HTTP server.
- Chapter 10 walks through implementing an async HTTP client.

Part 5 discusses optimizations:

- Chapter 11 dives into the details of Rust optimizations.

About the code

This book contains many examples of source code both in numbered listings and in line with normal text. In both cases, source code is formatted in a `fixed-width font like this` to separate it from ordinary text. Sometimes code is also **in bold** to highlight code that has changed from previous steps in the chapter, such as when a new feature adds to an existing line of code.

In many cases, the original source code has been reformatted; we've added line breaks and reworked indentation to accommodate the available page space in the book. In some cases, even this was not enough, and listings include line-continuation markers (➥). Additionally, comments in the source code have often been removed from the listings when the code is described in the text. Code annotations accompany many of the listings, highlighting important concepts.

You can get executable snippets of code from the liveBook (online) version of this book at https://livebook.manning.com/book/code-like-a-pro-in-rust. The complete code for the examples in the book is available for download from the Manning website at https://www.manning.com/books/code-like-a-pro-in-rust, and from GitHub at https://github.com/brndnmtthws/code-like-a-pro-in-rust-book.

You can clone a copy of the book's code locally on your computer by running the following command with Git:

```
$ git clone https://github.com/brndnmtthws/code-like-a-pro-in-rust-book
```

The book's code is organized into directories by chapter and section within the repository, organized within each section by topic. The code is licensed under the MIT license, which is a permissive license that allows you to copy the code samples and use them as you see fit, even as the basis for your own work.

Throughout this book, there are many references to open source projects which are used as teaching aids. The source code for most of these projects (or crates) can be obtained from their respective project repositories—for reference, see the following table.

List of projects referenced in this book

Name	Description	Home page	Repository URL
dryoc	Cryptography library	https://crates.io/crates/dryoc	https://github.com/brndnmtthws/dryoc.git
rand	Provides random values	https://rust-random.github.io/book	https://github.com/rust-random/rand.git
Rocket	HTTP/web framework	https://rocket.rs	https://github.com/SergioBenitez/Rocket.git
num_cpus	Returns the number of logical CPU cores	https://crates.io/crates/num_cpus	https://github.com/seanmonstar/num_cpus.git
zlib	Compression library	https://zlib.net/	https://github.com/madler/zlib.git

List of projects referenced in this book *(continued)*

Name	Description	Home page	Repository URL
lazy_static	Global static variable library	https://crates.io/crates/lazy_static	http://mng.bz/E9rD
Tokio	Async runtime	https://tokio.rs	https://github.com/tokio-rs/tokio
Syn	Rust code parser	https://crates.io/crates/syn	https://github.com/dtolnay/syn
axum	Async web framework	https://docs.rs/axum/latest/axum/	https://github.com/tokio-rs/axum

liveBook discussion forum

Purchase of *Code Like a Pro in Rust* includes free access to liveBook, Manning's online reading platform. Using liveBook's exclusive discussion features, you can attach comments to the book globally or to specific sections or paragraphs. It's a snap to make notes for yourself, ask and answer technical questions, and receive help from the author and other users. To access the forum, go to https://livebook.manning.com/book/code-like-a-pro-in-rust. You can also learn more about Manning's forums and the rules of conduct at https://livebook.manning.com/discussion.

Manning's commitment to our readers is to provide a venue where a meaningful dialogue between individual readers and between readers and the author can take place. It is not a commitment to any specific amount of participation on the part of the author, whose contribution to the forum remains voluntary (and unpaid). We suggest you try asking him some challenging questions lest his interest stray! The forum and the archives of previous discussions will be accessible from the publisher's website as long as the book is in print.

about the author

BRENDEN MATTHEWS is a software engineer, entrepreneur, and prolific open source contributor. He has been using Rust since the early days of the language and has contributed to several Rust tools and open source projects, in addition to using Rust professionally. He's the author of Conky, a popular system monitor, and a member of the Apache Software Foundation, with over 25 years of industry experience. Brenden is also a YouTube contributor and instructor as well as an author of many articles on Rust and other programming languages. He has given talks at several technology conferences, including QCon, LinuxCon, ContainerCon, MesosCon, All Things Open, and Rust meetups. He has been a GitHub contributor for over 13 years, has multiple published Rust crates, has contributed to several open source Rust projects, and has built production-grade Rust applications professionally. Brenden is also the author of *Rust Design Patterns*, a follow-up to *Code Like a Pro in Rust*.

about the cover illustration

The figure on the cover of *Code Like a Pro in Rust* is "Femme de l'Argou," or "Woman of Aargau, Switzerland," taken from a collection by Jacques Grasset de Saint-Sauveur, published in 1797. Each illustration is finely drawn and colored by hand.

In those days, it was easy to identify where people lived and what their trade or station in life was just by their dress. Manning celebrates the inventiveness and initiative of the computer business with book covers based on the rich diversity of regional culture centuries ago, brought back to life by pictures from collections such as this one.

Feelin' Rusty

This book will help beginner-to-intermediate Rust developers get up to speed on the language, tooling, data structures, memory management, testing, asynchronous programming, and best practices as quickly as possible. By the end of this book, you should feel confident building production-grade software systems with idiomatic—or *Rustaceous*—Rust. This book is not an exhaustive reference of the Rust language or its tooling; instead, it focuses solely on the good stuff.

Rust offers compelling features for those looking to build fast, safe programs. Some people find Rust's learning curve a bit steep, and this book can help overcome the challenging parts, clarify Rust's core concepts, and provide actionable advice.

The book is written for those already familiar with the Rust programming language. Additionally, it will be of much benefit to the reader to have experience with other system-level programming languages, such as C, C++, and Java. You need not be an expert in Rust to get value out of this book, but I won't spend much time reviewing basic syntax, history, or programming concepts.

Many of the code samples in this book are partial listings, but the full working code samples can be found on GitHub at http://mng.bz/BA70. The code is made available under the MIT license, which permits usage, copying, and modifications without restriction. I recommend you follow along the full code listings if you can, to get the most out of this book. The code samples are organized by chapter within the repository; however, some examples may span multiple sections or chapters and are, thus, named based on their subject matter.

1.1   *What's Rust?*

Rust (figure 1.1) is a modern programming language with a focus on performance and safety. It has all the features you would likely want or expect from a modern programming language, including closures, generics, asynchronous I/O, powerful tooling, IDE integrations, linters, and style-checking tools. Alongside Rust's robust set of features, it boasts a vibrant, growing community of developers and contributors.

Rust is a powerful language with several applications, including web development. While it was written with the intention of being a systems-level language, it also fits quite well in domains that are well outside system-level programming, such as web programming with WebAssembly (Wasm), a web stan-

Figure 1.1   Rust language logo (Source: Rust core team. Licensed under CC BY 4.0.)

dard for executing bytecode. In figure 1.2, I've illustrated where Rust generally sits in the language stack, but this is by no means definitive.

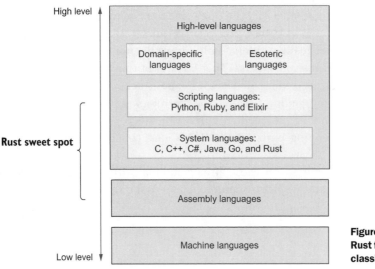

Figure 1.2   Where Rust fits in language classifications

Rust's creators envisioned its primary use as building system-level code and libraries that are safety and performance critical. Rust's safety guarantees don't come for free; the cost of those features comes in terms of added language and compilation-time complexity.

Rust *can* compete with higher-level languages, like Python or Ruby; however, its main drawback here is Rust's lack of a runtime interpreter, as it is compiled to platform-dependent binaries. Thus, one must distribute their Rust programs as binaries (or somehow provide a compiler). There are a few cases in which Rust is likely a much better choice than a scripting language, like Python or Ruby, such as embedded or resource-constrained environments.

Rust can also be compiled for web browsers directly, through the use of Wasm, which has grown significantly in popularity recently. Wasm is simply treated as yet another CPU target, much like x86-64 or AArch64, except the CPU in this case is a web browser.

Some highlights of the Rust language include the following:

- Rust features a core suite of tools for working with the language, including, but not limited to, the following:
  - `rustc`, the official Rust compiler
  - `cargo`, a package manager and build tool
  - https://crates.io, a package registry
- Rust has many modern programming language features, including the following:
  - The borrow checker, which enforces Rust's memory-management model
  - Static typing
  - Asynchronous I/O
  - Closures
  - Generics
  - Macros
  - Traits
- Rust offers several community tools for improving code quality and productivity:
  - `rust-clippy`, an advanced linter and style tool
  - Rustfmt, an opinionated code formatter
  - `sccache`, a compiler cache for `rustc`
  - `rust-analyzer`, a full-featured IDE integration for the Rust language

The most loved language

At the time of writing, Rust has won the most loved programming language category of Stack Overflow's annual developer survey every year since 2016. In the 2021 survey, out of 82,914 responses, Rust was loved by 86.98% of those using it ("2021 Developer Survey," http://mng.bz/ddON). The second-place language, Clojure, came in at 81.12% loved, and the third-place language, TypeScript, was 72.73% loved.

1.2 *What's unique about Rust?*

Rust addresses common programming mistakes with a unique set of abstractions—some of which you may have never encountered before. In this section, I'll provide a quick tour of the features that make Rust different.

1.2.1 *Rust is safe*

Safety is one of Rust's hallmarks, and its safety features are what differentiates it most from other languages. Rust can provide strong safety guarantees thanks to a feature called the *borrow checker*.

In languages like C and C++, memory management is a somewhat manual process, and developers must be aware of the implementation details when considering memory management. Languages like Java, Go, and Python use automatic memory management, or garbage collection, which obfuscates the details of allocating and managing memory with the tradeoff of incurring some performance overhead.

Rust's borrow checker works by validating references at *compile time*, rather than reference counting or performing garbage collection at run time. It's a unique feature that also introduces challenges when writing software, especially if you've never encountered the borrow checker.

The borrow checker is part of Rust's compiler `rustc`, which verifies that for any given object or variable, there can be no more than one mutable reference at a time. It's possible to have multiple immutable references (i.e., read-only references) to objects or variables, but you can never have more than a single active mutable reference. As shown in figure 1.3, Rust guarantees memory safety by checking that there's never an overlap between mutable and immutable references.

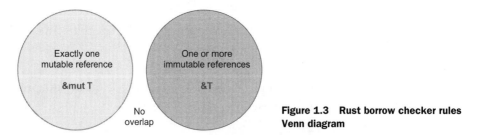

Figure 1.3 Rust borrow checker rules
Venn diagram

Rust uses *resource acquisition is initialization* (RAII) to keep track of when variables and all their references are in and out of scope. Once they are out of scope, memory can be released. The borrow checker will not allow references to out-of-scope variables, and it only allows one mutable reference or multiple immutable references but never both.

The borrow checker provides safety for concurrent programming, too. Race conditions may arise when sharing data, such as between separate threads. In most cases, the root cause is the same: simultaneous shared mutable references. With Rust, it's not possible to have more than one mutable reference, thereby ensuring data synchronization problems are avoided, or at least not created unintentionally.

Rust's borrow checker is tricky to master at first, but soon, you'll find it's the best feature of Rust. Similar to languages like Haskell, once you manage to make your code compile, that's often enough (when combined with adequate testing) to guarantee your code will work and never crash (testing is covered in chapters 6 and 7). There are exceptions to this, but by and large, code written in Rust will not crash from common memory errors, like reading past the end of a buffer or mishandling memory allocations and deallocations.

1.2.2   Rust is modern

The Rust language developers have paid special attention to supporting modern programming paradigms. Coming from other languages, you may notice Rust's out-with-the-old, in-with-the-new approach. Rust largely eschews paradigms like object-oriented programming in favor of traits, generics, and functional programming.

Notably, Rust emphasizes the following paradigms and features:

- *Functional programming*—Closures, anonymous functions, and iterators
- *Generics*
- *Traits*—Sometimes referred to as *interfaces* in other languages
- *Lifetimes*—For handling references
- *Metaprogramming*—Through its macro system
- *Asynchronous programming*—Via async/await
- *Package and dependency management*—Via Cargo
- *Zero-cost abstractions*

Traditional object-oriented features are notably absent from Rust. And while it's true that you can model patterns similar to classes and inheritance in Rust, the terminology is different, and Rust lends itself to functional programming. For those coming from an object-oriented background, such as C++, Java, or C#, it may take some time to get used to. Once they adjust to the new patterns, many programmers find a certain delight and freedom in being liberated from the rigidness of object-oriented ideology.

1.2.3   Rust is pure open source

When considering languages and platforms to build upon, community governance is important to consider when thinking about the long-term maintenance of any project. Some languages and platforms that are open source but mostly governed by large companies, such as Go (Google), Swift (Apple), and .NET (Microsoft), come with certain risks, such as making technology decisions that favor their products.

Rust is a community-driven project, led primarily by the not-for-profit Mozilla Foundation. The Rust programming language itself is dual licensed under the Apache and MIT licenses. Individual projects within the Rust ecosystem are individually licensed, but most key components and libraries exist under open source licenses, such as MIT or Apache.

There is strong support among large technology companies for Rust. Amazon, Facebook, Google, Apple, Microsoft, and others have made plans to use or pledge support for Rust. By not being tied to any particular entity, Rust is a good long-term choice with minimal potential for conflict of interest.

NOTE The Rust team maintains a list of production users on the official Rust language website: https://www.rust-lang.org/production.

1.2.4 Rust vs. other popular languages

Table 1.1, while not exhaustive, provides a summary of the differences between Rust and other popular programming languages.

Table 1.1 Rust compared to other languages

Language	Paradigms	Typing	Memory model	Key features
Rust	Concurrent, functional, generic, imperative	Static, strong	RAII, explicit	Safety, performance, async
C	Imperative	Static, weak	Explicit	Efficiency, portability, low-level memory management, widely supported
C++	Imperative, object-oriented, generic, functional	Static, mixed	RAII, explicit	Efficiency, portability, low-level memory management, widely supported
C#	Object-oriented, imperative, event-driven, functional, reflective, concurrent	Static, dynamic, strong	Garbage collected	Supported on Microsoft platforms, large ecosystem, advanced language features
JavaScript	Prototypes, functional, imperative	Dynamic, duck, weak	Garbage collected	Widely supported, async
Java	Generic, object-oriented, imperative, reflective	Static, strong	Garbage collected	Bytecode-based, production-grade Java Virtual Machine, widely supported, large ecosystem
Python	Functional, imperative, object-oriented, reflective	Dynamic, duck, strong	Garbage collected	Interpreted, highly portable, widely used
Ruby	Functional, imperative, object-oriented, reflective	Dynamic, duck, strong	Garbage collected	Syntax, everything's an expression, simple concurrency model
TypeScript	Functional, generic, imperative, object-oriented	Static, dynamic, duck, mixed	Garbage collected	Types, JavaScript compatibility, async

1.3 **When should you use Rust?**

Rust is a systems programming language, generally meant to be used for lower-level system programming, in situations similar to where you'd use C or C++. Rust may not be well suited for use cases in which you want to optimize for developer productivity, as writing Rust is often trickier than writing code with popular languages like Go, Python, Ruby, or Elixir.

Rust is also a great candidate for web programming with the onset of Wasm. You can build applications and libraries with Rust, compile them for Wasm, and take advantage of the benefits of Rust's safety model with the portability of the web.

There is no specific use case for Rust—you should use it where it makes sense. I have personally used Rust for many small one-off projects, simply because it's a joy to write, and once the code compiles, you can generally count on it working. With proper use of the Rust compiler and tooling, your code is considerably less likely to have errors or behave in undefined ways—which are desirable properties for *any* project.

> **TIP** Using the right tool for the job is important for any endeavor to succeed, but to know *which* tools are the right tools, you must first gain experience using a variety of different tools for different tasks.

1.3.1 **Rust use cases**

The following is a list of example use cases for which Rust is well suited:

- *Code acceleration*—Rust can accelerate functions from other languages, like Python, Ruby, or Elixir.
- *Concurrent systems*—Rust's safety guarantees apply to concurrent code. This makes Rust ideal for use in high-performance concurrent systems.
- *Cryptography*—Rust is ideally suited for implementing cryptography algorithms.
- *Embedded programming*—Rust generates binaries that bundle all dependencies, excluding the system C library or any third-party C libraries. This lends itself to a relatively straightforward binary distribution, particularly on embedded systems. Additionally, Rust's memory-management model is great for systems that demand minimal memory overhead.
- *Hostile environments*—In situations where safety is of utmost concern, Rust's guarantees are a perfect fit.
- *Performance critical*—Rust is optimized for safety *and* performance. It's easy to write code that's extremely fast, without compromising on safety, with Rust.
- *String processing*—String processing is an incredibly tricky problem, and Rust is particularly well suited for the task because it makes it easy to write code that can't overflow.
- *Replacing legacy C or C++*—Rust is an excellent choice for replacing legacy C or C++.
- *Safe web programming*—Rust can target Wasm, allowing us to build web applications with Rust's safety and strong type checking.

1.4   *Tools you'll need*

Included as part of this book is a collection of code samples, freely available under the MIT license. To obtain a copy of the code, you will need an internet-connected computer with a supported operating system and the tools discussed in table 1.2 installed. For details on installing these tools, refer to the appendix.

Table 1.2   Required tools

Name	Description
`git`	The source code for this book is stored in a public Git repository, hosted on GitHub at http://mng.bz/BA70.
`rustup`	This is Rust's tool for managing Rust components. `rustup` will manage your installation of `rustc` and other Rust components.
`gcc` or `clang`	You must have a copy of GNU Compiler Collection (GCC) or Clang installed to build certain code samples, but it's not required for most. Clang is likely the best choice for most people, and thus, it's referred to by default. In cases where the `clang` command is specified, you may freely substitute `gcc` if you prefer.

Summary

- Rust is a modern system-level programming language with advanced safety features and zero-cost abstractions.
- Rust's steep learning curve can be an initial deterrent, but this book helps you move beyond these hurdles.
- Rust has many similarities to—and borrows concepts from—other languages, but it's unique, as explained throughout this book.
- Rust's vibrant community and mature package repository provide a rich ecosystem to build atop.
- To get the most out of this book, follow along the code samples from http://mng.bz/BA70.

## Part 1

Pro Rust

Rust offers a great deal of value: speed, safety, and a rich set of tools for working with the language. Learning the language is important, but having command of the tools provided by both the core Rust project and the wider community will help you achieve mastery quickly.

Tooling makes all the difference between a good and a bad programming language—as does your effectiveness with the tooling. Merely having awareness about what tooling is available and some of the capabilities it provides will place you head and shoulders above developers who don't take the time to learn the tools.

In the first part of the book, we'll spend some time introducing (or reviewing, depending on your level of expertise) the basics of the language and, in particular, the tools you'll need to work with it. You don't need to be a Rust Pro to use its tools, but you do need to understand the tools to effectively use the language.

Project management with Cargo

This chapter covers

- Introducing Cargo and how to manage Rust projects with Cargo
- Handling dependencies in Rust projects
- Linking to other (non-Rust) libraries
- Publishing Rust applications and libraries
- Documenting Rust code
- Following the Rust community's best practices for managing and publishing projects
- Structuring Rust projects with modules and workspaces
- Considerations for using Rust in embedded environments

Before we can jump into the Rust language itself, we need to familiarize ourselves with the basic tools required to work with Rust. This may seem tedious, but I can assure you that mastering tooling is critical to success. The tools were created by the language creators for the language users to make your life easier, so understanding their purpose will forever pay dividends.

Rust's package management tool is called *Cargo*, and it's the interface to Rust's compiler `rustc`, the https://crates.io registry, and many other Rust tools (which we cover in more detail in chapter 3). Strictly speaking, it's possible to use Rust and `rustc` *without* using Cargo, but it's not something I'd recommend for most people.

When working with Rust, you'll likely spend a lot of time using Cargo and tools that work with Cargo. It's important to familiarize yourself with its use and best practices. In chapter 3, I'll provide recommendations and details on how to further increase the usefulness of Cargo with community crates.

2.1 Cargo tour

To demonstrate Cargo's features, let's take a tour of Cargo and its typical usage. I implore you to follow along (ideally by running the commands as demonstrated in the chapter). In doing so, you may discover new features even if you're already familiar with Cargo and its usage.

2.1.1 Basic usage

To start, run `cargo help` to list the available commands:

```
$ cargo help
Rust's package manager

USAGE:
    cargo [+toolchain] [OPTIONS] [SUBCOMMAND]

OPTIONS:
    -V, --version           Print version info and exit
        --list              List installed commands
        --explain <CODE>    Run `rustc --explain CODE`
    -v, --verbose           Use verbose output (-vv very verbose/build.rs
                            output)
    -q, --quiet             No output printed to stdout
        --color <WHEN>      Coloring: auto, always, never
        --frozen            Require Cargo.lock and cache are up to date
        --locked            Require Cargo.lock is up to date
        --offline           Run without accessing the network
    -Z <FLAG>...            Unstable (nightly-only) flags to Cargo, see
    'cargo -Z help' for details
    -h, --help              Prints help information

Some common cargo commands are (see all commands with --list):
    build, b    Compile the current package
    check, c    Analyze the current package and report errors, but don't
    build object files
    clean       Remove the target directory
    doc         Build this package's and its dependencies' documentation
    new         Create a new cargo package
    init        Create a new cargo package in an existing directory
```

```
run, r      Run a binary or example of the local package
test, t     Run the tests
bench       Run the benchmarks
update      Update dependencies listed in Cargo.lock
search      Search registry for crates
publish     Package and upload this package to the registry
install     Install a Rust binary. Default location is $HOME/.cargo/bin
uninstall   Uninstall a Rust binary

See 'cargo help <command>' for more information on a specific command.
```

If you run this yourself, your output may differ slightly, depending on the version of Cargo you have installed. If you don't see output similar to the preceding code, you may need to verify your Cargo installation is working. Refer to the appendix for details on installing Cargo.

2.1.2 *Creating a new application or library*

Cargo has a built-in boilerplate generator, which can create a *Hello, world!* application or library, saving you time on getting started. To get started, run the following command in your shell from a development directory (I personally like to use ~/dev):

```
$ cargo new dolphins-are-cool
     Created binary (application) `dolphins-are-cool` package
```

This command creates a new boilerplate application called dolphins-are-cool (you can change the name to anything you want). Let's quickly examine the output:

```
$ cd dolphins-are-cool/
$ tree
.
├── Cargo.toml
└── src
    └── main.rs

1 directory, 2 files
```

In this code, we see Cargo has created two files:

- Cargo.toml, which is the Cargo configuration file for the new application, in TOML format
- main.rs inside the src directory, which represents the entry point for our new application

   TIP *Tom's obvious minimal language* (TOML) is a configuration file format used by many Rust-related tools. For details on TOML, refer to https://toml.io.

Next, use cargo run to compile and execute the newly created application:

```
$ cargo run
   Compiling dolphins-are-cool v0.1.0 (/Users/brenden/dev/dolphins-are-cool)
    Finished dev [unoptimized + debuginfo] target(s) in 0.59s
     Running `target/debug/dolphins-are-cool`
Hello, world!
```
◁——— **This is the Rust program output.**

Running the `cargo new` command like this but with the `--lib` argument will create a new library:

```
$ cargo new narwhals-are-real --lib
     Created library `narwhals-are-real` package
$ cd narwhals-are-real/
$ tree
.
├── Cargo.toml
└── src
    └── lib.rs

1 directory, 2 files
```

The code generated from `cargo new --lib` is slightly different, as it contains a single-unit test in src/lib.rs rather than a `main` function. You can run the tests with `cargo test`:

```
$ cargo test
    Finished test [unoptimized + debuginfo] target(s) in 0.00s
     Running target/debug/deps/narwhals_are_real-3265ca33d2780ea2

running 1 test
test tests::it_works ... ok

test result: ok. 1 passed; 0 failed; 0 ignored; 0 measured; 0 filtered out;
finished in 0.00s

   Doc-tests narwhals-are-real

running 0 tests

test result: ok. 0 passed; 0 failed; 0 ignored; 0 measured; 0 filtered out;
finished in 0.00s
```

> **TIP** Applications use src/main.rs as their entrypoint, and libraries use src/lib.rs as their entrypoint.

When using `cargo new`, Cargo will automatically initialize the new directory as a Git repository (*except* when already inside a repository), including a .gitignore file. Cargo also supports hg, Pijul, and Fossil with the `--vcs` flag.

2.1.3 *Building, running, and testing*

The Cargo commands you'll likely spend the most time working with are `build`, `check`, `test`, and `run`. These commands are summarized in table 2.1.

Table 2.1 Cargo build and run commands

Cargo command	Summary
build	Compiles and links your package, creating all final targets
check	Similar to build, except does not actually generate any targets or objects—merely checks the validity of code
test	Compiles and runs all tests
run	Compiles and runs the target binary

The commands you will likely spend a great deal of time working with are `cargo check` and `cargo test`. By using `check`, you can save time and iterate quickly while writing code, as it will validate syntax faster than `cargo build`. To illustrate this, let's time the compilation of the `dryoc` crate, available from https://github.com/brndnmtthws/dryoc, which I use throughout this book for examples:

```
$ cargo clean
$ time cargo build
...
    Finished dev [unoptimized + debuginfo] target(s) in 9.26s
cargo build  26.95s user 5.18s system 342% cpu 9.374 total
$ cargo clean
$ time cargo check
...
    Finished dev [unoptimized + debuginfo] target(s) in 7.97s
cargo check  23.24s user 3.80s system 334% cpu 8.077 total
```

In this case, the difference is not substantial: about 9.374 seconds for the `build` command versus 8.077 seconds for `check` (according to the wall-clock time given by the `time` command). However, on larger crates, the time saved can become substantial. Additionally, there's a multiplicative effect, as you often recompile (or recheck) the code several times when iterating on changes.

2.1.4 Switching between toolchains

A *toolchain* is a combination of an architecture, a platform, and a channel. One example is `stable-x86_64-apple-darwin`, which is the stable channel for x64-64 Darwin (equivalent to Apple's macOS on Intel CPUs). Rust is published as three different *channels*: stable, beta, and nightly. Stable is the least frequently updated, best tested channel. Beta contains features that are ready for stabilization but which require further testing and are subject to change. Nightly contains unreleased language features that are considered a work in progress.

When working with Rust, you'll often find yourself needing to switch between different toolchains. In particular, you may often need to switch between the stable and nightly channels. An easy way to do this directly with Cargo is to use the `+channel` option, like so:

```
# Runs tests with stable channel:
$ cargo +stable test
...
# Runs tests with nightly channel:
$ cargo +nightly test
...
```

> **NOTE** You may need to install the nightly toolchain with `rustup toolchain install nightly` *before* running any `cargo +nightly ...` commands, if you haven't already done so. If you install cargo via a system-level package manager (e.g., Debian's apt), this command may not work as expected.

This option works with all Cargo commands, and it's the quickest way to switch between toolchains. The alternative is to switch your default toolchain using `rustup`, covered in the appendix.

In many cases, you'll want to test your code with both stable and nightly before publishing, especially with open source projects, as many people use both toolchains. Additionally, many Rust projects are nightly *only*, which is discussed in greater detail in chapter 3.

You may also use the `override` option with `rustup`, which allows you to set the toolchain for a specific project or directory. The `rustup` tool stores this configuration in its settings.toml, which is located within $HOME/.rustup on UNIX-like systems. For example, you can set the current working directory to the nightly channel with the following code:

```
# Only applies to the current directory and its children
$ rustup override set nightly
```

This is quite handy, as it allows you to keep the stable channel by default, but switch to nightly for specific projects.

2.2   *Dependency management*

The `crates.io` package (or crate) registry is one of Rust's force multipliers. In the Rust community, packages are called *crates*, and they include both applications and libraries. As of the time of writing, there are more than 92,000 different crates available.

When referring to crates in this book, we're likely using libraries rather than applications. In chapter 3, we'll discuss more Rust tooling that can be installed from crates, but most of the time we'll be using libraries.

Rust has a unique approach compared to some programming languages, in that the core language itself does not include many features. By comparison, languages like Java, C#, and even C++, to some degree, include significant components as part of the core language (either in the runtime or as part of the compiler). For example, Rust's core data structures—compared to other languages—are quite minimal, and many are just wrappers around the core data resizable structure, `Vec`. Rust prefers to provide features through crates, rather than creating a large standard library.

The Rust language itself doesn't even include a random number generator, which is critical for many programming tasks. For that you need to use the rand crate, which is the most downloaded crate as of the time of writing (or write your own random number generator).

If you're coming from a language like JavaScript, Ruby, or Python, Rust's crates will be somewhat similar to their corresponding package management tools. Coming from languages like C or C++ is like discovering fire for the first time. Gone are the days of manually writing complicated build checks for third-party libraries or integrating third-party code and build systems into your own source repository.

Describing dependencies in Rust is done by listing them in Cargo.toml. A simple example using the rand crate looks as shown in the following listing.

Listing 2.1 A minimal Cargo.toml

```
[package]
name = "simple-project"
version = "0.1.0"
authors = ["Brenden Matthews <brenden@brndn.io>"]
edition = "2018"

[dependencies]
rand = "0.8"
```

In the preceding code, we're including the rand crate, using the latest 0.8 release of the library. When specifying dependency versions, you should follow semantic versioning (SemVer, https://semver.org), which uses the *major.minor.patch* pattern. By default, Cargo will use *caret* requirements if an operator is not specified, which permits updates to the least-specified version.

You can also add a dependency to a project with the cargo add command:

```
# Adds the rand crate as a dependency to the current project
$ cargo add rand
```

Cargo supports carets (^x.y.z), tildes (~x.y.z), wildcards (*, x.*), comparison requirements (>=x, <x.y, =x.y.z), and combinations thereof (see table 2.2). In practice, you would specify the library version as major.minor (allows compatible upgrades under the caret rules) or =major.minor.patch (pinned to a specific version). Refer to http://mng.bz/rjAB for more information on dependency specifications.

Table 2.2 Summary of SemVer dependency specification

Operator	Example	Min version	Max version	Updates?
Caret	^2.3.4	>=2.3.4	<3.0.0	Allowed
Caret	^2.3	>=2.3.0	<3.0.0	Allowed
Caret	^0.2.3	>=0.2.3	<0.3.0	Allowed

Table 2.2   Summary of SemVer dependency specification *(continued)*

Operator	Example	Min version	Max version	Updates?
Caret	^2	>=2.0.0	<3.0.0	Allowed
Tilde	~2.3.4	>=2.3.4	<2.4.0	Allowed
Tilde	~2.3	>=2.3.0	<2.4.0	Allowed
Tilde	~0.2	>=0.2.0	<0.3	Allowed
Wildcard	2.3.*	>=2.3.0	<2.4.0	Allowed
Wildcard	2.*	>=2.0.0	<3.0.0	Allowed
Wildcard	*	None	None	Allowed
Comparison	=2.3.4	=2.3.4	=2.3.4	No
Comparison	>=2.3.4	>=2.3.4	None	Allowed
Comparison	>=2.3.4,<3.0.0	>=2.3.4	<3.0.0	Allowed

Internally, Cargo uses the `semver` crate (https://crates.io/crates/semver) for parsing the versions specified. When you run `cargo update` within your project, Cargo will update the Cargo.lock file with the newest available crates, per your dependency specification.

> **TIP**   I prefer to avoid pinning dependency versions when possible, *especially* in libraries. It can cause headaches down the road when competing downstream packages require different versions of common libraries. While many advocate for version pinning, it's better to permit flexibility as needed.

How exactly to specify dependencies is a topic of much debate. There are no hard-and-fast rules, but you should generally assume other projects follow SemVer. Some projects adhere to SemVer rules strictly, and others do not. In most cases, it needs to be evaluated on a case-by-case basis. A reasonable default assumption is to allow upgrades to minor and patch versions by specifying the minimum required version with the caret operator, which is the default in Rust (if you don't explicitly specify an operator). For your own published crates, please follow SemVer, as it helps other developers build on your work and preserves compatibility.

2.2.1   *Handling the Cargo.lock file*

Handling Cargo.lock requires a bit of special consideration, at least with regard to version control systems. The file contains a list of the package dependencies (both direct and indirect dependencies), their versions, and checksums for verifying integrity.

   If you're coming from languages with similar package management systems, you've probably seen similar files before (npm uses package-lock.json, Ruby gems use Gemfile .lock, and Python Poetry uses poetry.lock). For libraries, it's recommended you *do not* include this file in your version control system. When using Git, you can do this by adding Cargo.lock to .gitignore. Leaving out the lock file allows downstream packages to update indirect dependencies as needed.

For applications, it's recommended you always include Cargo.lock alongside Cargo.toml. This helps to ensure consistent behavior in published releases, should third-party libraries change in the future.

This is a well-established convention and not unique to Rust. Lastly, Cargo will automatically create an appropriate .gitignore file for you and initialize a Git repository.

2.3   Feature flags

It's common practice when publishing software, particularly libraries, to have optional dependencies. This is usually for the purpose of keeping compile times low and binaries small, and, perhaps, providing performance improvements, with the tradeoff of some additional complexity at compile time.

In some cases, you may want to include optional dependencies as part of your crate. These can be expressed as feature flags with Cargo (table 2.3). There are some limitations with feature flags, notably that they only permit Boolean expressions (i.e., enabled or disabled). Feature flags are also passed through to crates in your dependency list, so you can enable features for underlying crates through top-level feature flags.

Table 2.3   Example feature flags from the `dryoc` crate

Flag	Description	Enabled by default?
serde	Enables an optional `serde` dependency	No
base64	Enables a `base64` dependency but only activates when `serde` is also enabled	No
simd_backend	Enables the SIMD and assembly features for `curve25519-dalek` and `sha2` crates	No
u64_backend	Enables the u64 backend for the `x25519-dalek` crate, which is mutually exclusive with `u32_backend`	Yes
u32_backend	Enables the u32 backend for the `x25519-dalek` crate, which is mutually exclusive with the `u64_backend`	No

I recommend not relying too heavily on feature flags. You may find yourself leaning toward creating supercrates with lots of feature flags, but if you find yourself doing this, you may want to instead break your crate into smaller, separate subcrates. This pattern is quite common; some good examples include the `serde`, `rand`, and `rocket` crates. There are some cases where you *must* use feature flags to express certain optional features, such as when providing optional trait implementations in the top-level crate.

To examine how feature flags are used in practice, let's look at the `dryoc` crate in the following listing. This crate uses a few flags to express some features: `serde`; `base64`, for binary encoding (with `serde`); and SIMD optimizations.

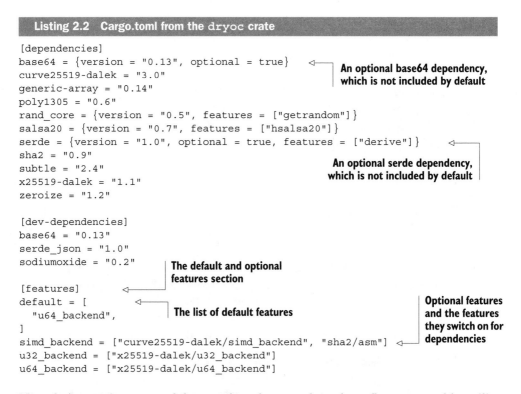

Listing 2.2 Cargo.toml from the `dryoc` crate

```toml
[dependencies]
base64 = {version = "0.13", optional = true}
curve25519-dalek = "3.0"
generic-array = "0.14"
poly1305 = "0.6"
rand_core = {version = "0.5", features = ["getrandom"]}
salsa20 = {version = "0.7", features = ["hsalsa20"]}
serde = {version = "1.0", optional = true, features = ["derive"]}
sha2 = "0.9"
subtle = "2.4"
x25519-dalek = "1.1"
zeroize = "1.2"

[dev-dependencies]
base64 = "0.13"
serde_json = "1.0"
sodiumoxide = "0.2"

[features]
default = [
  "u64_backend",
]
simd_backend = ["curve25519-dalek/simd_backend", "sha2/asm"]
u32_backend = ["x25519-dalek/u32_backend"]
u64_backend = ["x25519-dalek/u64_backend"]
```

An optional base64 dependency, which is not included by default

An optional serde dependency, which is not included by default

The default and optional features section

The list of default features

Optional features and the features they switch on for dependencies

Next, let's examine some of the crate's code to see how these flags are used by utilizing `cfg` and `cfg_attr`, which instruct the Rust compiler, `rustc`, how to use these flags. We'll look at src/message.rs, which demonstrates the use of feature flags, in the following listing.

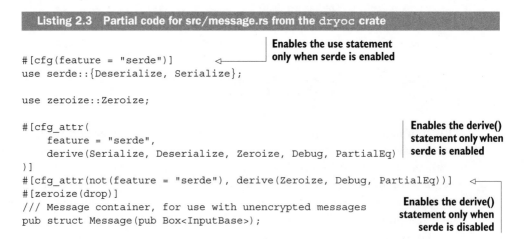

Listing 2.3 Partial code for src/message.rs from the `dryoc` crate

```rust
#[cfg(feature = "serde")]
use serde::{Deserialize, Serialize};

use zeroize::Zeroize;

#[cfg_attr(
    feature = "serde",
    derive(Serialize, Deserialize, Zeroize, Debug, PartialEq)
)]
#[cfg_attr(not(feature = "serde"), derive(Zeroize, Debug, PartialEq))]
#[zeroize(drop)]
/// Message container, for use with unencrypted messages
pub struct Message(pub Box<InputBase>);
```

Enables the use statement only when serde is enabled

Enables the derive() statement only when serde is enabled

Enables the derive() statement only when serde is disabled

The preceding code listing uses several conditional compilation attributes:

- cfg(*predicate*)—Instructs the compiler to only compile what it is attached to if the predicate is true
- cfg_attr(*predicate, attribute*)—Instructs the compiler to only enable the specified attribute (second argument) if the predicate (first argument) is true
- not(*predicate*)—Returns true if the predicate is false and vice versa

Additionally, you may use all(*predicate*) and any(*predicate*), which return true when all or any of the predicates are true. For more examples, see src/lib.rs, src/b64.rs, src/dryocbox.rs, and src/dryocsecretbox.rs within the dryoc crate.

> **TIP** When you generate documentation for a project with rustdoc, it automatically provides a feature flag listing for you. We'll explore rustdoc in detail later in this chapter.

2.4 Patching dependencies

One problem you may encounter from time to time is the need to patch an upstream crate (i.e., a crate you depend on from *outside* your project). I have encountered many instances where I needed to update another crate I was depending on, usually for some minor problem. It's rarely worth the trouble of replacing the functionality of upstream crates just to fix one or two minor bugs. In some cases, you may be able to simply switch to the prerelease version of the crate, or else you have to patch it yourself.

The process for patching an upstream crate goes something like this:

1 Create a fork on GitHub.
2 Patch the crate in your fork.
3 Submit a pull request to the upstream project.
4 Change your Cargo.toml to point to your fork while waiting for the pull request to be merged and released.

This process is not without problems. One obstacle is keeping track of changes to the upstream crate and integrating them as needed. Another problem is that your patch may never be accepted upstream—in which case, you can get stuck on a fork. When working with upstream crates, you should try to avoid forking when possible.

Cargo provides a way for you to patch crates using the preceding fork method without too much fuss; however, there are some caveats. To illustrate, let's walk through the typical process for patching a crate. For this example, I'll make a local copy of the source code rather than creating a forked project on GitHub.

Let's modify the num_cpus crate, to replace it with our own patched version. I chose this crate for its simplicity; it returns the number of logical CPU cores. Start by creating an empty project:

```
$ cargo new patch-num-cpus
...
$ cd patch-num-cpus
$ cargo run
...
Hello, world!
```

Next, add the `num_cpus` dependency to Cargo.toml:

```
[dependencies]
num_cpus"= "".0"
```

Update src/main.rs to print the number of CPUs:

```
fn main() {
    printl"!("There are {} C"Us", num_cpus::get());
}
```

Finally, run the new crate:

```
$ cargo run
    Finished dev [unoptimized + debuginfo] target(s) in 0.00s
     Running `target/debug/patch-num-cpus`
There are 4 CPUs
```

At this point, we haven't patched or modified anything. Let's create a new library within the same working directory, where we'll reimplement the same API:

```
$ cargo new num_cpus --lib
...
```

Next, we'll patch the default src/lib.rs to implement `num_cpus::get()`. Update src/lib.rs from the num_cpus directory to the following:

```
pub fn get() -> usize {
    100                    ⊲──── Return some arbitrary value, for test purposes.
}
```

Now, we have `num_cpus` with our own implementation, which returns a rather pointless hardcoded value (100, in this case). Go back up a directory to the original `patch-num-cpus` project, and modify Cargo.toml to use the replacement crate:

```
[dependencies]
num_cpus = { path = "num_cpus" }
```

Run the same code with the patched crate:

```
$ cargo run
   Compiling patch-num-cpus v0.1.0
    Finished dev [unoptimized + debuginfo] target(s) in 0.33s
     Running `target/debug/patch-num-cpus`
There are 100 CPUs
```

This example is fairly pointless, but it effectively illustrates the process. If you want to patch a dependency using a fork from GitHub, for example, you would point your dependency directly to your GitHub repository, like this (in Cargo.toml):

```
[dependencies]
num_cpus = { git = "https://github.com/brndnmtthws/num_cpus",
  rev = "b423db0a698b035914ae1fd6b7ce5d2a4e727b46" }
```

If you execute `cargo run` now, you should again see the correct number of CPUs reported (as I created the fork above but without any changes). `rev` in the preceding example is referring to a Git hash for the latest commit at the time of writing. When you compile the project, Cargo will fetch the source code from the GitHub repository, check out the particular revision specified (which could be a commit, branch, or tag), and compile that version as a dependency.

2.4.1   *Indirect dependencies*

Sometimes, you need to patch dependencies of dependencies. That is to say, you might depend on a crate that depends on another crate that requires patching. Using `num_cpus` as an example, the crate currently depends on `libc = "0.2.26"` (but only on non-Windows platforms). For the sake of this example, we can patch that dependency to a newer release by updating Cargo.toml like so:

```
[patch.crates-io]
libc = { git = "https://github.com/rust-lang/libc", tag = "0.2.88" }
```

In this example, we're going to point to the Git repository for `libc` and specify the `0.2.88` tag explicitly. The patch section in Cargo.toml serves as a way to patch the crates.io registry itself, rather than patching a package directly. You are, in effect, replacing all upstream dependencies for `libc` with your own version.

Use this feature carefully, and only under special circumstances. It does not affect downstream dependencies, meaning any crates that depend on your crate won't inherit the patch. This is a limitation of Cargo that currently does not have a reasonable workaround. In cases in which you need more control over second- and third-order dependencies, you'll need to either fork all the projects involved or include them directly in your own project as subprojects using workspaces (discussed later in this chapter).

2.4.2   *Best practices for dependency patching*

There are a few rules we should try to follow when it comes to patching dependencies, as outlined here:

- Patching dependencies should be a last resort, as patches are difficult to maintain over time.

- When patching is necessary, submit patches upstream with the required changes for open source projects, especially when required by licenses (i.e., GPL-licensed code).
- Avoid forking upstream crates, and in cases where it's unavoidable, try to get back onto the main branch as quickly as possible. Long-lived forks will diverge and can eventually become a maintenance nightmare.

2.5   *Publishing crates*

For projects you wish to publish to crates.io, the process is simple. Once your crate is ready to go, you can run `cargo publish`, and Cargo takes care of the details. There are a few requirements for publishing a crate, such as specifying a license, providing certain project details like documentation and a repository URL, and ensuring all dependencies are also available to crates.io.

It is possible to publish to a private registry; however, at the time of writing, Cargo's support for private registries is quite limited. Thus, it's recommended to use private Git repositories and tags instead of relying on crates.io for private crates.

2.5.1   *CI/CD integration*

For most crates, you'll want to set up a system for publishing releases to crates.io automatically. Continuous integration/continuous deployment (CI/CD) systems are a common component of modern development cycles. They're usually composed of two distinct steps:

- *Continuous integration (CI)*—A system that compiles, checks, and verifies each commit to a VCS repository
- *Continuous deployment (CD)*—A system that automatically deploys each commit or release, provided it passes all necessary checks from the CI

To demonstrate this, I will walk through the `dryoc` project, which uses GitHub Actions (https://github.com/features/actions), freely available for open source projects.

Before looking at the code, let's describe the release process with a typical Git workflow once you've decided it's time to publish a release:

1 If needed, update the `version` attribute within Cargo.toml to the version you want to release.
2 The CI system will run, verifying all the tests and checks pass.
3 You'll create and push a tag for the release (use a version prefix, such as `git tag -s vX.Y.Z`).
4 The CD system will run, build the tagged release, and publish to crates.io with `cargo publish`.
5 Update the `version` attribute in Cargo.toml for the *next* release cycle in a new commit.

NOTE Published crates are immutable, so any changes will require rolling forward. There is no way to roll back or make changes to a crate once published to crates.io.

Let's examine the `dryoc` crate, which implements this pattern using GitHub Actions. There are two Actions to look at:

- *.github/workflows/build-and-test.yml*—Builds and runs tests for a combination of features, platforms, and toolkits (http://mng.bz/VRmP)
- *.github/workflows/publish.yml*—Builds and runs tests for a tagged release matching the v* pattern, publishing the crate to crates.io (http://mng.bz/xjAW)

Listing 2.4 shows the build job parameters, including the feature, channel, and platform matrix. These jobs use the brndnmtthws/rust-action all-in-one GitHub Action (http://mng.bz/A87z) to set up the Rust environment.

Listing 2.4 Partial code for .github/workflows/build-and-test.yml

```yaml
name: Build & test
on:                              ◁──┐ Builds will only run on Git pushes and
  push:                              │ pull requests for the main branch.
    branches: [main]
  pull_request:
    branches: [main]
env:
  CARGO_TERM_COLOR: always
concurrency:
  group: ${{ github.workflow }}-${{ github.ref }}
  cancel-in-progress: true
jobs:
  build:
    strategy:
      matrix:                   ┌ Runs with stable, beta,
        rust:         ◁─────────┘ and nightly channels
          - stable
          - beta
          - nightly           ┌ Runs tests with different
        features:     ◁───────┘ features enabled separately
          - serde
          - base64
          - simd_backend
          - default           ┌ Runs on Linux,
        os:           ◁───────┘ macOS, and Windows
          - ubuntu-latest
          - macos-latest
          - windows-latest    ┌ Some build combinations don't
        exclude:      ◁───────┘ work, so they're disabled here.
          - rust: stable
            features: simd_backend
          - rust: beta
            features: simd_backend
          - os: windows-latest
            features: simd_backend
```

The following listing shows the individual steps to build, test, format, and run Clippy (discussed in chapter 3).

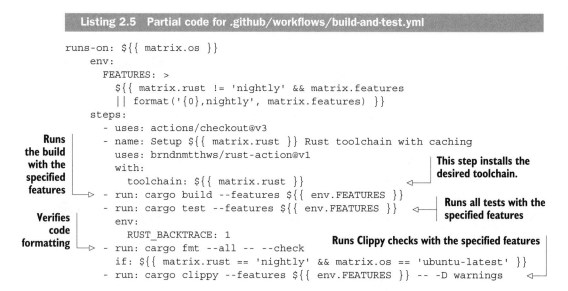

Listing 2.5   Partial code for .github/workflows/build-and-test.yml

```
runs-on: ${{ matrix.os }}
    env:
      FEATURES: >
        ${{ matrix.rust != 'nightly' && matrix.features
        || format('{0},nightly', matrix.features) }}
    steps:
      - uses: actions/checkout@v3
      - name: Setup ${{ matrix.rust }} Rust toolchain with caching
        uses: brndnmtthws/rust-action@v1
        with:
          toolchain: ${{ matrix.rust }}
      - run: cargo build --features ${{ env.FEATURES }}
      - run: cargo test --features ${{ env.FEATURES }}
        env:
          RUST_BACKTRACE: 1
      - run: cargo fmt --all -- --check
        if: ${{ matrix.rust == 'nightly' && matrix.os == 'ubuntu-latest' }}
      - run: cargo clippy --features ${{ env.FEATURES }} -- -D warnings
```

Runs the build with the specified features

This step installs the desired toolchain.

Runs all tests with the specified features

Verifies code formatting

Runs Clippy checks with the specified features

The following listing shows the steps involved to publish our crate.

Listing 2.6   Code for .github/workflows/publish.yml

```
name: Publish to crates.io
on:
  push:
    tags:
      - v*
env:
  CARGO_TERM_COLOR: always
jobs:
  build-test-publish:
    runs-on: ubuntu-latest
    steps:
      - uses: actions/checkout@v3
      - uses: brndnmtthws/rust-action@v1
        with:
          toolchain: stable
      - run: cargo build
      - run: cargo test
      - run: cargo login -- ${{ secrets.CRATES_IO_TOKEN }}
      - run: cargo publish
      - name: Create Release
        id: create_release
        uses: softprops/action-gh-release@v1
        if: startsWith(github.ref, 'refs/tags/')
        with:
          draft: false
```

Only runs when tag matches v*

Log in to crates.io using the secret stored in the repository's secrets configuration. This token is stored using GitHub's secret storage feature, which must be supplied ahead of time.

Creates a release on GitHub

Publishes the crate to https://crates.io

```
prerelease: false
discussion_category_name: General
generate_release_notes: true
```

NOTE GitHub's Actions doesn't currently support any way to gate a release when using separate stages (i.e., wait until the build stage succeeds before proceeding with the deploy stage). To accomplish this, you must verify the build stage succeeds before pushing any tags.

In the final publish step, you'll need to provide a token for https://crates.io. This can be done by creating a crates.io account, generating a token from the crates.io account settings, and then adding it to GitHub's secret storage in the settings for your GitHub repository.

2.6 Linking to C libraries

You may occasionally find yourself needing to use external libraries from non-Rust code. This is usually accomplished with a foreign function interface (FFI). FFI is a fairly standard way to accomplish cross-language interoperability. We'll revisit FFI again in greater detail in chapter 4.

Let's walk through a simple example of calling functions from one of the most popular C libraries: zlib. Zlib was chosen because it's nearly ubiquitous, and this example should work easily out of the box on any platform where zlib is available. We'll implement two functions in Rust: `compress()` and `uncompress()`. Here are the definitions from the zlib library (which has been simplified for the purposes of this example).

Listing 2.7 Simplified code listing from zlib.h

```
int compress(void *dest, unsigned long *destLen,
             const void *source, unsigned long sourceLen);

unsigned long compressBound(unsigned long sourceLen);

int uncompress(void *dest, unsigned long *destLen,
               const void *source, unsigned long sourceLen);
```

First, we'll define the C interface in Rust using `extern`.

Listing 2.8 Code for zlib utility functions

```
use libc::{c_int, c_ulong};

#[link(name = "z")]
extern "C" {
    fn compress(
        dest: *mut u8,
        dest_len: *mut c_ulong,
        source: *const u8,
        source_len: c_ulong,
    ) -> c_int;
```

```
    fn compressBound(source_len: c_ulong) -> c_ulong;
    fn uncompress(
        dest: *mut u8,
        dest_len: *mut c_ulong,
        source: *const u8,
        source_len: c_ulong,
    ) -> c_int;
}
```

We've included `libc` as a dependency, which provides C-compatible types in Rust. Whenever you're linking to C libraries, you'll want to use types from `libc` to maintain compatibility. Failure to do so may result in undefined behavior. We've defined three utility functions from zlib: `compress`, `compressBound`, and `uncompress`.

The `link` attribute tells `rustc` that we need to link these functions to zlib. This is equivalent to adding the `-lz` flag at link time. On macOS, you can verify this with `otool -L`, as shown in the following code (on Linux, use `ldd`, and on Windows, use `dumpbin`):

```
$ otool -L target/debug/zlib-wrapper
target/debug/zlib-wrapper:
    /usr/lib/libz.1.dylib (compatibility version 1.0.0, current version
    1.2.11)
    /usr/lib/libiconv.2.dylib (compatibility version 7.0.0, current version
    7.0.0)
    /usr/lib/libSystem.B.dylib (compatibility version 1.0.0, current version
    1292.60.1)
    /usr/lib/libresolv.9.dylib (compatibility version 1.0.0, current version
    1.0.0)
```

Next, we need to write Rust functions that wrap the C functions and can be called from Rust code. Calling C functions directly is considered unsafe in Rust, so you must wrap the call in an `unsafe {}` block.

Listing 2.9 Code for `zlib_compress`

```
pub fn zlib_compress(source: &[u8]) -> Vec<u8> {          Returns the upper
    unsafe {                                              bound of the length
        let source_len = source.len() as c_ulong;         of the compressed
                                                          output
        let mut dest_len = compressBound(source_len);  ◄──┘
        let mut dest = Vec::with_capacity(dest_len as usize);  ◄──┐
                                                                  Allocates
        compress(                    ◄──── Calls zlib C function   dest_len bytes
            dest.as_mut_ptr(),                                    on the heap
            &mut dest_len,                                        using a Vec
            source.as_ptr(),
            source_len,
        );
        dest.set_len(dest_len as usize);
        dest     ◄──┐
    }             │  Returns the result as a Vec
}
```

The `zlib_uncompress` version of the preceding function is nearly identical, except we need to provide our own length for the destination buffer. Finally, we can demonstrate the usage as shown in the following listing.

Listing 2.10 Code for `main()`

```
fn main() {
    let hello_world = "Hello, world!".as_bytes();
    let hello_world_compressed = zlib_compress(&hello_world);
    let hello_world_uncompressed =
        zlib_uncompress(&hello_world_compressed, 100);
    assert_eq!(hello_world, hello_world_uncompressed);
    println!(
        "{}",
        String::from_utf8(hello_world_uncompressed)
            .expect("Invalid characters")
    );
}
```

The biggest challenge when dealing with FFI is the complexity of some C APIs and mapping the various types and functions. To work around this, you can use the rust `bindgen` tool, which is discussed in greater detail in chapter 4.

2.7 *Binary distribution*

Rust's binaries are composed of all Rust dependencies for a given platform included as a single binary—excluding the C runtime—in addition to any non-Rust libraries that may have been dynamically linked. You can build binaries that are statically linked to the C runtime, but, by default, this is optional. Thus, when distributing Rust binaries, you'll need to consider whether you want to statically link the C runtime or rely on the system's runtime.

The binaries themselves *are* platform dependent. They can be cross-compiled for different platforms, but you cannot mix different architectures or platforms with the same Rust binary. A binary compiled for Intel-based x64-64 CPUs will not run on ARM-based platforms, like AArch64 (also known as ARMv8) without some type of emulation. A binary compiled for macOS won't run on Linux.

Some OS vendors, notably Apple's macOS, provide emulation for other CPU platforms. It's possible to run x86-64 binaries automatically on ARM using Apple's Rosetta tool, which should happen automatically. For more detail on macOS binary distribution, consult Apple's developer documentation at http://mng.bz/ZRvP. In most cases, you'll want to stick with the defaults for the platform you're using, but there are some exceptions to this rule.

If you're coming from a language such as Go, you may have become accustomed to distributing precompiled binaries without worrying about the C runtime. Unlike Go, Rust requires a C runtime, and it uses dynamic linking by default.

2.7.1 *Cross compilation*

You can use Cargo to cross-compile binaries for different targets but only where compiler support is available for that target. For example, you can easily compile Linux binaries on Windows, but compiling Windows binaries on Linux is not as easy (but not impossible).

You can list the available targets on your host platform using `rustup`:

```
$ rustup target list
rustup target list
aarch64-apple-darwin
aarch64-apple-ios
aarch64-fuchsia
aarch64-linux-android
aarch64-pc-windows-msvc
..
```

You can install different targets with `rustup target add <target>` and then use `cargo build --target <target>` to build for a particular target. For example, on my Intel-based macOS machine, I can run the following to compile binaries for AArch64 (used by the M1 chip):

```
$ rustup target add aarch64-apple-darwin
info: downloading component 'rust-std' for 'aarch64-apple-darwin'
info: installing component 'rust-std' for 'aarch64-apple-darwin'
info: using up to 500.0 MiB of RAM to unpack components
 18.3 MiB /  18.3 MiB (100 %)  14.7 MiB/s in  1s ETA:  0s
$ cargo build --target aarch64-apple-darwin
...
    Finished dev [unoptimized + debuginfo] target(s) in 3.74s
```

However, if I try to run the binary, it will fail:

```
$ ./target/aarch64-apple-darwin/debug/simple-project
-bash: ./target/aarch64-apple-darwin/debug/simple-project: Bad CPU type in
executable
```

If I had access to an AArch64 macOS device, I could copy this binary to that machine and run it there successfully.

2.7.2 *Building statically linked binaries*

Normal Rust binaries include all the compiled dependencies, *except* the C runtime library. On Windows and macOS, it's normal to distribute precompiled binaries and link to the OS's C runtime libraries. On Linux, however, most packages are compiled from source by the distributions' maintainers, and the distributions take responsibility for managing the C runtime.

When distributing Rust binaries on Linux, you can use either glibc or musl, depending on your preference. Glibc is the default C library runtime on most Linux distributions. However, I recommend statically linking to musl when you want to distribute

Linux binaries for maximum portability. In fact, when trying to statically link on certain targets, Rust assumes you want to use musl.

> **NOTE** Musl behaves slightly differently from glibc in certain cases. These differences are documented on the musl wiki at http://mng.bz/Rm7K.

You can instruct `rustc` to use a static C runtime with the `target-feature` flag like this:

```
$ RUSTFLAGS="-C target-feature=+crt-static" cargo build
    Finished dev [unoptimized + debuginfo] target(s) in 0.01s
```

In this code, we're passing `-C target-feature=+crt-static` to `rustc` via the `RUSTFLAGS` environment variable, which is interpreted by Cargo and passed to `rustc`.

We use the following code to link statically to musl on x86-64 Linux:

```
$ rustup target add x86_64-unknown-linux-musl     ⊲—— Make sure musl target is installed.
...
$ RUSTFLAGS="-C target-feature=+crt-static" cargo build --target
x86_64-unknown-linux-musl     ⊲
...                                      Compile using musl target
                                         and force static C runtime.
```

To explicitly disable static linking, use `RUSTFLAGS="-C target-feature=-crt-static"` instead (by flipping the plus `[+]` to minus `[-]`). This may be desirable on targets that default to static linking—if unsure, use the default parameters.

Alternatively, you can specify `rustc` flags for Cargo with ~/.cargo/config:

```
[target.x86_64-pc-windows-msvc]
rustflags = ["-Ctarget-feature=+crt-static"]
```

The preceding code, when added to ~/.cargo/config, will instruct `rustc` to link statically when using the `x86_64-pc-windows-msvc` target.

2.8 Documenting Rust projects

Rust's tool for documenting code, which ships with Rust by default, is called `rustdoc`. If you've used code documentation tools from other projects (e.g., Javadoc, docstring, or RDoc), `rustdoc` will come naturally.

Using `rustdoc` is as simple as adding comments in your code and generating docs. Let's run through a quick example. Start by creating a library:

```
$ cargo new rustdoc-example --lib
    Created library `rustdoc-example` package
```

Now, let's edit src/lib.rs to add a function called `mult`, which takes two integers (a and b) and multiplies them. We'll also add a test:

```
pub fn mult(a: i32, b: i32) -> i32 {
    a * b
}
```

```
#[cfg(test)]
mod tests {
    use super::*;
    #[test]
    fn it_works() {
        assert_eq!(2 * 2, mult(2, 2));
    }
}
```

We haven't added any documentation yet. Before we do, let's generate some empty documentation using Cargo:

```
$ cargo doc
 Documenting rustdoc-example v0.1.0
 (/Users/brenden/dev/code-like-a-pro-in-rust/code/c2/2.8/rustdoc-example)
    Finished dev [unoptimized + debuginfo] target(s) in 0.89s
```

Now, you should see the generated HTML docs in target/. If you want to open the docs in a browser, you can open target/doc/src/rustdoc_example/lib.rs.html to view them. The result should look like figure 2.1. The default docs are empty, but you can see the public function `mult` listed in the docs.

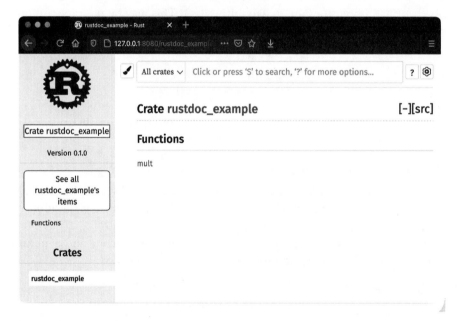

Figure 2.1   Screenshot of empty `rustdoc` HTML output

Next, let's add a compiler attribute and some docs to our project. Update src/lib.rs so that it looks like this:

This is a crate-level doc string, which appears
on the front page for the crate's docs.

```
//! # rustdoc-example
//!
//! A simple project demonstrating the use of rustdoc with the function
//! [`mult`].

#![warn(missing_docs)]          ◁—    This compiler attribute tells rustc to generate a warning when
                                      docs are missing for public functions, modules, or types.

/// Returns the product of `a` and `b`.   ◁—
pub fn mult(a: i32, b: i32) -> i32 {           This comment provides the
    a * b                                      documentation for the function mult.
}
```

TIP   Rust documentation is formatted using *CommonMark*, a subset of Markdown. A reference for CommonMark can be found at https://commonmark
.org/help.

If you rerun `cargo doc` with the newly created code documentation and open it in a
browser, you will see the output shown in figure 2.2. For crates published to crates.io,
there's a companion `rustdoc` site that automatically generates and hosts documentation for crates at https://docs.rs. For example, the docs for the `dryoc` crate are available at https://docs.rs/dryoc.

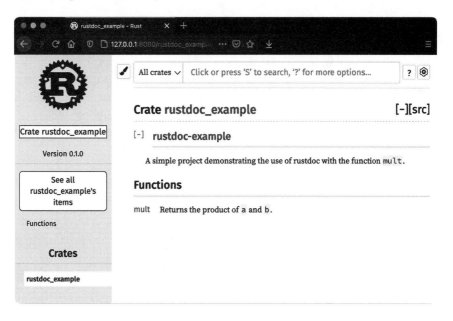

Figure 2.2   Screenshot of `rustdoc` HTML output with comments

In documented crates, you should update Cargo.toml to include the `documentation`
property, which links to the documentation for the project. This is helpful for those

who find their crate on sources like crates.io. For example, the `dryoc` crate has the following in Cargo.toml:

```
[package]
name = "dryoc"
documentation = "https://docs.rs/dryoc"
```

You don't have to do anything else to use docs.rs. The website automatically generates updated docs when new releases are published to crates.io. Table 2.4 serves as a reference for `rustdoc` syntax.

Table 2.4 **Quick reference for `rustdoc` usage**

Syntax	Type	Description
`//!`	Doc string	Crate- or module-level documentation, which belongs at the top of a crate or module. Uses CommonMark.
`///`	Doc string	Documents the module, function, trait, or type following the comment. Uses CommonMark.
`[func], [`func`], [Foo](Bar)`	Link	Links to a function, module, or other type in the docs. The keyword must be in scope for `rustdoc` to link correctly. Many options are available for linking; consult the `rustdoc` documentation for details.

2.8.1 *Code examples in documentation*

One handy feature of `rustdoc` is that code included as examples within documentation is compiled and executed as integration tests. Thus, you can include code samples with assertions, which are tested when you run `cargo test`. This helps you maintain high-quality documentation with working code samples.

One such example might look like this (appended to the crate-level docs in src/lib.rs from the previous example):

```
//! # Example
//!
//! -----
//! use rustdoc_example::mult;
//! assert_eq!(mult(10, 10), 100);
//! -----
```

Running the tests with the preceding example using `cargo test` yields the following:

```
cargo test
   Compiling rustdoc-example v0.1.0
   (/Users/brenden/dev/code-like-a-pro-in-rust/code/c2/2.8/rustdoc-example)
    Finished test [unoptimized + debuginfo] target(s) in 0.42s
     Running target/debug/deps/rustdoc_example-bec4912aee60500b

running 1 test
```

```
test tests::it_works ... ok

test result: ok. 1 passed; 0 failed; 0 ignored; 0 measured; 0 filtered out;
  finished in 0.00s

  Doc-tests rustdoc-example

running 1 test
test src/lib.rs - (line 7) ... ok

test result: ok. 1 passed; 0 failed; 0 ignored; 0 measured; 0 filtered out;
  finished in 0.23s
```

For more information about `rustdoc`, refer to the official documentation at https://doc.rust-lang.org/rustdoc. For more information about CommonMark, refer to CommonMark's help page at https://commonmark.org/help.

2.9   *Modules*

Rust *modules* provide a way to organize code hierarchically, into a set of distinct units, which can optionally be split into separate source files. Rust's modules combine two features into one: the inclusion of code from other source files and namespacing of publicly visible symbols. In Rust, all symbols are declared as private by default, but they can be exported (or made publicly visible) with the `pub` keyword. If we were to export too many symbols, we might eventually have a name collision. Thus, we can organize our code by modules to prevent namespace pollution.

A module declaration block uses the `mod` keyword, with an optional `pub` visibility specifier, and is followed immediately by a code block in braces:

```
mod private_mod {
  // ...             ◁──── Private code goes here.
}
pub mod public_mod {
  // ...            ◁──── Public code to be exported goes here.
}
```

The terms *module* and *mod* are sometimes used interchangeably when talking about Rust code. By convention, module names typically use snake case, whereas most other names use camel case (structs, enums, traits). Primitive types (`i32`, `str`, `u64`, etc.) are usually short, single words and sometimes snake case. Constants are typically upper-case, which is also the convention in most other languages. Following these patterns makes it easier to determine what's being imported just by glancing at `use` statements.

We can include a module with the same `mod` keyword, except, instead of a code block, it simply ends with a semicolon:

```
mod private_mod;
pub mod public_mod;
```

Modules can be deeply nested:

```
mod outer_mod {
  mod inner_mod {
    mod super_inner_mod {
      ...
    }
  }
}
```

> ## Visibility specifiers
>
> In Rust, everything is private by default with respect to visibility, except for public traits and public enums, where associated items are public by default. Privately scoped declarations are bound to a module, meaning they can be accessed from within the module (and submodules) they're declared in.
>
> Using the `pub` keyword changes the visibility to public, with an optional modifier: we can use `pub(modifier)` with `crate`, `self`, `super`, or `in path` with a path to another module. In other words, `pub(crate)` specifies an item is public within the crate but not accessible outside the crate.
>
> Items declared within a module aren't exported outside the scope of a crate unless the module itself is also public. For example, in the following code, we have two public functions, but in this case, only `public_mod_fn()` would be visible outside the crate:
>
> ```
> mod private_mod {
>   pub fn private_mod_fn() {}
> }
> pub mod public_mod {
>   pub fn public_mod_fn() {}
> }
> ```
>
> Additionally, a privately scoped item within a public module is still private and can't be accessed outside its crate.
>
> Rust's visibility is quite intuitive and also helps to prevent accidentally leaky abstractions. For more detail on Rust's visibility, refer to the language reference at http://mng.bz/2710.

When we include a symbol or module from another crate, we do so with the `use` statement like so:

```
use serde::ser::{Serialize, Serializer};
```
← **Includes the Serialize and Serializer symbols from the ser module within the serde crate**

When we include code with a `use` statement, the first name is usually the name of the crate we want to include code from followed by a module, specific symbols, or a wildcard (*) to include all symbols from that module.

Modules can be organized using the file system, too. We can create the same hierarchy as in the previous example using paths within our crate's source directory, but we still need to tell cargo which files to include in the crate. To do this, we use the mod *statement*, rather than a block. Consider a crate with the following structure:

```
$ tree .
.
├── Cargo.lock
├── Cargo.toml
└── src
    ├── lib.rs
    ├── outer_module
    │   └── inner_module
    │       ├── mod.rs
    │       └── super_inner_module.rs
    └── outer_module.rs

3 directories, 6 files
```

In this code, we have a crate with three nested inner modules, like in the earlier example. In our top-level lib.rs, we'll include the outer module, which is defined in outer_ module.rs:

```
mod outer_module;
```

The compiler will look for the mod declaration in either outer_module.rs or outer_ module/mod.rs. In our case, we supplied outer_module.rs at the same level as lib.rs. Within outer_module.rs, we have the following to include the inner module:

```
mod inner_module;
```

The compiler next looks for inner_module.rs or inner_module/mod.rs within the outer module. In this case, it finds inner_module/mod.rs, which contains the following:

```
mod super_inner_module;
```

This includes super_inner_module.rs within the inner_module directory. This seems quite a bit more complex than the example from earlier in this section, but for larger projects, it's much better to use modules than to include all the source code for a crate in either lib.rs or main.rs. If modules seem a bit confusing, try recreating similar structures from scratch to understand how the pieces fit together. You can start with the example included in this book's source code under c02/modules. We'll also explore module structures again in chapter 9.

2.10 Workspaces

Cargo's *workspace* feature allows you to break a large crate into multiple separate crates and group those crates together within a workspace that shares a single Cargo.lock lockfile. Workspaces have a few important features, which we'll discuss in this section, but their main feature is allowing you to share parameters from Cargo.toml and the resolved dependency tree from a single Cargo.lock. Each project within a workspace shares the following:

- A top-level Cargo.lock file
- The target/ output directory, containing project targets from all workspaces
- [patch], [replace], and [profile.*] sections from the top-level Cargo.toml

To use workspaces, you'll create projects with Cargo as you normally would, within subdirectories that don't overlap with the top-level crate's directories (i.e., they shouldn't be in src/, target/, tests/, examples/, benches/, etc.). You can then add these dependencies as you normally would, except that rather than specifying a version or repository, you simply specify a path or add each project to the workspace.members list in Cargo.toml.

Let's walk through an example project using workspaces. Start by creating a top-level application, and change into the newly created directory:

```
$ cargo new workspaces-example
     Created binary (application) `workspaces-example` package
$ cd workspaces-example
```

Now, create a subproject, which will be a simple library:

```
$ cargo new subproject --lib
```

The newly created directory structure should look like this:

```
$ tree
.
├── Cargo.toml
├── src
│   └── main.rs
└── subproject
    ├── Cargo.toml
    └── src
        └── lib.rs

3 directories, 4 files
```

Next, let's update the top-level Cargo.toml to include the subproject by adding it as a dependency (you still need to define dependencies within workspaces):

```
[dependencies]
subproject = { path = "./subproject" }
```

In the preceding example, we're adding the subproject by specifying it as a dependency and using the `path` property on it. To include the project in the workspace, we also need to add it to [workspace.members], which holds a list of paths or a glob pattern for the workspace members. For larger projects, using a glob may be easier than listing each path explicitly, provided you use a consistent path hierarchy. For this example, the workspace code in Cargo.toml would look like this:

```
[workspace]
members = ["subproject"]
```

You can now run `cargo check` to make sure everything compiles without any errors. Currently, our top-level project doesn't use the code from the subproject, so let's add a function that returns `"Hello, world!"` and call that from our application. First, update subproject/src/lib.rs to include our `hello_world` function:

```
pub fn hello_world() -> String {
    String::from("Hello, world!")
}
```

Now, update src/main.rs in the top-level application to call this function:

```
fn main() {
    println!("{}", subproject::hello_world());
}
```

Finally, we run our new code:

```
$ cargo run
   Compiling subproject v0.1.0
   (/Users/brenden/dev/code-like-a-pro-in-rust/code/c2/2.9/workspaces-examp
   le/subproject)
   Compiling workspaces-example v0.1.0 (/Users/brenden/dev/
   ➥ code-like-a-pro-in-rust/code/c2/2.9/workspaces-example)
    Finished dev [unoptimized + debuginfo] target(s) in 0.85s
     Running `target/debug/workspaces-example`
Hello, world!
```

You can repeat these steps with as many subprojects as desired by substituting a different name for each occurrence of `subproject` in the preceding code. The full code for this example can be found under c02/workspaces-example.

> **TIP** Cargo also supports *virtual* manifests, which are top-level crates that do not specify a [package] section in Cargo.toml and only contain subprojects. This is useful when you want to publish a collection of packages under one top-level crate.

Many crates use workspaces to break out projects. An additional feature of workspaces is that each subproject may be published as its own individual crate for others to use.

A couple of notable examples of projects that make use of the workspaces feature include the `rand` (https://crates.io/crates/rand) crate and the Rocket (https://rocket.rs/) crate—the latter of which uses a virtual manifest. For a complete reference on Cargo workspaces, see http://mng.bz/1JRj.

2.11 *Custom building scripts*

Cargo provides a build-time feature that allows one to specify build-time operations in a Rust script. The script contains a single rust `main` function plus any other code you'd like to include, including build dependencies, which are specified in a special [build-dependencies] section of Cargo.toml. The script communicates with Cargo by printing specially formatted commands to stdout, which Cargo will interpret and act upon.

> **NOTE** It's worth noting that although it's called a *script*, it's not a script in the sense of being interpreted code. That is to say, the code is still compiled by `rustc` and executed from a binary.

A few common uses for build scripts include the following:

- Compiling C or C++ code
- Running custom preprocessors on Rust code before compiling it
- Generating Rust protobuf code using `protoc-rust` (https://crates.io/crates/protoc-rust)
- Generating Rust code from templates
- Running platform checks, such as verifying the presence of and finding libraries

Cargo normally reruns the build script every time you run a build, but this can be modified using `cargo:rerun-if-changed`.

Let's walk through a simple `"Hello, world!"` example using a tiny C library. First, create a new Rust application and change into the directory:

```
$ cargo new build-script-example
$ cd build-script-example
```

Next, let's make a tiny C library with a function that returns the string `"Hello, world!"`. Create a file called src/hello_world.c:

```
const char *hello_world(void) {
    return "Hello, world!";
}
```

Now, update Cargo.toml to include the `cc` crate as a build dependency and the `libc` crate for C types:

```
[dependencies]
libc = "0.2"
[build-dependencies]
cc = "1.0"
```

Let's create the actual build script by creating the file build.rs at the top-level directory (*not* inside src/, where the other source files are):

```
fn main() {
    println!("cargo:rerun-if-changed=src/hello_world.c");
    cc::Build::new()
        .file("src/hello_world.c")
        .compile("hello_world");
}
```

Instructs Cargo to only rerun the build script when src/hello_world.c is modified

Compiles the C code into a library using the cc crate

Finally, let's update src/main.rs to call the C function from our tiny library:

```
use libc::c_char;
use std::ffi::CStr;

extern "C" {
    fn hello_world() -> *const c_char;
}

fn call_hello_world() -> &'static str {
    unsafe {
        CStr::from_ptr(hello_world())
            .to_str()
            .expect("String conversion failure")
    }
}

fn main() {
    println!("{}", call_hello_world());
}
```

Defines the external interface of the C library

A wrapper around the external library that extracts the static C string

Finally, compile and run the code:

```
$ cargo run
   Compiling cc v1.0.67
   Compiling libc v0.2.91
   Compiling build-script-example v0.1.0 (/Users/brenden/dev/
   code-like-a-pro-in-rust/code/c2/2.10/build-script-example)
    Finished dev [unoptimized + debuginfo] target(s) in 2.26s
     Running `target/debug/build-script-example`
Hello, world!
```

The full code for this example can be found under c02/build-script-example.

2.12   *Rust projects in embedded environments*

As a systems-level programming language, Rust is an excellent candidate for embedded programming. This is especially true in cases where memory allocation is explicit and safety is paramount. In this book, I won't explore embedded Rust in depth—that's a subject that warrants its own book entirely—but it's worth mentioning in case you're considering Rust for embedded projects.

Rust's static analysis tooling is especially powerful in embedded domains, where it can be more difficult to debug and verify code at run time. Compile-time guarantees can make it easy to verify resource states, pin selections, and safely run concurrent operations with shared state.

If you'd like to experiment with embedded Rust, there is excellent support for Cortex-M device emulation using the popular QEMU project (https://www.qemu.org). Sample code is available at https://github.com/rust-embedded/cortex-m-quickstart.

At the time of writing, embedded Rust resources for non-ARM architectures are limited, but one notable exception is the Arduino Uno platform. The `ruduino` crate (https://crates.io/crates/ruduino) provides reusable components specifically for Arduino Uno, which is an affordable, low-power, embedded platform that can be acquired for the cost of dinner for two. More information on the Arduino platform can be found at https://www.arduino.cc.

Rust's compiler (`rustc`) is based on the LLVM project (https://llvm.org); therefore, any platform for which LLVM has an appropriate backend is technically supported, although peripherals may not necessarily work. For example, there is early support for RISC-V, which is supported by LLVM, but hardware options for RISC-V are limited. To learn more about embedded Rust, *The Embedded Rust Book* is available online at https://docs.rust-embedded.org/book.

2.12.1 *Memory allocation*

For cases where dynamic memory allocation isn't necessary, you can use the `heapless` crate to provide data structures with fixed sizes and no dynamic allocation. If dynamic memory allocation is desired, it's relatively easy to create your own allocator by implementing the `GlobalAlloc` trait (http://mng.bz/PR7n). For some embedded platforms, such as the popular Cortex-M processors, there already exists a heap allocator implementation with the `alloc-cortex-m` crate.

Summary

- Cargo is the primary tool used for building, managing, and publishing Rust projects.
- In Rust, packages are known as *crates*, and crates can be published as libraries or applications to the https://crates.io registry.
- Cargo is used to install crates from crates.io.
- Cargo can be used to automate build, test, and publish steps of a continuous integration and deployment system.
- The `cargo doc` command will automatically generate documentation for a Rust project using `rustdoc`. Documentation can be formatted using the CommonMark format (a specification of Markdown).
- As with crates.io, https://docs.rs provides free documentation hosting automatically for open source crates published to crates.io.
- Rust can generate binaries for distribution that include all dependencies, *excluding* the C library. On Linux systems, you should statically link to musl rather than using the system's C library for maximum portability when distributing precompiled binaries.
- Crates can be organized into modules and workspaces, which provides a way to separate code into its parts.

Rust tooling 3

This chapter covers

- Introducing core Rust language tools: rust-analyzer, rustfmt, Clippy, and sccache
- Integrating Rust tools with Visual Studio Code
- Using stable versus nightly toolchains
- Exploring additional tools you may find useful

Mastery of any language depends on mastering its tooling. In this chapter, we'll explore some of the critical tools you need to be effective with Rust.

Rust offers several tools to improve productivity and reduce the amount of busy work required to produce high-quality software. Rust's compiler, `rustc`, is built upon *LLVM*, so Rust inherits the rich tools included with LLVM, such as LLVM's debugger, *LLDB*. In addition to the tools you would expect to find from other languages, Rust includes a number of its own Rust-specific tools, which are discussed in this chapter.

The main tools discussed in this chapter are rust-analyzer, rustfmt, Clippy, and sccache. These are tools you'll likely use every time you work with Rust. Additionally, I have included instructions for a few other tools, which you may find yourself using occasionally: `cargo-update`, `cargo-expand`, `cargo-fuzz`, `cargo-watch`, and `cargo-tree`.

3.1 Overview of Rust tooling

In chapter 2, we focused on working with Cargo, which is Rust's project management tool. Additionally, there are several tools you may want to use when working with Rust. Unlike Cargo, these tools are optional and can be used at your own discretion. However, I find them to be extremely valuable, and I use them on nearly all of my Rust projects. Projects may require some of these tools, so it's worthwhile to familiarize yourself with them.

The tools discussed in this chapter are normally used via a text editor, or as command-line tools. In table 3.1, I've listed a summary of the core Rust language tools, and in table 3.2, I've summarized a few popular editors and their support for Rust.

Table 3.1 Summary of Rust's core language tools

Name	Description
Cargo	Rust's project management tool for compiling, testing, and managing dependencies (covered in chapter 2)
Rust-analyzer	Provides Rust support for text editors that implement the language server protocol
Rustfmt	Rust's opinionated code style tool, which provides automatic code formatting and checking and can be integrated into CI/CD systems
Clippy	Rust's code quality tool, which provides a plethora of code quality checks (called *lints*) and can be integrated into CI/CD systems
Sccache	General-purpose compiler cache tool to improve compilation speed for large projects

Table 3.2 Summary of Rust editors

Editor	Extension	Summary	References
Emacs	Rust-analyzer	Rust support via LSP	http://mng.bz/Jd7V
Emacs	Rust-mode	Native Emacs extensions for Rust	https://github.com/rust-lang/rust-mode
IntelliJ IDEA	IntelliJ Rust	JetBrains-native integration for Rust	https://www.jetbrains.com/rust/
Sublime	Rust-analyzer	Rust support via LSP	https://github.com/sublimelsp/LSP-rust-analyzer
Sublime	Rust enhanced	Native Sublime package for Rust	https://github.com/rust-lang/rust-enhanced
Vim	Rust-analyzer	Rust support via LSP	https://rust-analyzer.github.io/manual.html#vimneovim
Vim	Rust.vim	Native Vim configuration for Rust	https://github.com/rust-lang/rust.vim
VS Code	Rust-analyzer	Rust support via LSP	https://rust-analyzer.github.io/manual.html#vs-code

3.2 *Using rust-analyzer for Rust IDE integration*

The rust-analyzer tool is the most mature and full-featured editor for the Rust language. It can be integrated with any editor that implements the Language Server Protocol (LSP, https://microsoft.github.io/language-server-protocol). The following are some of the features provided by rust-analyzer:

- Code completions
- Import insertion
- Jumping to definitions
- Renaming symbols
- Documentation generation
- Refactorings
- Magic completions
- Inline compiler errors
- Inlay hints for types and parameters
- Semantic syntax highlighting
- Displaying inline reference documentation

With VS (Visual Studio) Code, rust-analyzer can be installed using the CLI (see figure 3.1):

```
$ code --install-extension rust-lang.rust-analyzer
```

Once installed, VS Code will look as shown in figure 3.1 when working with Rust code. Note the Run | Debug buttons at the top of `fn main()`, which allow you to run or debug code with one click.

If you use IntelliJ Rust, there is no need to install a separate extension for Rust support. However, it's worth noting that IntelliJ Rust shares some code with rust-analyzer, specifically for its macro support (http://mng.bz/wjAP).

Figure 3.1   VS Code with rust-analyzer showing inferred type annotations

3.2.1   *Magic completions*

Rust-analyzer has a postfix text completion feature that provides quick completions for common tasks, such as debug printing or string formatting. Becoming familiar with *magic completions* can save you a lot of repetitive typing. Additionally, you only need to remember the completion expressions rather than memorizing syntax. I recommend practicing magic completions, as you'll find yourself using them frequently once you get the hang of the syntax.

Magic completions are similar to *snippets* (a feature of VS Code and other editors) but with a few Rust-specific features that make them a bit like "snippets++." Magic completions also work in any editor that supports the language server protocol, not just VS Code.

Using magic completions is as simple as typing an expression and using the editor's completion dropdown menu. For example, to create a test module in the current source file, you can type `tmod` and select the first completion result, which will create a test module template like so:

```
tmod ->
#[cfg(test)]
mod tests {
    use super::*;

    #[test]
    fn test_name() {

    }
}
```

The `tmod` completion creates a test module with a single test function, which can be filled out accordingly. In addition to `tmod`, there's a `tfn` completion, which creates a test function.

Another useful magic completion is for string printing. Rust versions prior to 1.58.0 did not support string interpolation. To help with the lack of string interpolation, rust-analyzer provides several completions for printing, logging, and formatting strings.

> **NOTE** While string interpolation was added in Rust 1.58.0, this section has been left in the book because it provides a good demonstration of the features of rust-analyzer.

Type the following into your editor:

```
let bananas = 5.0;
let apes = 2.0;

"bananas={bananas} apes={apes} bananas_per_ape={bananas / apes}"
```

At this point, placing the cursor at the end of the string quote and typing `.print` will convert the string to the `println` completion option, as shown in figure 3.2.

If you select the `println` option by pressing the Enter key once, the option is selected from the drop-down menu that appears, and then rust-analyzer converts the code into the following:

```
let bananas = 5.0;
let apes = 2.0;

println!(
    "bananas={} apes={} bananas_per_ape={}",
    bananas,
    apes,
    bananas / apes
)
```

Table 3.3 contains several important magic completions to take note of. The list is not exhaustive, and the full list of magic completions and other features of rust-analyzer is available in the manual at https://rust-analyzer.github.io/manual.html.

Figure 3.2   VS Code with rust-analyzer showing `println` magic completion

Table 3.3   Magic completions to remember

Expression	Result	Description
`"str {arg}".format`	`format!("str {}", arg)`	Formats a string with arguments
`"str {arg}".println`	`println!("str {}", arg)`	Prints a string with arguments
`"".log`*L*	`log::`*level*`!("str {}", arg)` where *level* is one of `debug`, `trace`, `info`, `warn`, or `error`	Logs a string with arguments at the specified level
`pd`	`eprintln!("arg = {:?}", arg)`	Debugs print (prints to `stderr`) snippet
`ppd`	`eprintln!("arg = {:#?}", arg)`	Debugs pretty-print (prints to `stderr`) snippet
`expr.ref`	`&expr`	Borrows `expr`
`expr.refm`	`&mut expr`	Mutably borrows `expr`
`expr.if`	`if expr {}`	Converts an expression to an if statement, which is especially useful with `Option` and `Result`

3.3 *Using rustfmt to keep code tidy*

Source code formatting can be a source of frustration, especially in a Rust project with multiple developers. For single-contributor projects, it's not such a big deal, but once you have more than one contributor, there can be a divergence in coding style. *Rustfmt* is Rust's answer to coding style, providing an idiomatic, automatic, and opinionated styling tool. It's similar in nature to gofmt if you're coming from Golang or an equivalent formatting tool of other languages. The idea of opinionated formatting is relatively new, and—in my humble opinion—it is a wonderful addition to modern programming languages.

Example output from running `cargo fmt---check -v` is shown in figure 3.3, which enables verbose mode and check mode. Passing `--check` will cause the command to return nonzero if the formatting is not as expected, which is useful for checking the code format on continuous integration systems.

```
●  ●  ●    ⌥⌘2                     brenden@MacBook-Pro:~/dev/dryoc
→ dryoc git:(main) cargo fmt -- --check -v
Using rustfmt config file /Users/brenden/dev/dryoc/.rustfmt.toml for /Users/brenden/dev/dryoc/src/lib.rs
Formatting /Users/brenden/dev/dryoc/src/argon2.rs
Formatting /Users/brenden/dev/dryoc/src/auth.rs
Formatting /Users/brenden/dev/dryoc/src/blake2b/blake2b_simd.rs
Formatting /Users/brenden/dev/dryoc/src/blake2b/blake2b_soft.rs
Formatting /Users/brenden/dev/dryoc/src/blake2b/mod.rs
Formatting /Users/brenden/dev/dryoc/src/bytes_serde.rs
Formatting /Users/brenden/dev/dryoc/src/classic/crypto_auth.rs
Formatting /Users/brenden/dev/dryoc/src/classic/crypto_box.rs
Formatting /Users/brenden/dev/dryoc/src/classic/crypto_box_impl.rs
Formatting /Users/brenden/dev/dryoc/src/classic/crypto_core.rs
Formatting /Users/brenden/dev/dryoc/src/classic/crypto_generichash.rs
Formatting /Users/brenden/dev/dryoc/src/classic/crypto_hash.rs
Formatting /Users/brenden/dev/dryoc/src/classic/crypto_kdf.rs
Formatting /Users/brenden/dev/dryoc/src/classic/crypto_kx.rs
Formatting /Users/brenden/dev/dryoc/src/classic/crypto_onetimeauth.rs
Formatting /Users/brenden/dev/dryoc/src/classic/crypto_pwhash.rs
Formatting /Users/brenden/dev/dryoc/src/classic/crypto_secretbox.rs
Formatting /Users/brenden/dev/dryoc/src/classic/crypto_secretbox_impl.rs
Formatting /Users/brenden/dev/dryoc/src/classic/crypto_secretstream_xchacha20poly1305.rs
Formatting /Users/brenden/dev/dryoc/src/classic/crypto_shorthash.rs
Formatting /Users/brenden/dev/dryoc/src/classic/crypto_sign.rs
Formatting /Users/brenden/dev/dryoc/src/classic/crypto_sign_ed25519.rs
Formatting /Users/brenden/dev/dryoc/src/classic/generichash_blake2b.rs
Formatting /Users/brenden/dev/dryoc/src/constants.rs
Formatting /Users/brenden/dev/dryoc/src/dryocbox.rs
Formatting /Users/brenden/dev/dryoc/src/dryocsecretbox.rs
Formatting /Users/brenden/dev/dryoc/src/dryocstream.rs
Formatting /Users/brenden/dev/dryoc/src/error.rs
Formatting /Users/brenden/dev/dryoc/src/generichash.rs
Formatting /Users/brenden/dev/dryoc/src/kdf.rs
Formatting /Users/brenden/dev/dryoc/src/keypair.rs
Formatting /Users/brenden/dev/dryoc/src/kx.rs
Formatting /Users/brenden/dev/dryoc/src/lib.rs
Formatting /Users/brenden/dev/dryoc/src/onetimeauth.rs
Formatting /Users/brenden/dev/dryoc/src/poly1305/mod.rs
Formatting /Users/brenden/dev/dryoc/src/poly1305/poly1305_soft.rs
Formatting /Users/brenden/dev/dryoc/src/protected.rs
Formatting /Users/brenden/dev/dryoc/src/pwhash.rs
Formatting /Users/brenden/dev/dryoc/src/rng.rs
Formatting /Users/brenden/dev/dryoc/src/scalarmult_curve25519.rs
Formatting /Users/brenden/dev/dryoc/src/sha512.rs
Formatting /Users/brenden/dev/dryoc/src/sign.rs
Formatting /Users/brenden/dev/dryoc/src/siphash24.rs
Formatting /Users/brenden/dev/dryoc/src/types.rs
Formatting /Users/brenden/dev/dryoc/src/utils.rs
Spent 0.018 secs in the parsing phase, and 0.098 secs in the formatting phase
Using rustfmt config file /Users/brenden/dev/dryoc/.rustfmt.toml for /Users/brenden/dev/dryoc/tests/integration_tests.rs
Formatting /Users/brenden/dev/dryoc/tests/integration_tests.rs
Spent 0.001 secs in the parsing phase, and 0.008 secs in the formatting phase
→ dryoc git:(main) ▮
```

Figure 3.3 Rustfmt in action on the `dryoc` **crate**

I can't count the number of hours of my life I've lost debating code formatting on pull requests. This problem can be solved instantly by using rustfmt and simply mandating code contributions follow the defined style. Rather than publishing and maintaining lengthy style guideline documents, you can use rustfmt and save everyone a lot of time.

3.3.1 *Installing rustfmt*

Rustfmt is installed as a `rustup` component:

```
$ rustup component add rustfmt
...
```

Once installed, it can be used by running Cargo:

```
$ cargo fmt
# Rustfmt will now have formatted your code in-place
```

3.3.2 *Configuring rustfmt*

While the default rustfmt configuration is adequate for most people, you may want to tweak settings slightly to suit your preferences. This can be done by adding a .rustfmt .toml configuration file to your project's source tree.

Listing 3.1 Example .rustfmt.toml configuration

```
format_code_in_doc_comments = true
group_imports = "StdExternalCrate"
imports_granularity = "Module"
unstable_features = true
version = "Two"
wrap_comments = true
```

I've listed a few rustfmt options in table 3.4, which illustrates some of the configurations permitted.

Table 3.4 Partial listing of rustfmt options

Setting	Default	Recommendation	Description
`imports_granularity`	`Preserve`	`Module`	Defines granularity of import statements
`group_imports`	`Preserve`	`StdExternalGroup`	Defines the ordering of import grouping
`unstable_features`	`false`	`true`	Enables nightly-only features (unavailable on the stable channel)
`wrap_comments`	`false`	`true`	Automatically word wraps comments in addition to code

Table 3.4 Partial listing of rustfmt options *(continued)*

Setting	Default	Recommendation	Description
`format_code_in_doc_comments`	`false`	`true`	Applies rustfmt to source code samples in documentation
`version`	One	Two	Selects the rustfmt version to use. Some rustfmt features are only available in version 2.

At the time of writing, some notable rustfmt options are nightly-only features. An up-to-date listing of the available style options can be found on the rustfmt website at https://rust-lang.github.io/rustfmt/.

> **TIP** If you're coming from the C or C++ world and want to apply the same opinionated formatting pattern there, be sure to check out the `clang-format` tool as part of LLVM.

3.4 *Using Clippy to improve code quality*

Clippy is Rust's code quality tool, which provides more than 450 checks at the time of writing. If you've ever been frustrated by a colleague who likes to chime in on your code reviews and point out minor syntax, formatting, and other stylistic improvements, then Clippy is for you. Clippy can do the same job as your colleague but without any snark, and it will even give you the code change, in many cases.

Clippy can often find real problems in your code. However, the real benefit of Clippy is that it obviates the need for arguing over code style problems because it enforces idiomatic style and patterns for Rust. Clippy is related to, but a little more advanced than, rustfmt, which is discussed in the previous section.

3.4.1 *Installing Clippy*

Clippy is distributed as a `rustup` component; thus, it's installed as follows:

```
$ rustup component add clippy
...
```

Once installed, you can run Clippy on any Rust project using Cargo:

```
$ cargo clippy
...
```

When run, Clippy will produce output that looks similar to the `rustc` compiler output, as shown in figure 3.4.

```
● ● ●    ⌥⌘2                        brenden@MacBook-Pro:~/dev/dryoc
→ dryoc git:(main) ✗ cargo clippy
warning: unreachable statement
   ──→ src/auth.rs:128:9
       |
127 |           loop {}
       |           ------- any code following this expression is unreachable
128 |           let mut output = Output::new_byte_array();
       |           ^^^^^^^^^^^^^^^^^^^^^^^^^^^^^^^^^^^^^^^^^^ unreachable statement
       |
    = note: `#[warn(unreachable_code)]` on by default

warning: unused variable: `key`
   ──→ src/auth.rs:124:9
       |
124 |           key: Key,
       |           ^^^ help: if this is intentional, prefix it with an underscore: `_key`
       |
    = note: `#[warn(unused_variables)]` on by default

warning: unused variable: `input`
   ──→ src/auth.rs:125:9
       |
125 |           input: &Input,
       |           ^^^^^ help: if this is intentional, prefix it with an underscore: `_input`

warning: empty `loop {}` wastes CPU cycles
   ──→ src/auth.rs:127:9
       |
127 |           loop {}
       |           ^^^^^^^
       |
    = help: you should either use `panic!()` or add `std::thread::sleep(..);` to the loop body
    = help: for further information visit https://rust-lang.github.io/rust-clippy/master/index.html#empty_loop
    = note: `#[warn(clippy::empty_loop)]` on by default
warning: `dryoc` (lib) generated 4 warnings
    Finished dev [unoptimized + debuginfo] target(s) in 0.02s
→ dryoc git:(main) ✗ ▊
```

Figure 3.4   Clippy in action on the `dryoc` crate, with an intentional error added

3.4.2   Clippy's lints

With more than 450 code quality checks (known as *lints*), one could write an entire book about Clippy. Lints are categorized by their severity level (allow, warn, deny, and deprecated) and grouped according to their type, which can be one of the following: correctness, restriction, style, deprecated, pedantic, complexity, perf, cargo, and nursery.

One such lint is the `blacklisted_name` lint, which disallows the use of variable names such as `foo`, `bar`, or `quux`. The lint can be configured to include a custom list of variable names you wish to disallow.

Another example of a lint is the `bool_comparison` lint, which checks for unnecessary comparisons between expressions and Booleans. For example, the following code is considered invalid:

```
if function_returning_boolean() == true {}      ◁──── Clippy will complain here.
```

On the other hand, the following code is valid:

```
if function_returning_boolean() {}              ◁──── The == true is not necessary.
```

Most of Clippy's lints are style related, but it can also help find performance bugs. For example, the `redundant_clone` lint can find situations where a variable is unnecessarily cloned. Typically, this case looks something like this:

```
let my_string = String::new("my string");
println!("my_string='{}'", my_string.clone());
```

In the preceding code, the call to `clone()` is entirely unnecessary. If you run Clippy with this code, you'll get the following warning:

```
$ cargo clippy
warning: redundant clone
  --> src/main.rs:3:37
   |
3  |  println!("my_string='{}'", my_string.clone());
   |                                       ^^^^^^^^ help: remove this
   |
   = note: `#[warn(clippy::redundant_clone)]` on by default
note: this value is dropped without further use
  --> src/main.rs:3:28
   |
3  |  println!("my_string='{}'", my_string.clone());
   |                             ^^^^^^^^^
   = help: for further information visit
   https://rust-lang.github.io/rust-clippy/master/index.html#redundant_clone

warning: 1 warning emitted
```

Clippy is frequently updated, and an up-to-date list of the lints for stable Rust can be found in the Clippy documentation at http://mng.bz/qjAr.

3.4.3 Configuring Clippy

Clippy can be configured either by adding a .clippy.toml file to the project source tree or placing attributes within your Rust source files. In most cases, you'll want to use attributes to disable Clippy lints on an as-needed basis. There are many cases in which Clippy may generate a warning but the code is as intended.

Notably, some complexity warnings from Clippy may need to be tweaked or disabled when there's no better alternative. For example, the `too_many_arguments` warning will trigger when you have a function with more than the default limit of seven arguments. You could increase the default value or simply disable it for the specific function:

```
#[allow(clippy::too_many_arguments)]
fn function(
  a: i32, b: i32, c: i32, d: i32, e: i32, f: i32, g: i32, h: i32
) {
  // ...              ⟵——— Your code goes here.
}
```

The `allow()` attribute in the preceding code is specific to Clippy and instructs it to allow an exception for the `too_many_arguments` lint on the next line of code.

Alternatively, to change the argument threshold for the entire project, you could add the following into your .clippy.toml:

```
too-many-arguments-threshold = 10
```
◁—————— Sets the argument threshold
to 10, up from the default of 7

The .clippy.toml file is a normal TOML file, which should contain a list of `name = value` pairs, according to your preferences. Each lint and its corresponding configuration parameters are described in detail in the Clippy documentation at https://rust-lang .github.io/rust-clippy/stable/index.html.

3.4.4   *Automatically applying Clippy's suggestions*

Clippy can, in some cases, automatically fix code. In particular, when Clippy is able to provide a precise suggestion for you to fix the code, it can generally apply the fix automatically as well. To fix the code automatically, run Clippy with the `--fix` flag:

```
$ cargo clippy --fix -Z unstable-options
...
```

Note that we pass the `-Z unstable-options` option as well because at the time of writing, the `--fix` feature is nightly only.

3.4.5   *Using Clippy in CI/CD*

I recommend enabling Clippy as part of your CI/CD system, provided you have one. You would typically run Clippy as a step after build, test, and format. Additionally, you may want to instruct Clippy to fail on warnings, run for all features, as well as check tests:

```
$ cargo clippy
...
$ cargo clippy -- -D warnings
...
$ cargo clippy --all-targets --all-features -- -D warnings
...
```

This command runs Clippy
with the default settings.

This command runs Clippy, but
instructs it to fail on warnings
(rather than allowing warnings).

This command runs Clippy, fails on warnings, enables all crate
features, and also checks tests (by default, Clippy ignores tests).

If you maintain an open source project, enabling Clippy as part of the CI/CD checks will make it easier for others to contribute high-quality code to your project, and it also makes it easier to confidently maintain the code and accept code changes.

Listing 3.2   Brief example using Clippy with GitHub Actions

```
on: [push]

name: CI
```

```
jobs:
  clippy:
    name: Rust project
    runs-on: ubuntu-latest
    steps:
      - uses: actions/checkout@v2
      - name: Install Rust toolchain with Clippy
        uses: actions-rs/toolchain@v1
        with:
          toolchain: stable
          components: clippy
      - name: Run Clippy
        uses: actions-rs/cargo@v1
        with:
          command: clippy
          args: --all-targets --all-features -- -D warnings
```

Chapter 2 contains a full example of using Clippy and rustfmt together with GitHub's Actions CI/CD system.

3.5   Reducing compile times with sccache

The *sccache* tool is a general-purpose compiler cache that can be used with Rust projects. Rust compile times can grow significantly for large projects, and sccache helps reduce compile times by caching unchanged objects produced by the compiler. The sccache project was created by the nonprofit organization Mozilla specifically to help with Rust compilation, but it's generic enough to be used with most compilers. It was inspired by the ccache tool, which you may have encountered from the C or C++ world.

Even if your project is not large, installing sccache and using it locally can save you a lot of time recompiling code. To illustrate, compiling the `dryoc` crate from a clean project takes 8.891 seconds on my computer, normally. On the other hand, compiling from a clean project with sccache enabled takes 5.839 seconds. That's 52% more time to compile a relatively small project without sccache versus with it! That time accumulates and can become significant for larger projects.

Note that sccache only helps in cases in which code has been previously compiled. It will not speed up fresh builds.

3.5.1   Installing sccache

Sccache is written in Rust and can be installed using Cargo:

```
$ cargo install sccache
```

Once installed, sccache is enabled by using it as a `rustc` wrapper with Cargo. Cargo accepts the `RUSTC_WRAPPER` argument as an environment variable. You can compile and build any Rust project using sccache by exporting the wrapper environment variable as follows:

```
$ export RUSTC_WRAPPER=`which sccache`
$ cargo build
...
```

The which sccache command
returns the path of sccache,
assuming it's available in $PATH.

3.5.2 *Configuring sccache*

If you've previously used ccache, then sccache will be familiar to you. Sccache has some noteworthy features that ccache lacks: it can be used directly with a number of networked storage backends, which makes it ideally suited for use with CI/CD systems. It supports the vendor-neutral S3 protocol, a couple of vendor storage services, as well as the open source Redis and Memcached protocols.

To configure sccache, you can specify environment variables, but it can also be configured through platform-dependent configuration files. By default, sccache uses up to 10 GiB of local storage. To configure sccache to use the Redis backend, you can set the address for Redis as an environment variable:

```
$ export SCCACHE_REDIS=redis://10.10.10.10/sccache
```

Assuming a Redis instance running
on the default port at 10.10.10.10,
with a database named sccache.

For details on sccache configuration and usage, consult the official project documentation at https://github.com/mozilla/sccache.

3.6 *Integration with IDEs, including Visual Studio Code*

This is a topic I won't cover in detail, but it's worth mentioning some features for working with Rust in text editors. These days, I prefer to use VS Code, but it is possible to use tools like rust-analyzer, Clippy, rustfmt, and more with any editor.

For rust-analyzer, there are installation instructions provided in the rust-analyzer manual to integrate with Vim, Sublime, Eclipse, Emacs, and others. Rust-analyzer *should* work with any editor that supports the Language Server API, which includes many popular editors in addition to those mentioned here.

In the case of VS Code, using rust-analyzer is as simple as installing the extension. From the command line, you need to first make sure you have the `rust-src` component installed, which you can do with `rustup`:

```
$ rustup component add rust-src
```

Next, install the VS Code extension from the command line:

```
$ code --install-extension matklad.rust-analyzer
```

Using the extension in VS Code is as simple as opening any Rust project in VS Code. It will automatically recognize the Cargo.toml file in your project directory and load the project.

> **TIP** You can open VS Code directly from any project directory using the command line by running `code .`, where . is shorthand for the current working directory.

3.7 Using toolchains: Stable vs. nightly

You may start out using Rust on the stable toolchain and slowly find yourself discovering features you want to use but cannot because they aren't available in the stable channel. Those features, however, *are* available in the nightly channel. This is a common problem in Rust and something many have balked at. In fact, a number of popular crates are *nightly-only* crates. That is, they can only be used with the nightly channel.

There are, in a sense, two Rusts: stable Rust and nightly Rust. This may sound confusing or cumbersome, but in practice, it's not so bad. In most cases, you should be fine using stable, but in some cases, you'll want to use nightly. If you're publishing public crates, you may find that you have certain features behind a `nightly` feature flag, which is a common pattern.

You may eventually find yourself asking this: Why not just use nightly exclusively to get all the benefits of Rust? Practically speaking, this isn't such a bad idea. The only caveat is the case where you want to publish crates for others to use, and your potential customers are only able to use stable Rust. In that case, it makes sense to try and maintain stable support, with nightly features behind a feature flag.

3.7.1 Nightly-only features

You may need to use nightly-only features, and to do so, you must tell `rustc` which features you want to use. For example, to enable the `allocator_api`, a feature available only in nightly Rust at the time of writing, you need to enable the `allocator_api`.

> **Listing 3.3 Code for lib.rs from `dryoc`**

any() returns true if any of the predicates are true, and all() returns true if all predicates are true. The doc attribute is set automatically whenever the code is being analyzed with rustdoc.

```
#![cfg_attr(
    any(feature = "nightly", all(feature = "nightly", doc)),
    feature(allocator_api, doc_cfg)
)]
```

If the predicate evaluates to true, the allocator_api and doc_cfg features are enabled.

In the preceding code listing, I've enabled two nightly-only features: `allocator_api` and `doc_cfg`. One feature provides custom memory allocation in Rust, and the other enables the `doc` compiler attribute, which allows one to configure `rustdoc` from within the code.

> **TIP** Rust's built-in attributes are documented at https://doc.rust-lang.org/reference/attributes.html. The `any()` and `all()` predicates are specific to `cfg` and `cfg_attr`, which are the conditional compilation attributes. These are documented at http://mng.bz/7vRv.

Also note that in listing 3.3, we're using a feature flag, which means we need to build this crate with the `nightly` feature enabled. At the moment, there isn't a way to detect which channel your code is being compiled with, so we have to specify feature flags instead.

3.7.2 *Using nightly on published crates*

In the `dryoc` crate, I use this pattern to provide a protected memory feature. *Protected memory*, in the case of the `dryoc` crate, is a feature whereby data structures that use a custom allocator (which is a nightly-only API in Rust, at the time of writing) to implement memory locking and protection. The feature gating within the crate is shown in the following listing.

Listing 3.4 Code from src/lib.rs

```
#[cfg(any(feature = "nightly", all(doc, not(doctest))))]
#[cfg_attr(all(feature = "nightly", doc), doc(cfg(feature = "nightly")))]
#[macro_use]
pub mod protected;
```

There are a few things going on in this code, which I'll explain. First, you'll notice the `doc` and `doctest` keywords. Those are included because I want to make sure the `protected` module is included when building the documentation but *not* when running the doctests if `feature = "nightly"` isn't enabled (i.e., testing the code samples within the crate documentation). The first line translates to the following: enable the next block of code (which is `pub mod protected`) only if `feature = "nightly"` is enabled or `doc` is enabled and we're *not* running the doctests. `doc` and `doctests` are special attributes that are enabled only while running either `cargo doc` or `cargo test`.

  The second line enables a `rustdoc`-specific attribute that tells `rustdoc` to mark all the content within the module as `feature = "nightly"`. In other words, if you look at the docs for the `dryoc` crate at http://mng.bz/mjAa, you will see a note that says the following:

> *Available on* **crate feature** `nightly` *only*.

For details about the allocator API feature in Rust, refer to the GitHub tracking issue at https://github.com/rust-lang/rust/issues/32838. For details about the `doc` attribute feature, refer to the GitHub tracking issue at https://github.com/rust-lang/rust/issues/43781.

3.8 *Additional tools: cargo-update, cargo-expand, cargo-fuzz, cargo-watch, cargo-tree*

There are a few more Cargo tools worth mentioning, which I will summarize in the following subsections. Each of them is supplemental to the tools already discussed, and they may be mentioned elsewhere in the book.

3.8.1   Keeping packages up to date date with cargo-update

Packages installed with Cargo may need to be updated occasionally, and `cargo-update` provides a way to keep them up to date. This is different from project dependencies, which are updated with the `cargo update` command. The `cargo-update` crate is for managing Cargo's own dependencies, separately from a project.

Run the following to install `cargo-update`:

```
$ cargo install cargo-update
```

Do the following using cargo-update:

```
$ cargo help install-update          ◁─── Prints help
...
$ cargo install-update -a            ◁─── Updates all installed packages.
...
```

3.8.2   Debugging macros with cargo-expand

At some point, you may encounter macros you need to debug in other crates, or you may need to implement your own macro. `rustc` provides a way to generate the resulting source code with the macro applied, and `cargo-expand` is a wrapper around that feature.

Run the following to install cargo-expand:

```
$ cargo install cargo-expand
```

Using `cargo-expand`, from a project you're working on, do the following:

```
$ cargo help expand          ◁─── Prints help.
...
$ cargo expand outermod::innermod          ◁─┐ Shows the expanded form
...                                           │ of "outermod::innermod"
```

For a simple `"Hello, world!"` Rust project, the output of `cargo expand` would look like this:

```
#![feature(prelude_import)]
#[prelude_import]
use std::prelude::rust_2018::*;
#[macro_use]
extern crate std;
fn main() {
    {
        ::std::io::_print(::core::fmt::Arguments::new_v1(
            &["Hello, world!\n"],
            &match () {
                () => [],
            },
        ));
    };
}
```

You can run `cargo-expand` for an entire project or filter by item name, as shown in the preceding example. It's worth experimenting with `cargo-expand` to see how other code looks once its macros are expanded. For any moderately large project, the expanded code can become very large, so I recommend filtering by specific functions or modules. I have found `cargo-expand` especially useful when using libraries with macros, as it helps me understand what's happening in other people's code.

3.8.3 *Testing libFuzzer*

Fuzz testing is one strategy for finding unexpected bugs, and `cargo-fuzz` provides fuzzing support based on LLVM's *libFuzzer* (https://llvm.org/docs/LibFuzzer.html). Do the following to install `cargo-fuzz`:

```
$ cargo install cargo-fuzz
```

Using `cargo-fuzz` from a project you're working on, run the following:

```
$ cargo help fuzz        ⟵─── Prints help.
 ...
```

Using `cargo-fuzz` requires creating tests using the libFuzzer API. This can be accomplished with the `cargo-fuzz` tool by running the `cargo fuzz add` command, followed by the name of the test. For example, run the following to create a boilerplate test (with `cargo-fuzz`):

```
$ cargo fuzz new myfuzztest       ⟵─── Creates a new fuzz test called myfuzztest
 $ cargo fuzz run myfuzztest      ⟵─── Runs the newly created test, which may take a long time
```

The resulting test (created by `cargo-fuzz` in fuzz/fuzz_targets/myfuzztest.rs) looks like so:

```
#![no_main]
use libfuzzer_sys::fuzz_target;

fuzz_target!(|data: &[u8]| {
    // ...              ⟵─── Fuzzed code goes here.
});
```

Fuzz testing is covered in greater detail in chapter 7. If you're already familiar with lib-Fuzzer or fuzz testing in general, you should have no trouble getting up to speed on your own with cargo-fuzz.

3.8.4 *Iterating with cargo-watch*

`Cargo-watch` is a tool that continuously watches your project's source tree for changes and executes a command when the there's a change. Common use cases for `cargo-watch` are automatically running tests, generating documentation with `rustdoc`, or simply recompiling your project.

To install `cargo-watch`, run the following:

```
$ cargo install cargo-watch
```

Using `cargo-watch` from a project you're working on, run the following:

```
$ cargo help watch      ⟵───  Prints help.
...
$ cargo watch           ⟵───  Runs cargo check continuously.
$ cargo watch -x doc          ⟵─┐
                                 │ Continuously rebuilds documentation on changes.
```

3.8.5 Examining dependencies with cargo-tree

As projects grow in complexity, you may find yourself perplexed by dependencies, either because there are too many, there are conflicts, or there is some other combination thereof. One tool that's useful for figuring out where dependencies come from is `cargo-tree`.

To install `cargo-tree`, run the following:

```
$ cargo install cargo-tree
```

Using `cargo-tree` from a project you're working on, do the following:

```
$ cargo help tree       ⟵───  Prints help.
    ...
```

As an example, if I run `cargo-tree` on the `dryoc` crate, I will see the dependency tree, as shown in the following listing.

Listing 3.5 Partial output of `cargo-tree` for `dryoc` crate

```
$ cargo tree
dryoc v0.3.9 (/Users/brenden/dev/dryoc)
├── bitflags v1.2.1
├── chacha20 v0.6.0
│   ├── cipher v0.2.5
│   │   └── generic-array v0.14.4
│   │       └── typenum v1.12.0
│   │       [build-dependencies]
│   │       └── version_check v0.9.2
│   └── rand_core v0.5.1
│       └── getrandom v0.1.16
│           ├── cfg-if v1.0.0
│           └── libc v0.2.88
├── curve25519-dalek v3.0.2
│   ├── byteorder v1.3.4
│   ├── digest v0.9.0
│   │   └── generic-array v0.14.4 (*)
│   ├── rand_core v0.5.1 (*)
│   ├── subtle v2.4.0
```

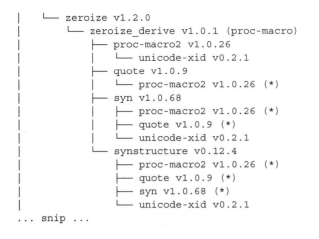

```
|     └── zeroize v1.2.0
|         └── zeroize_derive v1.0.1 (proc-macro)
|             ├── proc-macro2 v1.0.26
|             |   └── unicode-xid v0.2.1
|             ├── quote v1.0.9
|             |   └── proc-macro2 v1.0.26 (*)
|             ├── syn v1.0.68
|             |   ├── proc-macro2 v1.0.26 (*)
|             |   ├── quote v1.0.9 (*)
|             |   └── unicode-xid v0.2.1
|             └── synstructure v0.12.4
|                 ├── proc-macro2 v1.0.26 (*)
|                 ├── quote v1.0.9 (*)
|                 ├── syn v1.0.68 (*)
|                 └── unicode-xid v0.2.1
... snip ...
```

We can see the preceding hierarchy of regular and dev-only dependencies for the crate. Packages marked with (*) are shown with duplicates removed.

Summary

- Many popular editors include Rust support, either via the Language Server Protocol (LSP) or native extensions.
- Rust-analyzer is the canonical Rust language IDE tool, and it can be used with any editor that provides support for LSP.
- Using rustfmt and Clippy can boost productivity and improve code quality.
- There are cases when you may want to use nightly-only features in published crates. When doing so, you should place these features behind a feature flag to support stable users.
- `cargo-update` makes it easy to update your Cargo packages.
- `cargo-expand` lets you expand macros to see the resulting code.
- `cargo-fuzz` let's you easily integrate with libFuzzer for fuzz testing.
- `cargo-watch` automates rerunning Cargo commands on code changes.
- `cargo-tree` allows you to visualize project dependency trees.

Part 2

Core data

When we build software, we spend a lot of time working with data structures. Sometimes, we need to write custom data structures, but more often than not, we use the built-in structures provided by each programming language for the majority of the work. Rust provides a rich set of flexible data structures that provide a good balance of performance, convenience, features, and customizability.

Before you go about implementing your own custom data structures, it's worth taking the time to understand the ins and outs of the core structures included with the Rust standard library. You may find they provide enough in terms of features and flexibility to meet the needs of nearly any application. In cases where Rust's built-in structures are insufficient, foundational knowledge of Rust's existing data structures will be of much benefit when designing your own.

In part 2, we'll dive into the details of Rust's core data structures and memory management, which will provide you with some of the essential knowledge required for writing highly effective Rust. Once you learn to effectively utilize Rust's data structures and memory management features, working with Rust gets a lot easier, too.

Data structures

Up to this point in the book, we haven't spent much time talking about the Rust *language* itself. In the previous two chapters, we discussed tooling. With that out of the way, we can start diving into the Rust language and its features, which we'll focus on for the rest of this book. In this chapter, we'll cover the most important part of Rust after its basic syntax: data structures.

When working with Rust, you'll spend a great deal of time interacting with its data structures, as you would any other language. Rust offers most of the features you'd expect from data structures, as you'd expect with any modern programming language, but it does so while offering exceptional safety and performance. Once you get a handle on Rust's core data types, you'll find the rest of the language comes into great clarity, as the patterns often repeat themselves.

In this chapter, we'll discuss how Rust differs from other languages in its approach to data, review the core data types and structures, and discuss how to effectively use them. We'll also discuss how Rust's primitive types map to C types, which allows you to integrate with non-Rust software.

When working with Rust, you'll likely spend most of your time working with three core data structures: strings, vectors, and maps. The implementations included with Rust's standard library are fast and full featured and will cover the majority of your typical programming use cases. We'll begin by discussing strings, which are commonly used to represent a plethora of data sources and sinks.

4.1 Demystifying String, str, &str, and &'static str

In my first encounters with Rust, I was a little confused by the string types. If you find yourself in a similar position, worry not, for I have good news: while they *seem* complicated, largely due to Rust's concepts of borrowing, lifetimes, and memory management, I can assure you it's all very straightforward once you get a handle on the underlying memory layout.

Sometimes, you may find yourself with a str when you want a String, or you may end up with String but have a function that wants a &str. Getting from one to the other isn't hard, but it may seem confusing at first. We'll discuss all that and more in this section.

It's important to separate the underlying data (a contiguous sequence of characters) from the interface you're using to interact with them. There is only one kind of string in Rust, but there are multiple ways to handle a string's allocation and references to that string.

4.1.1 String vs str

Let's start by clarifying a few things: first, there are, indeed, two separate core string types in Rust (String and str). And while they are technically different types, they are—for the most part—the same thing. They both represent a UTF-8 sequence of characters of arbitrary length, stored in a contiguous region of memory. The only practical difference between String and str is how the memory is managed. Additionally, to understand *all* core Rust types, it's helpful to think about them in terms of how memory is managed. Thus, the two Rust string types can be summarized as

- str—A stack-allocated UTF-8 string, which can be borrowed but cannot be moved or mutated (note that &str *can* point to heap-allocated data; we'll talk more about this later)
- String—A heap-allocated UTF-8 string, which can be borrowed and mutated

In languages like C and C++, the difference between heap- and stack-allocated data can be blurry, as C pointers don't tell you *how* memory was allocated. At best, they tell you that there's a region of memory of a specific type, which might be valid and may be anywhere from 0 to N elements in length. In Rust, memory allocation is explicit; thus your *types*, themselves, usually define *how* memory is allocated, in addition to the number of elements.

In C, you can allocate strings on the stack and mutate them, but this is not allowed in Rust without using the `unsafe` keyword. Not surprisingly, this is a major source of programming errors in C.

Let's illustrate some C strings:

```
char *stack_string = "stack-allocated string";
char *heap_string  = strndup("heap-allocated string");
```

In this code, we have two identical pointer types, pointing to different *kinds* of memory. The first, `stack_string`, is a pointer to stack-allocated memory. Memory allocated on the stack is usually handled by the compiler, and the allocation is essentially instantaneous. `heap_string` is a pointer of the same type, to a *heap*-allocated string. `strndup()` is a standard C library function that allocates a region of memory on the heap using `malloc()`, copies the input into that region, and returns the address of the newly allocated region.

> **NOTE** If we're being pedantic, we might say that heap-allocated string in the preceding example is initially stack allocated but converted into a heap-allocated string after the call to `strndup()`. You can prove this by examining the binary generated by the compiler, which would contain the literal heap-allocated string in the binary.

Now, as far as C is concerned, all strings are the same: they're just contiguous regions of memory of arbitrary length, terminated by a null character (hex byte value `0x00`). So if we switch back to thinking about Rust, we can think of `str` as equivalent to the first line, `stack_string`. `String` is equivalent to the second line, `heap_string`. While this is somewhat of an oversimplification, it's a good model to help us understand strings in Rust.

4.1.2 *Using strings effectively*

Most of the time, when working in Rust, you're going to be working with either a `String` or `&str` but never a `str`. The Rust standard library's *immutable* string functions are implemented for the `&str` type, but the *mutable* functions are only implemented for the `String` type.

It's not possible to create a `str` directly; you can only borrow a reference to one. The `&str` type serves as a convenient lowest common denominator, such as when used as a function argument because you can always borrow a `String` as `&str`.

Let's quickly discuss static lifetimes: In Rust, `'static` is a special lifetime specifier that defines a reference (or borrowed variable) that is valid for the entire life of a process. There are a few special cases in which you may need an explicit `&'static str`, but in practice, it's something infrequently encountered.

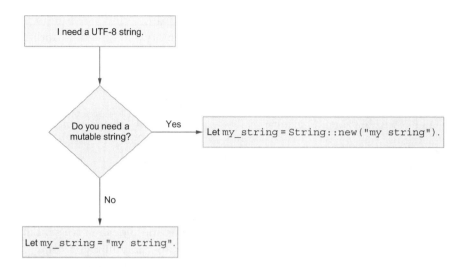

Figure 4.1   Deciding when to use `str` or a `String`, in a very simple flowchart

Deciding to use `String` or a static string comes down to mutability, as shown in figure 4.1. If you don't require mutability, a static string is almost always the best choice.

The only real difference between `&'static str` and `&str` is that, while a `String` can be borrowed as `&str`, `String` can never be borrowed as `&'static str` because the life of a `String` is never as long as the process. When a `String` goes out of scope, it's released with the `Drop` trait (we'll explore traits in greater detail in chapter 8).

Under the hood, a `String` is actually just a `Vec` of UTF-8 characters. We'll discuss `Vec` in greater detail later in the chapter. Additionally, a `str` is just a slice of UTF-8 characters, and we'll discuss slices more in the next section. Table 4.1 summarizes the core string types you will encounter and how to differentiate them.

Table 4.1   String types summarized

Type	Kind	Components	Use
`str`	Stack-allocated UTF-8 string slice	A pointer to an array of characters plus its length	Immutable string, such as logging or debug statements or anywhere else you may have an immutable stack-allocated string
`String`	Heap-allocated UTF-8 string	A vector of characters	Mutable, resizable string, which can be allocated and deallocated as needed
`&str`	Immutable string reference	A pointer to either borrowed `str` or `String` plus its length	Can be used anywhere you want to borrow *either* a `str` or a `String` immutably
`&'static str`	Immutable static string reference	A pointer to a `str` plus its length	A reference to a `str` with an explicit `static` lifetime

Another difference between `str` and `String` is that `String` can be moved, whereas `str` cannot. In fact, it's not possible to own a variable of type `str`—it's only possible to hold reference to a `str`. To illustrate, consider the following listing.

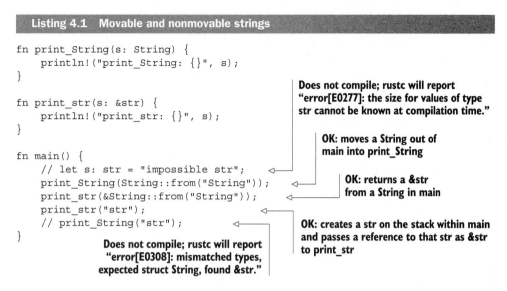

Listing 4.1   Movable and nonmovable strings

```
fn print_String(s: String) {
    println!("print_String: {}", s);
}

fn print_str(s: &str) {
    println!("print_str: {}", s);
}

fn main() {
    // let s: str = "impossible str";
    print_String(String::from("String"));
    print_str(&String::from("String"));
    print_str("str");
    // print_String("str");
}
```

Does not compile; rustc will report "error[E0277]: the size for values of type str cannot be known at compilation time."

OK: moves a String out of main into print_String

OK: returns a &str from a String in main

OK: creates a str on the stack within main and passes a reference to that str as &str to print_str

Does not compile; rustc will report "error[E0308]: mismatched types, expected struct String, found &str."

The preceding code, when run, prints the following output:

```
print_String: String
print_str: String
print_str: str
```

4.2   Understanding slices and arrays

Slices and *arrays* are special types in Rust. They represent a sequence of arbitrary values of the same type. You can also have multidimensional slices or arrays (i.e., slices of slices, arrays of arrays, arrays of slices, or slices of arrays).

Slices are a somewhat new programming concept, as you generally won't find the term *slice* used when discussing sequences in the language syntax for Java, C, C++, Python, or Ruby. Typically, sequences are referred to as either *arrays* (as in Java, C, C++, and Ruby), *lists* (as in Python), or simply *sequences* (as in Scala). Other languages may provide equivalent behavior, but *slices* are not necessarily a first-class language concept or type in the way they are in Rust or Go (although the slice abstraction has been catching on in other languages). C++ does have `std::span` and `std::string_view`, which provide equivalent behavior, but the term *slice* is not used in C++ when describing these.

NOTE   The term *slices* appears to have originated with the Go language, as described in this blog post from 2013 by Rob Pike: https://go.dev/blog/slices.

In Rust, specifically, slices and arrays differ subtly. An array is a fixed-length sequence of values, and a slice is a sequence of values with an arbitrary length. That is, a slice can be of a variable length, determined at run time, whereas an array has a fixed length known at compile time. Slices have another interesting property, which is that you can destructure slices into as many nonoverlapping subslices as desired; this can be convenient for implementing algorithms that use divide-and-conquer or recursive strategies.

Working with arrays can, at times, be tricky in Rust because knowing the length of a sequence at compile time requires the information to be passed to the compiler at compile time and present in the type signature. As of Rust 1.51, it's possible to use a feature called *const generics* (discussed in greater detail in chapter 10) to define generic arrays of arbitrary length but only at compile time.

Let's illustrate the difference between slices and arrays with the following code.

Listing 4.2   Creating an array and a slice

```
let array = [0u8; 64];
    let slice: &[u8] = &array;
```
The type signature here is [u8; 64], an array, initialized with zeroes.

This borrows a slice of the array.

In this code, we've initialized a byte array containing 64 elements, all of which are zero. `0u8` is shorthand for an unsigned integral type, 8 bits in length, with a value of `0`. `0` is the value, and `u8` is the type.

On the second line, we're borrowing the array as a slice. Up until now, this hasn't been particularly interesting. You can do some slightly more interesting things with slices, such as borrowing twice:

```
let (first_half, second_half) = slice.split_at(32);
println!(
    "first_half.len()={} second_half.len()={}",
    first_half.len(),
    second_half.len()
);
```
Splits and borrows a slice twice, destructuring it into two separate, nonoverlapping subslices

The preceding code is calling the `split_at()` function, which is part of Rust's core library and implemented for all slices, arrays, and vectors. `split_at()` *destructures* the slice (which is already borrowed from `array`) and gives us two nonoverlapping slices that correspond to the first and second half of the original array.

This concept of destructuring is important in Rust because you may find yourself in situations where you need to borrow a portion of an array or slice. In fact, you can borrow the same slice or array multiple times using this pattern, as slices don't overlap. One common use case for this is parsing or decoding text or binary data. For example:

```
let wordlist = "one,two,three,four";
for word in wordlist.split(',') {
    println!("word={}", word);
}
```

Looking at the preceding code, it may be immediately obvious that we've taken a string, split it on `,`, and then printed each word within that string. The output from this code prints the following:

```
word=one
word=two
word=three
word=four
```

What's worth noting about the preceding code is that there's no heap allocation happening. All of the memory is allocated on the stack, of a fixed length known at compile time, with no calls to `malloc()` under the hood. This is the equivalent of working with raw C pointers, but there's no reference counting or garbage collection involved; therefore, there is none of the overhead. And unlike C pointers, the code is succinct, safe, and not overly verbose.

Slices, additionally, have a number of optimizations for working with contiguous regions of memory. One such optimization is the `copy_from_slice()` method, which works on slices. A call to `copy_from_slice()` from the standard library uses the `memcpy()` function to copy memory, as shown in the following listing.

Listing 4.3   Snippet of slice/mod.rs, from http://mng.bz/5oRO

```
pub fn copy_from_slice(&mut self, src: &[T])
where
    T: Copy,
{
                    ◁——— Code intentionally omitted

    // SAFETY: `self` is valid for `self.len()` elements by definition,
    // and `src` was checked to have the same length. The slices cannot
    // overlap because mutable references are exclusive.
    unsafe {
        ptr::copy_nonoverlapping(
           src.as_ptr(),
           self.as_mut_ptr(),
           self.len()
        );
    }
}
```

In the preceding listing, which comes from Rust's core library, `ptr::copy_nonoverlapping()` is just a wrapper around the C library's `memcpy()`. On some platforms, `memcpy()` has additional optimizations beyond what you might be able to accomplish with normal code. Other optimized functions are `fill()` and `fill_with()`, which both use `memset()` to fill memory.

Let's review the core attributes of arrays and slices:

- An array is a fixed-length sequence of values, with the value known at compile time.
- Slices are pointers to contiguous regions of memory, including a length, representing an arbitrary-length sequence of values.
- Both slices and arrays can be recursively destructured into nonoverlapping subslices.

4.3   Vectors

Vectors are, arguably, Rust's most important data type (the next most important being `String`, which is based on `Vec`). When working with data in Rust, you'll find yourself frequently creating vectors when you need a resizable sequence of values. If you're coming from C++, you've likely heard the term *vectors* before, and in many ways Rust's vector type is very similar to what you'd find in C++. Vectors serve as a general-purpose container for just about any kind of sequence.

Vectors are one of the ways to allocate memory on the heap in Rust (another being smart pointers, like `Box`; smart pointers are covered in greater detail in chapter 5). Vectors have a few internal optimizations to limit excessive allocations, such as allocating memory in blocks. Additionally, in nightly Rust, you can supply a custom allocator (discussed in greater detail in chapter 5) to implement your own memory allocation behavior.

4.3.1   Diving deeper into Vec

`Vec` inherits the methods of slices because we can obtain a slice reference from a vector. Rust does not have inheritance in the sense of object-oriented programming, but rather `Vec` is a special type that is both a `Vec` and a slice at the same time. For example, let's take a look at the standard library implementation for `as_slice()`.

> **Listing 4.4   Snippet of vec/mod.rs, from http://mng.bz/6nRe**

```
pub fn as_slice(&self) -> &[T] {
    self
}
```

The preceding code listing is performing a special conversion that (under normal circumstances) wouldn't work. It's taking `self`, which is `Vec<T>` in the preceding code, and simply returning it as `&[T]`. If you try to compile the same code yourself, it will fail.

How does this work? Rust provides a trait called `Deref` (and its mutable companion `DerefMut`), which may be used by the compiler to coerce one type into another, implicitly. Once implemented for a given type, that type will also automatically implement all the methods of the dereferenced type. In the case of `Vec`, `Deref` and `DerefMut` are implemented in the Rust standard library, as shown in the following listing.

Listing 4.5   Snippet of the `Deref` implementation for `Vec`, from http://mng.bz/6nRe

```
impl<T, A: Allocator> ops::Deref for Vec<T, A> {
    type Target = [T];

    fn deref(&self) -> &[T] {
        unsafe { slice::from_raw_parts(self.as_ptr(), self.len) }
    }
}

impl<T, A: Allocator> ops::DerefMut for Vec<T, A> {
    fn deref_mut(&mut self) -> &mut [T] {
        unsafe { slice::from_raw_parts_mut(self.as_mut_ptr(), self.len) }
    }
}
```

In the preceding code listing, dereferencing the vector will coerce it into a slice from its raw pointer and length. It should be noted that such an operation is temporary—that is to say, a slice cannot be resized, and the length is provided to the slice at the time of dereferencing.

If, for some reason, you took a slice of a vector and resized the vector, the slice's size would not change. This would only be possible in unsafe code, however, because the borrow checker will not let you borrow a slice from a vector and change the vector at the same time. Take the following to illustrate:

```
let mut vec = vec![1, 2, 3];          | Returns &[i32] because vec is borrowed here
let slice = vec.as_slice();       ◄── | This is a mutable operation.
vec.resize(10, 0);                ◄──┘
println!("{}", slice[0]);         ◄──── This fails to compile.
```

The preceding code will fail to compile, as the borrow checker returns this error:

```
error[E0502]: cannot borrow `vec` as mutable because it is also borrowed as
immutable
  --> src/main.rs:4:5
   |
3  |     let slice = vec.as_slice();
   |                 --- immutable borrow occurs here
4  |     vec.resize(10, 0);
   |     ^^^^^^^^^^^^^^^^^^ mutable borrow occurs here
5  |     println!("{}", slice[0]);
   |                    -------- immutable borrow later used here
```

4.3.2   *Wrapping vectors*

Some types in Rust merely wrap a `Vec`, such as `String`. The `String` type is a `Vec<u8>` and dereferences (using the previously mentioned `Deref` trait) into a `str`.

Listing 4.6   Snippet of string.rs, from http://mng.bz/orAZ

```
pub struct String {
    vec: Vec<u8>,
}
```

Wrapping vectors is a common pattern, as `Vec` is the preferred way to implement a resizable sequence of any type.

4.3.3   *Types related to vectors*

In 90% of cases, you'll want to use a `Vec`. In the other 10% of cases, you'll probably want to use a `HashMap` (discussed in the next section). Container types other than `Vec` or `HashMap` may make sense in certain situations, or cases when you need special optimization, but most likely, a `Vec` will be sufficient, and using another type will not provide noticeable performance improvements. A quote comes to mind:

> *Programmers waste enormous amounts of time thinking about, or worrying about, the speed of noncritical parts of their programs, and these attempts at efficiency actually have a strong negative impact when debugging and maintenance are considered. We should forget about small efficiencies, say about 97% of the time: premature optimization is the root of all evil. Yet we should not pass up our opportunities in that critical 3%.*
>
> —Donald Knuth

In cases where you are concerned about allocating excessively large regions of contiguous memory or about *where* the memory is located, you can easily get around this problem by simply stuffing a `Box` into a `Vec` (i.e, using `Vec<Box<T>>`). With that said, there are several other collection types in Rust's standard library, some of which wrap a `Vec` internally, and you may occasionally need to use them:

- `VecDeque`—A double-ended queue that can be resized, based on `Vec`
- `LinkedList`—A doubly linked list
- `HashMap`—A hash map, discussed in more detail in the next section
- `BTreeMap`—A map based on a B-tree
- `HashSet`—A hash set, based on `HashMap`
- `BTreeSet`—A B-tree set, based on `BTreeMap`
- `BinaryHeap`—A priority queue, implemented with a binary heap, using a `Vec` internally

Additional recommendations, including up-to-date performance details of Rust's core data structures, can be found in the Rust standard library collections reference at https://doc.rust-lang.org/std/collections/index.html.

> **TIP** It's also reasonable to build your own data structures on top of `Vec`, should you need to. For an example of how to do this, the `BinaryHeap` from Rust's standard library provides a complete example, which is documented at http://mng.bz/n1A5.

4.4   *Maps*

`HashMap` is the other container type in Rust that you'll find yourself using. If `Vec` is the preferred resizable type of the language, `HashMap` is the preferred type for cases where you need a collection of items that can be retrieved in constant time, using a key. Rust's `HashMap` is not much different from hash maps you may have encountered in other languages, but Rust's implementation is likely faster and safer than what you might find in other libraries, thanks to some optimizations Rust provides.

HashMap uses the Siphash-1-3 function for hashing, which is also used in Python (starting from 3.4), Ruby, Swift, and Haskell. This function provides good tradeoffs for common cases, but it may be inappropriate for very small or very large keys, such as integral types or very large strings.

It's also possible to supply your own hash function for use with HashMap. You may want to do this in cases where you want to hash very small or very large keys, but for most cases, the default implementation is adequate.

4.4.1 Custom hashing functions

To use a HashMap with a custom hashing function, you need to first find an existing implementation or write a hash function that implements the necessary traits. HashMap requires that std::hash::BuildHasher, std::hash::Hasher, and std::default::Default are implemented for the hash function you wish to use. Traits are discussed in greater detail in chapter 8.

Let's examine the implementation of HashMap from the standard library in the following listing.

Listing 4.7 Snippet of `HashMap`, from http://mng.bz/vPAp

```
impl<K, V, S> HashMap<K, V, S>
where
    K: Eq + Hash,
    S: BuildHasher,
{
                              ⊲─── Code intentionally omitted
}
```

In this listing, you can see BuildHasher specified as a trait requirement on the S type parameter. Digging a little deeper, in the following listing, you can see BuildHasher is just a wrapper around the Hasher trait.

Listing 4.8 Snippet of `BuildHasher`, from http://mng.bz/46RR

```
pub trait BuildHasher {
    /// Type of the hasher that will be created.        Here, there's a requirement
    type Hasher: Hasher;                            ⊲─┘ on the Hasher trait.

              ⊲─── Code intentionally omitted
}
```

The BuildHasher and Hasher APIs leave most of the implementation details up to the author of the hash function. For BuildHasher, only a build_hasher() method is required, which returns the new Hasher instance. The Hasher trait only requires two methods: write() and finish(). write() takes a byte slice (&[u8]), and finish() returns an unsigned 64-bit integer representing the computed hash. The Hasher trait also provides a number of blanket implementations, which you inherit for free if you implement the `Hasher` trait. It's worth examining the documentation for the traits themselves at http://mng.bz/QR76 and http://mng.bz/Xqo9 to get a clearer picture of how they work.

Many crates are available on https://crates.io that already implement a wide variety of hash functions. As an example, in the following listing, let's construct a `HashMap` with MetroHash, an alternative to SipHash, designed by J. Andrew Rogers, described at https://www.jandrewrogers.com/2015/05/27/metrohash/. The MetroHash crate already includes the necessary implementation of the `std::hash::BuildHasher` and `std::hash::Hasher` traits, which makes this very easy.

Listing 4.9   Code listing for using `HashMap` with MetroHash

```
use metrohash::MetroBuildHasher;                    Creates a new HashMap
use std::collections::HashMap;                      instance, using MetroHash

let mut map = HashMap::<String, String,                 Inserts a key and value pair into
    MetroBuildHasher>::default();          ◄────        the map, using the Into trait for
map.insert("hello?".into(), "Hello!".into());    ◄──   conversion from &str to String

println!("{:?}", map.get("hello?"));    ◄──  Retrieves the value from the map, which
                                             returns an Option; the {:?} argument to the
                                             println! macro tells it to format this value
                                             using the fmt::Debug trait.
```

4.4.2   Creating hashable types

`HashMap` can be used with arbitrary keys and values, but the keys must implement the `std::cmp::Eq` and `std::hash::Hash` traits. Many traits, such as `Eq` and `Hash`, can be automatically derived using the `#[derive]` attribute. Consider the following example.

Listing 4.10   Code listing for a compound key type

```
#[derive(Hash, Eq, PartialEq, Debug)]
struct CompoundKey {
    name: String,
    value: i32,
}
```

The preceding code represents a compound key composed of a name and value. We're using the `#[derive]` attribute to derive four traits: `Hash`, `Eq`, `PartialEq`, and `Debug`. While `HashMap` only requires `Hash` and `Eq`, we need to also derive `PartialEq` because `Eq` depends on `PartialEq`. I've also derived `Debug`, which provides automatic debug print methods. This is extremely convenient for debugging and testing code.

We haven't discussed `#[derive]` much in this book yet, but it's something you'll use frequently in Rust. We'll go into more detail on traits and `#[derive]` in chapters 8 and 9. For now, you should just think of it as an automatic way to generate trait implementations. These trait implementations have the added benefit in that they're composable: so long as they exist for any subset of types, they can also be derived for a superset of types.

4.5 Rust types: Primitives, structs, enums, and aliases

Being a strongly typed language, Rust provides several ways to model data. At the bottom are primitive types, which handle our most basic units of data, like numeric values, bytes, and characters. Moving up from there, we have structs and enums, which are used to encapsulate other types. Finally, aliases let us rename and combine other types into new types.

To summarize, in Rust, there are four categories of types:

- *Primitives*—These include strings, arrays, tuples, and integral types.
- *Structs*—A compound type composed of any arbitrary combination of other types, similar to C structs, for example.
- *Enums*—A special type in Rust, which is somewhat similar to enum from C, C++, Java, and other languages.
- *Aliases*—Syntax sugar for creating new type definitions based on existing types.

4.5.1 Using primitive types

Primitive types are provided by the Rust language and core library. These are equivalent to the primitives you'd find in any other strongly typed language, with a few exceptions, which we'll review in this section. The core primitive types are summarized in table 4.2, which includes integers, floats, tuples, and arrays.

Table 4.2 Summary of primitive types in Rust

Class	Kind	Description
Scalar	Integers	Can be either a signed or unsigned integer, anywhere from 8–128 bits in length (bound to a byte; i.e., 8 bits)
Scalar	Sizes	An architecture-specific size type, which can be signed or unsigned
Scalar	Floating point	32- or 64-bit floating point numbers
Compound	Tuples	Fixed-length collection of types or values, which can be destructured.
Sequence	Arrays	Fixed-length sequence of values of a type that can be sliced.

INTEGER TYPES

Integer types can be recognized by their signage designation (either i or u for signed and unsigned, respectively), followed by the number of bits. Sizes begin with i or u, followed by the word size. Floating-point types begin with f, followed by the number of bits. Table 4.3 summarizes the primitive integer types.

Table 4.3 Summary of integer-type identifiers

Length	Signed identifier	Unsigned identifier	C equivalent
8 bits	i8	u8	char and uchar
16 bits	i16	u16	short and unsigned short

Table 4.3 Summary of integer-type identifiers *(continued)*

Length	Signed identifier	Unsigned identifier	C equivalent
32 bits	i32	u32	`int` and `unsigned int`
64 bits	i64	u64	`long`, `long long`, `unsigned long`, and `unsigned long long`, depending on the platform
128 bits	i128	u128	Extended integers are nonstandard C but provided as `_int128` or `_uint128` with GCC and Clang

The type for an integer literal can be specified by appending the type identifier. For example, `0u8` denotes an unsigned 8-bit integer with a value of `0`. Integer values can be prefixed with `0b`, `0o`, `0x`, or `b` for binary, octal, hexadecimal, and byte literals. Consider the following listing, which prints each value as a decimal (base 10) integer.

Listing 4.11 Code listing with integer literals

```
let value = 0u8;
println!("value={}, length={}", value, std::mem::size_of_val(&value));
let value = 0b1u16;
println!("value={}, length={}", value, std::mem::size_of_val(&value));
let value = 0o2u32;
println!("value={}, length={}", value, std::mem::size_of_val(&value));
let value = 0x3u64;
println!("value={}, length={}", value, std::mem::size_of_val(&value));
let value = 4u128;
println!("value={}, length={}", value, std::mem::size_of_val(&value));

println!("Binary (base 2)        0b1111_1111={}", 0b1111_1111);
println!("Octal (base 8)         0o1111_1111={}", 0o1111_1111);
println!("Decimal (base 10)         1111_1111={}", 1111_1111);
println!("Hexadecimal (base 16)  0x1111_1111={}", 0x1111_1111);
println!("Byte literal           b'A'={}", b'A');
```

When we run this code, we get the following output.

Listing 4.12 Output from listing 4.11

```
value=0, length=1
value=1, length=2
value=2, length=4
value=3, length=8
value=4, length=16
Binary (base 2)        0b1111_1111=255
Octal (base 8)         0o1111_1111=2396745
Decimal (base 10)         1111_1111=11111111
Hexadecimal (base 16)  0x1111_1111=286331153
Byte literal           b'A'=65
```

SIZE TYPES

For size types, the identifiers are `usize` and `isize`. These are platform-dependent sizes, which are typically 32 or 64 bits in length for 32- and 64-bit systems, respectively. `usize` is equivalent to C's `size_t`, and `isize` is provided to permit signed arithmetic with sizes. In the Rust standard library, functions returning or expecting a length parameter expect a `usize`.

ARITHMETIC ON PRIMITIVES

Many languages permit unchecked arithmetic on primitive types. In C and C++, in particular, many arithmetic operations have undefined results and produce no errors. One such example is division by zero. Consider the following C program.

> **Listing 4.13 Code of `divide_by_zero.c`**

```c
#include <stdio.h>

int main() {
    printf("%d\n", 1 / 0);
}
```

If you compile and run this code with `clang divide_by_zero.c && ./a.out`, it will print a value that appears random. Both Clang and GCC happily compile this code, and they both print a warning, but there is no run-time check for an undefined operation.

In Rust, all arithmetic is checked by default. Consider the following Rust program:

```
// println!("{}", 1 / 0);      ◁——— Does not compile

let one = 1;
let zero = 0;
// println!("{}", one / zero);      ◁——— Does not compile

let one = 1;
let zero = one - 1;
// println!("{}", one / zero);      ◁——— Still doesn't compile

let one = { || 1 }();
let zero = { || 0 }();
println!("{}", one / zero);   ◁——— The code panics here!
```

In the preceding code, Rust's compiler is pretty good at catching errors at compile time. We need to trick the compiler to allow the code to compile and run. In the preceding code, we do this by initializing a variable from the return value of a closure. Another way to do it would be to just create a regular function that returns the desired value. In any case, running the problem produces the following output:

```
Running `target/debug/unchecked-arithmetic`
thread 'main' panicked at 'attempt to divide by zero', src/main.rs:14:20
note: run with `RUST_BACKTRACE=1` environment variable to display a
backtrace
```

If you need more control over arithmetic in Rust, the primitive types provide several methods for handling such operations. For example, to safely handle division by zero, you can use the `checked_div()` method, which returns an `Option`:

```
assert_eq!((100i32).checked_div(1i32), Some(100i32));     ◁———— 100 / 1 = 1
assert_eq!((100i32).checked_div(0i32), None);     ◁──┐
                                                     │ 100 / 0—the result is undefined.
```

For scalar types (integers, sizes, and floats), Rust provides a collection of methods that provide basic arithmetic operations (e.g., division, multiplication, addition, and subtraction) in checked, unchecked, overflowing, and wrapping forms.

When you want to achieve compatibility with the behavior from languages like C, C++, Java, C#, and others, the method you probably want to use is the *wrapping* form, which performs modular arithmetic and is compatible with the C-equivalent operations. Keep in mind that overflow on *signed* integers in C is undefined. Here's an example of modular arithmetic in Rust:

```
assert_eq!(0xffu8.wrapping_add(1), 0);
assert_eq!(0xffffffffu32.wrapping_add(1), 0);
assert_eq!(0u32.wrapping_sub(1), 0xffffffff);
assert_eq!(0x80000000u32.wrapping_mul(2), 0);
```

The full listing of arithmetic functions for each primitive is available in the Rust documentation. For `i32`, it can be found at https://doc.rust-lang.org/std/primitive.i32.html.

4.5.2   *Using tuples*

Rust's tuples are similar to what you'll find in other languages. A *tuple* is a fixed-length sequence of values, and the values can each have different types. Tuples in Rust are not reflective; unlike arrays, you can't iterate over a tuple, take a slice of a tuple, or determine the type of its components at run time. Tuples are essentially a form of syntax sugar in Rust, and while useful, they are quite limited.

Consider the following example of a tuple:

```
let tuple = (1, 2, 3);
```

This code looks somewhat similar to what you might expect for an array, except for the limitations mentioned above (you can't slice, iterate, or reflect tuples). To access individual elements within the tuple, you can refer to them by their position, starting at `0`:

```
                                                              │ This prints "tuple
println!("tuple = ({}, {}, {})", tuple.0, tuple.1, tuple.2);  ◁─┘ = (1, 2, 3)".
```

Alternatively, you can use `match`, which provides temporary destructuring, provided there's a pattern match (pattern matching is discussed in greater detail in chapter 8):

```
match tuple {
    (one, two, three) => println!("{}, {}, {}", one, two, three),
}
```
⟵ **This prints "1, 2, 3".**

We can also destructure a tuple into its parts with the following syntax, which moves the values *out* of the tuple:

```
let (one, two, three) = tuple;
println!("{}, {}, {}", one, two, three);
```
⟵ **This prints "1, 2, 3".**

In my experience, the most common use of tuples is returning multiple values from a function. For example, consider this succinct `swap()` function:

```
fn swap<A, B>(a: A, b: B) -> (B, A) {
    (b, a)
}

fn main() {
    let a = 1;
    let b = 2;

    println!("{:?}", swap(a, b));
}
```
⟵ **This prints "(2, 1)".**

TIP It's recommended that you don't make tuples with more than 12 arguments, although there is no strict upper limit to the length of a tuple. The standard library only provides trait implementations for tuples with up to 12 elements.

4.5.3 Using structs

Structs are the main building block in Rust. They are composite data types, which can contain any set types and values. They are similar in nature to C structs or classes in object-oriented languages. They can be composed generically in a fashion similar to templates in C++ or generics in Java, C#, or TypeScript (generics are covered in greater detail in chapter 8).

You should use a struct any time you need to

- Provide stateful functions (i.e., functions or methods that operate on internal-only state)
- Control access to internal state (i.e., private variables); or
- Encapsulate state behind an API.

You are not required to use structs. You can write APIs with functions only, if you desire, in a fashion similar to C APIs. Additionally, structs are only needed to define implementations—they are not for specifying interfaces. This differs from object-oriented languages, like C++, Java, and C#.

The simplest form of a struct is an empty struct:

```
struct EmptyStruct {}

struct AnotherEmptyStruct;
```
Unit struct, which ends with semicolon with no braces

Empty structs (or *unit structs*) are something you may encounter occasionally. Another form of struct is the *tuple struct,* which looks like this:

```
struct TupleStruct(String);

let tuple_struct = TupleStruct("string value".into());
println!("{}", tuple_struct.0);
```
Initializes the struct similarly to a tuple

The first tuple element can be accessed with .0, the second with .1, the third with .2, and so on.

A tuple struct is a special form of struct, which behaves like a tuple. The main difference between a tuple struct and a regular struct is that, in a tuple struct, the values have no names, only types. Notice how a tuple struct has a semicolon (;) at the end of the declaration, which is not required for regular structs (except for an empty declaration). Tuple structs can be convenient in certain cases by allowing you to omit the field names (thereby shaving a few characters off your source code), but they also create ambiguity.

A typical struct has a list of elements with names and types, like this:

```
struct TypicalStruct {
  name: String,
  value: String,
  number: i32,
}
```

Each element within a struct has *module* visibility by default. That means values within the struct are accessible anywhere within the scope of the current module. Visibility can be set on a per-element basis:

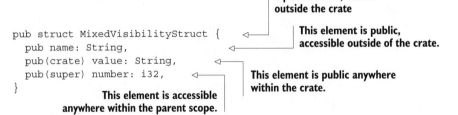

A public struct, visible outside the crate

This element is public, accessible outside of the crate.

```
pub struct MixedVisibilityStruct {
  pub name: String,
  pub(crate) value: String,
  pub(super) number: i32,
}
```

This element is public anywhere within the crate.

This element is accessible anywhere within the parent scope.

Most of the time, you shouldn't need to make struct elements public. An element within a struct can be accessed and modified by any code within the public scope for that struct element. The default visibility (which is equivalent to pub(self)) allows any code within the same module to access and modify the elements within a struct.

Visibility semantics also apply to the structs themselves, just like their member elements. For a struct to be visible outside of a crate (i.e., to be consumed from a library), it must be declared with `pub struct MyStruct { … }`. A struct that's not explicitly declared as public won't be accessible outside of the crate (this also applies generally to functions, traits, and any other declarations).

When you declare a struct, you'll probably want to derive a few standard trait implementations:

```
#[derive(Debug, Clone, Default)]
struct DebuggableStruct {
    string: String,
    number: i32,
}
```

In this code, we're deriving the `Debug`, `Clone`, and `Default` traits. These traits are summarized as follows:

- `Debug`—Provides a `fmt()` method, which formats (for printing) the content of the type
- `Clone`—Provides a `clone()` method, which creates a copy (or clone) of the type
- `Default`—Provides an implementation of `default()`, which returns a default (usually empty) instance of the type

You can derive these traits yourself if you wish (such as in cases where you want to customize their behavior), but so long as all elements within a struct implement each trait, you can derive them automatically and save a lot of typing.

With these three traits derived for the preceding example, we can now do the following:

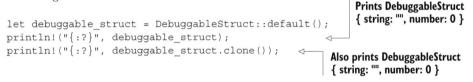

```
let debuggable_struct = DebuggableStruct::default();
println!("{:?}", debuggable_struct);
println!("{:?}", debuggable_struct.clone());
```

Prints DebuggableStruct { string: "", number: 0 }

Also prints DebuggableStruct { string: "", number: 0 }

To define methods for a struct, you will *implement* them using the `impl` keyword:

```
impl DebuggableStruct {
  fn increment_number(&mut self) {
    self.number += 1;
  }
}
```

A function that takes a mutable reference to self

This code takes a mutable reference of our struct and increments it by 1. Another way to do this would be to *consume* the struct and return it from the function:

```
impl DebuggableStruct {
  fn incremented_number(mut self) -> Self {
    self.number += 1;
```

A function that takes an owned mutable instance of self

```
        self
    }
}
```

There's a subtle difference between these two implementations, but they are functionally equivalent. There may be cases when you want to consume the input to a method to swallow it, but in most cases, the first version (using &mut self) is preferred.

4.5.4 *Using enums*

Enums can be thought of as a specialized type of struct that contains enumerated mutually exclusive *variants*. An enum can be *one* of its variants at a given time. With a struct, *all* elements of the struct are present. With an enum, only *one* of the variants is present. An enum can contain any kind of type, not just integral types. The types may be named or anonymous.

This is quite different from enums in languages like C, C++, Java, or C#. In those languages, enums are effectively used as a way to define constant values. Rust's enums can emulate enums, as you might expect from other languages, but they are conceptually different. While C++ has enums, Rust's enums are more similar to std::variant than C++'s enum.

Consider the following enum:

```
#[derive(Debug)]
enum JapaneseDogBreeds {
    AkitaKen,
    HokkaidoInu,
    KaiKen,
    KishuInu,
    ShibaInu,
    ShikokuKen,
}
```

For the preceding enum, JapaneseDogBreeds is the name of the enum type, and each of the elements within the enum is a unit-like type. Since the types in the enum don't exist outside the enum, they are created *within* the enum. We can run the following code now:

```
                                                            This prints "ShibaInu".
println!("{:?}", JapaneseDogBreeds::ShibaInu);           ⟵┘
println!("{:?}", JapaneseDogBreeds::ShibaInu as u32);                         ⟵┐

                            This prints "4", the 32-bit unsigned
                         integer representation of the enum value. ┘
```

Casting the enum type to a u32 works because enum types are enumerated. Now, what if we want to go from the number 4 to the enum value? For that, there is no automatic conversion, but we can implement it ourselves using the From trait:

```
impl From<u32> for JapaneseDogBreeds {
    fn from(other: u32) -> Self {
```

```
        match other {
            other if JapaneseDogBreeds::AkitaKen as u32 == other => {
                JapaneseDogBreeds::AkitaKen
            }
            other if JapaneseDogBreeds::HokkaidoInu as u32 == other => {
                JapaneseDogBreeds::HokkaidoInu
            }
            other if JapaneseDogBreeds::KaiKen as u32 == other => {
                JapaneseDogBreeds::KaiKen
            }
            other if JapaneseDogBreeds::KishuInu as u32 == other => {
                JapaneseDogBreeds::KishuInu
            }
            other if JapaneseDogBreeds::ShibaInu as u32 == other => {
                JapaneseDogBreeds::ShibaInu
            }
            other if JapaneseDogBreeds::ShikokuKen as u32 == other => {
                JapaneseDogBreeds::ShikokuKen
            }
            _ => panic!("Unknown breed!"),
        }
    }
}
```

In the preceding code, we must cast the enum type to a `u32` to perform the comparison, and then we return the enum type if there's a match. In the case where no value matches, we call `panic!()`, which causes the program to crash. The preceding syntax uses the `match` guard feature, which lets us match using an `if` statement.

It's possible to specify the enumeration variant types in an enum as well. This can be used to achieve behavior similar to C enums:

```
enum Numbers {
    One = 1,
    Two = 2,
    Three = 3,
}

fn main() {
    println!("one={}", Numbers::One as u32);     ⟵──  This prints "one=1". Note that
}                                                     without the as cast, this does
                                                      not compile because One
                                                      doesn't implement std::fmt.
```

Enums may contain tuples, structs, and anonymous (i.e., unnamed) types as variants:

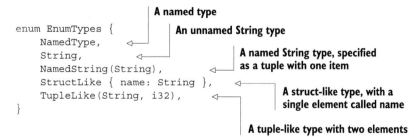

```
                          A named type
enum EnumTypes {          An unnamed String type
    NamedType,      ⟵
    String,         ⟵───┘
    NamedString(String),     ⟵─── A named String type, specified
    StructLike { name: String },  ⟵   as a tuple with one item
    TupleLike(String, i32),  ⟵──┐   A struct-like type, with a
}                                │   single element called name
                                 │
                          A tuple-like type with two elements
```

To clarify, an *unnamed* enum variant is a variant that's specified as a type, rather than with a name. A *named* enum variant is equivalent to creating a new type within the enum, which also happens to correspond to an enumerated integer value. In other words, if you want to emulate the behavior of enums from languages like C, C++, or Java, you'll be using named variants, which conveniently emulate the enumeration behavior by casting the value to an integer type, even though enum variants are also types (i.e., not just values).

As a general rule, it's good practice to avoid mixing named and unnamed variants within an enum, as it can be confusing.

4.5.5   *Using aliases*

Aliases are a special type in Rust that allows you to provide an alternative and equivalent name for any other type. They are equivalent to C and C++'s `typedef` or the C++ `using` keyword. Defining an alias does not create a new type.

Aliases have two common uses:

- Providing aliased type definitions for public types, as a matter of ergonomics and convenience for the user of a library
- Providing shorthand types that correspond to more complicated type compositions

For example, I may want to create a type alias for a hash map I frequently use within my crate:

```
pub(crate) type MyMap = std::collections::HashMap<String, MyStruct>;
```

Now, rather than having to type the full `std::collections::HashMap<String, MyStruct>`, I can use `MyMap` instead.

For libraries, it's common practice to export public type aliases with sensible defaults for type construction when generics are used. It can be difficult at times to determine which types are required for a given interface, and aliases provide one way for library authors to signal that information.

In the `dryoc` crate, I provide a number of type aliases, for convenience. The API makes heavy use of generics. One such example is shown in the following listing.

> **Listing 4.14   Snippet for kdf.rs, from http://mng.bz/yZAp**

```
/// Stack-allocated key type alias for key derivation with [`Kdf`].
pub type Key = StackByteArray<CRYPTO_KDF_KEYBYTES>;
/// Stack-allocated context type alias for key derivation with [`Kdf`].
pub type Context = StackByteArray<CRYPTO_KDF_CONTEXTBYTES>;
```

In the preceding code, the `Key` and `Context` type aliases are provided within this module, so the user of this library does not need to worry about implementation details.

4.6   *Error handling with Result*

Rust provides a few features to make error handling easier. These features are based on an enum called `Result`, defined in the following listing.

Listing 4.15   Snippet of `std::result::Result`, from http://mng.bz/M97Q

```
pub enum Result<T, E> {
    Ok(T),
    Err(E),
}
```

A `Result` represents an operation that can either succeed (returning a result) or fail (returning an error). You will quickly become accustomed to seeing `Result` as the return type for many functions in Rust.

You will likely want to create your own error type in your crate. That type could be either an enum containing all the different kinds of errors you expect or simply a struct with something actionable, such as an error message. I, being a simple person, prefer to just provide a helpful message and move on with my life. Here's a very simple error struct:

```
#[derive(Debug)]
struct Error {
    message: String,
}
```

Within your crate, you'll need to decide what type of errors you want your functions to return. My suggestion is to have your crate return its own error type. This is convenient for anyone else using your crate because it will be clear to them where the error originates from.

To make this pattern work, you'll need to implement the `From` trait to convert your error type into the target error type returned from the function where the `?` operator is used in cases where the types differ. Doing this is relatively easy because the compiler will tell you when it's necessary.

Now, within your crate, suppose you have a function that reads the contents of a file, like this:

```
fn read_file(name: &str) -> Result<String, Error> {
    use std::fs::File;
    use std::io::prelude::*;

    let mut file = File::open(name)?;          ⟵  Using the ? operator here
    let mut contents = String::new();              for implicit error handling
    file.read_to_string(&mut contents)?;       ⟵  Using the ?
    Ok(contents)                                   operator here too
}
```

In the preceding code, we have a function that opens a file, `name`; reads the contents into a string; and returns the contents as a result. We use the `?` operator twice, which works by returning the result of the function upon success or returning the error immediately. Both `File::open` and `read_to_string()` use the `std::io::Error` type, so we've provided the following `From` implementation, which permits this conversion automatically:

```
impl From<std::io::Error> for Error {
    fn from(other: std::io::Error) -> Self {
        Self {
            message: other.to_string(),
        }
    }
}
```

4.7 *Converting types with From/Into*

Rust provides two very useful traits as part of its core library: the `From` and `Into` traits. If you browse the Rust standard library, you may notice that `From` and `Into` are implemented for a great number of different types because of the usefulness of these traits. You will frequently encounter these traits when working with Rust.

These traits provide a standard way to convert between types. They are occasionally used by the compiler to automatically convert types on your behalf.

As a general rule, you only need to implement the `From` trait and almost never `Into`. The `Into` trait is the reciprocal of `From` and will be derived automatically by the compiler. There is one exception to this rule: versions of Rust prior to 1.41 had slightly stricter rules, which didn't allow implementing `From` when the conversion destination was an external type.

`From` is preferred because it doesn't require specifying the destination type, resulting in slightly simpler syntax. The signature for the `From` trait (from the standard library) is as follows:

```
pub trait From<T>: Sized {
    /// Performs the conversion.
    fn from(_: T) -> Self;
}
```

Let's create a very simple `String` wrapper and implement this trait for our type:

```
struct StringWrapper(String);

impl From<&str> for StringWrapper {
    fn from(other: &str) -> Self {
        Self(other.into())          ◁────┐  Returns a copy of the string,
    }                                     │  wrapped in a new StringWapper
}

fn main() {
    println!("{}", StringWrapper::from("Hello, world!").0);
}
```

In the preceding code, we're allowing conversion from a &str, a borrowed string, into a string. To convert the other string into our string, we just call into(), which comes from the Into trait implemented for String. In this example, we use *both* From and Into.

In practice, you will find yourself needing to convert between types for a variety of reasons. One such case is for handling errors when using Result. If you call a function that returns a result and use the ? operator within that function, you'll need to provide a From implementation if the error type returned by the inner function differs from the error type used by the Result.

Consider the following code:

```
use std::{fs::File, io::Read};

struct Error(String);

fn read_file(name: &str) -> Result<String, Error> {
    let mut f = File::open(name)?;
    let mut output = String::new();

    f.read_to_string(&mut output)?;

    Ok(output)
}
```

The preceding code attempts to read a file into a string and returns the result. We have a custom error type, which just contains a string. The code, as is, does not compile:

```
error[E0277]: `?` couldn't convert the error to `Error`
  --> src/main.rs:6:33
   |
5  | fn read_file(name: &str) -> Result<String, Error> {
   |                             -------------------- expected `Error`
   because of this
6  |     let mut f = File::open(name)?;
   |                                 ^ the trait `From<std::io::Error>` is
   not implemented for `Error`
   |
   = note: the question mark operation (`?`) implicitly performs a conversion
   on the error value using the `From` trait
   = note: required by `from`

error[E0277]: `?` couldn't convert the error to `Error`
  --> src/main.rs:9:34
   |
5  | fn read_file(name: &str) -> Result<String, Error> {
   |                             -------------------- expected `Error`
   because of this
...
9  |     f.read_to_string(&mut output)?;
   |                                  ^ the trait `From<std::io::Error>` is
   not implemented for `Error`
   |
```

```
= note: the question mark operation (`?`) implicitly performs a conversion
on the error value using the `From` trait
= note: required by `from`
```

To make it compile, we need to implement the `From` trait for `Error` such that the compiler knows how to convert `std::io::Error` into our own custom error. The implementation looks like this:

```
impl From<std::io::Error> for Error {
    fn from(other: std::io::Error) -> Self {
        Self(other.to_string())
    }
}
```

Now, if we compile and run the code, it works as expected.

4.7.1 *TryFrom and TryInto*

In addition to the `From` and `Into` traits, there are `TryFrom` and `TryInto`. These traits are nearly identical, except they are for cases in which the type conversion may fail. The conversion methods in these traits return `Result`, whereas with `From` and `Into`, there is no way to return an error aside from panicking, which causes the entire program to crash.

4.7.2 *Best practices for type conversion using From and Into*

We can summarize the best practices for type conversion with the `From` and `Into` traits as follows:

- Implement the `From` trait for types that require conversion to and from other types.
- Avoid writing custom conversion routines, and, instead, rely on the well-known traits where possible.

4.8 *Handling FFI compatibility with Rust's types*

You may, occasionally, need to call functions from non-Rust libraries (or vice versa), and in many cases, that requires modeling C structs in Rust. To do this, you must use Rust's foreign function interface features (FFI). Rust's structs are not compatible with C structs. To make them compatible, you should do the following:

- Structs should be declared with the `#[repr(C)]` attribute, which tells the compiler to pack the struct in a C-compatible representation.
- You should use C types from the `libc` crate, which provides mappings between Rust and C types. Rust types *are not* C types, and you can't always assume they'll be compatible, even when you think they're equivalent.

To make this whole process much easier, the Rust team provides a tool called `rust-bindgen`. With `rust-bindgen`, you can generate bindings to C libraries automatically from

C headers. Most of the time, you should use `rust-bindgen` to generate bindings, and you can follow the instructions at http://mng.bz/amgj to do so.

In some cases, I have found I need to call C functions for test purposes or some other reason, and dealing with `rust-bindgen` is not worth the trouble for simple cases. In those cases, the process for mapping C structs to Rust is as follows:

- Copy the C struct definition.
- Convert the C types to Rust types.
- Implement function interfaces.

Following up on the zlib example from chapter 2, let's quickly implement zlib's file struct, which looks like this in C:

```
struct gzFile_s {
    unsigned have;
    unsigned char *next;
    z_off64_t pos;
};
```

The corresponding Rust struct, after conversion, would look like this:

```
#[repr(C)]                           ◁─── Instructs rustc to align the memory in this struct
struct GzFileState {  ◁───                as a C compiler would, for compatibility with C
    have: c_uint,
    next: *mut c_uchar,
    pos: i64,                        A C struct representing a zlib
}                                    file state, as defined in zlib.h
```

Putting it all together, you can call C functions from zlib with the struct that zlib expects:

```
type GzFile = *mut GzFileState;
                                   Instructs rustc that these functions
#[link(name = "z")]                belong to the external z library
extern "C" {                  ◁───
    fn gzopen(path: *const c_char, mode: *const c_char) -> GzFile;     External
    fn gzread(file: GzFile, buf: *mut c_uchar, len: c_uint) -> c_int;  zlib
    fn gzclose(file: GzFile) -> c_int;                                 functions
    fn gzeof(file: GzFile) -> c_int;                                   as defined
}                                                                      in zlib.h

fn read_gz_file(name: &str) -> String {
    let mut buffer = [0u8; 0x1000];            Converts a Rust UTF-8 string into an ASCII
    let mut contents = String::new();          C string, raising an error if there's a failure
    unsafe {
        let c_name = CString::new(name).expect("CString failed");   ◁───
        let c_mode = CString::new("r").expect("CString failed");
        let file = gzopen(c_name.as_ptr(), c_mode.as_ptr());
        if file.is_null() {
            panic!(
                "Couldn't read file: {}",
                std::io::Error::last_os_error()
```

```
        );
    }
    while gzeof(file) == 0 {
        let bytes_read = gzread(
            file,
            buffer.as_mut_ptr(),
            (buffer.len() - 1) as c_uint,
        );
        let s = std::str::from_utf8(&buffer[..(bytes_read as usize)])
            .unwrap();
        contents.push_str(s);
    }
    gzclose(file);
}

contents
}
```

The `read_gz_file()` will open a gzipped file, read its contents, and return them as a string.

Summary

- `str` is Rust's stack-allocated UTF-8 string type. A `String` is a heap-allocated UTF-8 string, based on `Vec`.
- A `&str` is a string slice, which can be borrowed from both a `String` and `&'static str`.
- `Vec` is a heap-allocated, resizable sequence of values, allocated in a contiguous region of memory. In most cases, you should use a `Vec` when modeling a sequence of values.
- `HashMap` is Rust's standard hash map container type, which is suitable for most uses requiring constant-time lookups from a key.
- Rust also has `VecDeque`, `LinkedList`, `BTreeMap`, `HashSet`, `BTreeSet`, and `BinaryHeap` within its collections library.
- Structs are composable containers and Rust's primary building block. They are used to store state and implement methods that operate on that state.
- Enums are a special variant type in Rust, and they can emulate the behavior of `enum` from languages like C, C++, C#, and Java.
- Implementations of many standard traits can be derived using the `#[derive]` attribute. If needed, you can manually implement these traits, but most of the time, the automatically derived implementations are sufficient.

Working with memory 5

This chapter covers

- Learning about heap- and stack-based memory management details in Rust
- Understanding Rust's ownership semantics
- Using reference-counted pointers
- Effectively utilizing smart pointers
- Implementing custom allocators for specific use cases

In chapter 4, we discussed Rust's data structures, but to complete our understanding, we also need to discuss memory management and how it works with Rust's data structures. The core data structures provide nice abstractions for managing memory allocation and deallocation, but some applications may require more advanced features that require custom allocators, reference counting, smart pointers, or system-level features that are outside the scope of the Rust language.

It's possible to effectively use Rust without having a deep understanding of memory management, but there are many cases in which it's quite beneficial to know what's going on under the hood, so to speak. In this chapter, we'll get into the details of Rust's memory management.

5.1   *Memory management: Heap and stack*

Rust has very powerful and fine-grained memory management semantics. You may find when you're new to Rust that it seems somewhat opaque at first. For example, when you use a string or a vector, you likely aren't thinking too much about how the memory is allocated. In some ways, this is similar to scripting languages, such as Python or Ruby, where memory management is largely abstracted away and rarely something you need to think about.

Under the hood, Rust's memory management is not too different from languages like C or C++. In Rust, however, the language tries to keep memory management out of your way until you *need* to worry about memory management. And when you do, the language provides the tools you'll need to dial the complexity up or down, depending on what you're trying to accomplish. Let's quickly review the differences between the heap and the stack (figure 5.1).

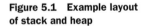

Figure 5.1   Example layout of stack and heap

The *heap* is a section of memory for dynamic allocation. This is typically a location in memory reserved for resizable data structures or anything where the size is only known at run time. That is not to say you cannot store static data in the heap; however, for static data, it's usually better to use the stack (the compiler will typically place static data into the program's static memory segment as an optimization, so it's not *actually* pushed onto the stack). The heap is typically managed by the underlying OS or core language libraries; however, programmers may—if they choose—implement their own heap. For systems that are memory constrained, such as embedded systems, it's common to write code without a heap.

The heap is usually managed by an allocator, and in most cases, the operating system, language runtime, or C library provides an allocator (e.g., `malloc()`). Data in the heap can be thought of as allocated randomly throughout the heap and can grow and shrink throughout the life of the process.

In Rust, allocating on the heap is accomplished by using any heap-allocated data structure, such as `Vec` or `Box` (`Box` is discussed in greater detail later in this chapter), as shown in the following listing.

Listing 5.1 Code showing heap-allocated values

```
let heap_integer = Box::new(1);
let heap_integer_vec = vec![0; 100];
let heap_string = String::from("heap string");
```

As noted in chapter 4, String is based on Vec, which makes this a heap-allocated string.

The *stack* is a thread-local memory space bound to the scope of a function. The stack is allocated using last in, first out (LIFO) order. When a function is entered, the memory is allocated and pushed onto the stack. When a function is exited, the memory is released and popped off the stack. For stack-allocated data, the size needs to be known at compile time. Allocating memory on the stack is normally much quicker than using the heap. There is one stack per thread of execution on operating systems that support it.

The stack is managed by the program itself based on the code generated by the compiler. When a function is entered, a new frame is pushed onto the stack (appended to the end of the stack) and the frame is popped off the stack when leaving the function. As a programmer, you don't have to worry about managing the stack—it's handled for you. The stack has some nice properties in that it's fast, and the function call stack can be used as a data structure by making recursive calls, as shown in the following listing; there's no need to worry about memory management.

Listing 5.2 Code showing stack-allocated values

```
let stack_integer = 69420;
let stack_allocated_string = "stack string";
```

Many languages obfuscate or abstract away the concepts of stack and heap, so you don't have to worry about them. In C and C++, you typically allocate memory on the heap using `malloc()` or the `new` keyword and simply declare a variable within a function to allocate it on the stack. Java also features the `new` keyword for allocating memory on the heap; however, in Java, memory is garbage collected, and you don't need to manage cleanup of the heap.

In Rust, the stack is managed by the compiler and platform implementation details. Allocating data on the heap, on the other hand, can be customized to suit your needs (we'll discuss custom allocators later in this chapter), which is similar to what you might find in C or C++.

The only types that can be allocated on the stack are primitive types, compound types (e.g., tuples and structs), `str`, and the container types themselves (but not necessarily their contents).

5.2   Understanding ownership: Copies, borrowing, references, and moves

Rust introduces a new programming concept called *ownership*, which is part of what makes it different from other languages. Ownership in Rust is where its safety guarantees come from—it's how the compiler knows when memory is in scope, being shared, has gone out of scope, or is being misused. The compiler's borrow checker is responsible for enforcing a small set of ownership rules. Every value has an owner; there can only be one owner at a time; and when the owner goes out of scope, the value is dropped.

If you're already comfortable with Rust's ownership, this section will serve as a review for you, or you can skip it if you wish. On the other hand, if you're still trying to get a handle on ownership in Rust, this section should help clarify those concepts in familiar terms.

Rust's ownership semantics are similar in some ways to C, C++, and Java, except that Rust has no concept of *copy constructors* (which create a copy of an object upon assignment), and you rarely interact with raw pointers in Rust. When you assign the value of one variable to another (i.e., `let a = b;`), it's called a *move*, which is a transfer of ownership (and a value can only have one owner). A move doesn't create a copy unless you're assigning a base type (i.e., assigning an integer to another value creates a copy).

Rather than using pointers, in Rust, we often pass data around using references. In Rust, a reference is created by borrowing. Data can be passed into functions by value (which is a move) or reference. While Rust does have C-like pointers, they aren't something you'll see very often in Rust, except, perhaps, when interacting with C code.

Borrowed data (i.e., a reference) can either be immutable or mutable. By default, when you borrow data, you do so immutably (i.e., you can't modify the data pointed to by the reference). If you borrow with the `mut` keyword, you can obtain a mutable reference, which allows you to modify data. You can borrow data immutably simultaneously (i.e., have multiple references to the same data), but you cannot borrow data mutably more than once at a time.

Borrowing is typically done using the `&` operator (or `&mut`, to borrow mutably); however, you'll sometimes see `as_ref()` or `as_mut()` methods being used instead, which are from the `AsRef` and `AsMut` traits, respectively. `as_ref()` and `as_mut()` are often used by container types to provide access to internal data, rather than obtaining a reference to the container itself (and we'll explore this in more detail later in this chapter). To clarify these concepts, consider the following code listing.

Listing 5.3   Code listing to demonstrate ownership

```
fn main() {
    let mut top_grossing_films =
```
⟵ Here, we create a mutable Vec and populate it with some values.

```
        vec!["Avatar", "Avengers: Endgame", "Titanic"];
    let top_grossing_films_mutable_reference =
        &mut top_grossing_films;
    top_grossing_films_mutable_reference
        .push("Star Wars: The Force Awakens");
    let top_grossing_films_reference = &top_grossing_films;
    println!(
        "Printed using immutable reference: {:#?}",
        top_grossing_films_reference
    );
    let top_grossing_films_moved = top_grossing_films;
    println!("Printed after moving: {:#?}", top_grossing_films_moved);

    // println!("Print using original value: {:#?}", top_grossing_films);
    // println!(
    //     "Print using mutable reference: {:#?}",
    //     top_grossing_films_mutable_reference
    // );
}
```

This borrows a mutable reference to the preceding Vec.

We can use this mutable reference to modify the data that was borrowed in the previous line.

Here, we print the contents of the Vec.

Now, we'll take an immutable reference of the same data, and by doing so, the previous mutable reference becomes invalid.

This assignment is a move, which transfers ownership of the Vec.

Here, we print the contents of the Vec after moving it.

The original variable is no longer valid, as it has been moved, so this code won't compile.

This code also won't compile because this reference was invalidated when we created the immutable reference.

Running the code in the preceding listing produces the following output:

```
Printed using immutable reference: [
    "Avatar",
    "Avengers: Endgame",
    "Titanic",
    "Star Wars: The Force Awakens",
]
Printed after moving: [
    "Avatar",
    "Avengers: Endgame",
    "Titanic",
    "Star Wars: The Force Awakens",
]
```

5.3 Deep copying

You may have encountered the concept of *deep copying* from other languages, such as Python or Ruby. The need for deep copying arises when the language or data structures implement optimizations to prevent copying data, typically through the use of pointers, references, and copy-on-write semantics.

Copies of data structures can either be *shallow* (copying a pointer or creating a reference) or *deep* (copying or cloning all the *values* within a structure, recursively). Some languages perform shallow copies by default when you make an assignment (a = b) or call a function. Thus, if you come from languages like Python, Ruby, or JavaScript, you may have needed to occasionally perform an explicit deep copy. Rust doesn't assume anything about your intentions; thus, you always need to explicitly instruct the compiler what to do. In other words, the concept of shallow copies does not exist in Rust, but rather, we have borrowing and references.

Languages that use implicit data references can create undesired side effects, and this may occasionally catch people off guard or create hard-to-find bugs. The problem occurs, generally speaking, when you intend to make a copy, but the language, instead, provides a reference. Lucky for you, Rust doesn't do any type of implicit data referencing magic but only so long as you stick to core data structures.

In Rust, the term *cloning* (rather than *copying*) is used to describe the process of creating a new data structure and copying (or, more correctly, cloning) all the data from the old structure into the new one. The operation is typically handled through the `clone()` method, which comes from the `Clone` trait and can be automatically derived using the `#[derive(Clone)]` attribute (traits and deriving traits are discussed in greater detail in chapters 8 and 9). Many data structures in Rust come with the `Clone` trait implemented for you, so you can usually count on `clone()` being available.

Consider the following code listing.

Listing 5.4 Code to demonstrate `clone()`

```
fn main() {                                            Here, we clone the original Vec.
    let mut most_populous_us_cities =
        vec!["New York City", "Los Angeles", "Chicago", "Houston"];
    let most_populous_us_cities_cloned = most_populous_us_cities.clone();
    most_populous_us_cities.push("Phoenix");
    println!("most_populous_us_cities = {:#?}", most_populous_us_cities);
    println!(
        "most_populous_us_cities_cloned = {:#?}",         We'll add a new city
        most_populous_us_cities_cloned                    to the list in the
    );                                                    original Vec.
}          When the cloned Vec is printed, it won't output
           "Phoenix" because it's an entirely distinct structure.
```

Running the code in the previous listing prints the following:

```
most_populous_us_cities = [
    "New York City",
    "Los Angeles",
    "Chicago",
    "Houston",
    "Phoenix",
]
most_populous_us_cities_cloned = [
    "New York City",
    "Los Angeles",
    "Chicago",
    "Houston",
]
```

The `Clone` trait, when derived, operates recursively. Thus, calling `clone()` on any top-level data structure, such as a `Vec`, is sufficient to create a deep copy of the contents of the `Vec`, provided they all implement `Clone`. Deeply nested structures can be easily cloned without needing to do anything beyond ensuring they implement the `Clone` trait.

5.4   Avoiding copies

There are certain cases where, perhaps unintentionally, data structures can end up being cloned or copied more often than needed. This can happen in string processing, for example, when many copies of a string are made repeatedly within algorithms that scan, mutate, or otherwise handle some arbitrary set of data.

One downside to `Clone` is that it can be too easy to copy data structures, and you may end up with many copies of the same data if applied too liberally. For most intents and purposes this isn't a problem, and you're unlikely to have problems until you start operating on very large sets of data.

Many core library functions in Rust return copies of objects, as opposed to modifying them in place. This is, in most cases, the preferred behavior; it helps maintain immutability of data, which makes it easier to reason about how algorithms behave, at the cost of duplicating memory—perhaps only temporarily. To illustrate, let's examine a few string operations from Rust's core library in table 5.1.

Table 5.1   Examining Rust core string functions for copies

Function	Description	Copies?	Algorithm	Identified by?
`pub fn replace<'a, P>(&'a self, from: P, to: &str) -> String where P: Pattern<'a>,`	Replaces all matches of a pattern with another string	Yes	Creates a new string, pushes updated contents into new string, returning the new string and leaving the original string untouched	`self` parameter is an *immutable* reference; function returns owned `String`
`pub fn to_lowercase(&self) -> String`	Returns the lowercase equivalent of this string slice, as a new `String`	Yes	Creates a new string, copies each character to the new string, converting uppercase characters to lowercase characters	`self` parameter is an immutable reference; function returns owned `String`
`pub fn make_ascii_lowercase (&mut self)`	Converts this string to its ASCII lowercase equivalent in place	No	Iterates over each character, applying a lowercase conversion on uppercase ASCII characters	Function takes a *mutable* `self` reference, modifying the memory in place
`pub fn trim(&self) -> &str`	Returns a string slice with leading and trailing whitespace removed	No	Uses a double-ended searcher to find the start and end of a substring *without* whitespace, returning a slice representing the trimmed result	Function returns reference, not an *owned* string

You'll notice a pattern in table 5.1, which is that you can often identify whether an algorithm creates a copy based on whether the function modifies the source data in place or returns a new copy. There's one more case to illustrate, which is what I call the *pass through*. Consider the following:

```
fn lowercased(s: String) -> String {
    s.to_lowercase()
}

fn lowercased_ascii(mut s: String) -> String {
    s.make_ascii_lowercase();
    s
}
```

A copy is created here, inside to_lowercase(), and the new string is returned.

The string is passed through directly, with the memory modified in place. The ownership is passed back to the caller by returning the same owned object, as the make_ascii_lowercase() function operates in place.

In the preceding code, the first function, `lowercased()`, takes an owned string but returns a new copy of that string by calling `to_lowercase()`. The second function takes a mutable owned string and returns a lowercased version using the *in-place* version (which only works on ASCII strings).

The following is a summary of what we've learned about functions:

- Functions that take immutable references and return a reference or slice are unlikely to make copies (e.g., `fn func(&self) -> &str`).
- Functions that take a reference (i.e., `&`) and return an owned object may be creating a copy (e.g., `fn func(&self) -> String`).
- Functions that take a mutable reference (i.e., `&mut`) may be modifying data in place (e.g., `fn func(&mut self)`).
- Functions that take an owned object and return an owned object of the same type are likely making a copy (e.g., `fn func(String) -> String`).
- Functions that take a mutable owned object and return an owned object of the same type may not be making a copy (e.g., `fn func(mut String) -> String`).

As a general rule, you should examine documentation and source code when you're unsure as to whether functions make copies, operate in place, or merely pass ownership. Rust's memory semantics do make it relatively easy to reason about how algorithms operate on data merely by examining the inputs and outputs, but this only works provided the functions being called follow these patterns. In cases when you have serious performance concerns, you should closely examine the underlying algorithms.

5.5   *To box or not to box: Smart pointers*

Rust's `Box` is a type of smart pointer, which we briefly discussed in chapter 4. `Box` is a bit different from smart pointers in languages like C++, as its main purpose is providing a way to allocate data on the heap. In Rust, the two main ways to allocate data on the heap are by using `Vec` or `Box`. `Box` is quite limited in terms of its capabilities; it only handles allocation and deallocation of memory for the object it holds, without providing much else in terms of features, but that's by design. `Box` is still very useful, and it should be the first thing you reach for in cases when you need to store data on the heap (aside from using a `Vec`).

TIP Since a `Box` cannot be empty (except in certain situations best left unexplored), we often hold a `Box` within an `Option` in any case when boxed data might not be present.

If the data or object is optional, you should put your `Box` in an `Option`. *Optional* types (or *maybe* types) aren't unique to Rust; you may have encountered them from Ada, Haskell, Scala, or Swift, to name a few languages. Optionals are a kind of *monad*—a functional design pattern whereby you wrap values that shouldn't have unrestricted access in a function. Rust provides some syntax sugar to make working with optionals more pleasant.

You will see `Option` used frequently in Rust; if you haven't encountered optionals before, you can think of them as a way to safely handle null values (e.g., pointers). Rust doesn't have null pointers (excluding unsafe code), but it does have `None`, which is functionally equivalent to a null pointer, without the safety problems.

The cool thing about `Box` and `Option` is that when both are used together, it's nearly impossible to have run-time errors (e.g., null pointer exceptions) due to invalid, uninitialized, or doubly freed memory. However, there is one caveat: heap allocations may fail. Handling this situation is tricky, outside the scope of this book, and somewhat dependent on the operating system and its settings.

One common cause of allocation failures is the system running out of free memory, and handling this (if you choose to handle it at all) is largely dependent on the application. Most of the time, the expected result for failed memory allocations is for the program to "fail fast" and exit with an out of memory error (OOM), which is almost always the default behavior (i.e., what will happen if you as a developer don't handle OOM errors). You have likely encountered such situations yourself. Some notable applications that provide their own memory management features are web browsers, which often have their own built-in task managers and memory management, much like the OS itself. If you're writing mission-critical software, such as a database or online transaction-processing system, you may want to handle memory allocation failures gracefully.

In situations when you suspect allocation might fail, `Box` provides the `try_new()` method, which returns a `Result`. This—like an `Option`—may be in either a success or failure state. The default `new()` method of `Box` will create a panic in case allocation fails, which will cause your program to crash. In most cases, crashing is the best way to handle failed allocations. Alternatively, you can catch allocation failures within a custom allocator (which is discussed later in this chapter).

TIP To better understand `Option` and `Result`, try implementing them yourself using an enum. In Rust, creating and using your own optionals is trivial with enums and pattern matching.

To illustrate the use of `Box`, consider a basic singly linked list in Rust.

Listing 5.5   Code for a basic, singly linked list in Rust

Data is boxed within each list item.
The data field can't be empty or null.

```rust
struct ListItem<T> {
    data: Box<T>,
    next: Option<Box<ListItem<T>>>,
}
```

next is optional; a None value
denotes the end of the list.

```rust
struct SinglyLinkedList<T> {
    head: ListItem<T>,
}
```

The struct for the list itself only contains the head; we don't
bother boxing the head because it must always be present.

New data is moved into the list within a
Box, allocating memory on the heap.

```rust
impl<T> ListItem<T> {
    fn new(data: T) -> Self {
        ListItem {
            data: Box::new(data),
            next: None,
        }
    }
    fn next(&self) -> Option<&Self> {
        if let Some(next) = &self.next {
            Some(next.as_ref())
        } else {
            None
        }
    }
    fn mut_tail(&mut self) -> &mut Self {
        if self.next.is_some() {
            self.next.as_mut().unwrap().mut_tail()
        } else {
            self
        }
    }
    fn data(&self) -> &T {
        self.data.as_ref()
    }
}
```

The next pointer is initialized as None because new
elements don't know where they are in the list yet.
Additionally, this implementation doesn't have an
insert operation, only append.

The next() method on each item returns an
optional reference to the next item, if it exists.
This function exists to help unwrap the nested
references for the sake of simplifying the code.

We're using a
code construct
to check if the
next pointer
points to
anything before
trying to
dereference it.

We return the inner reference to the
next item, equivalent to Some(&*next).

Using if let … won't work here, because we
can't borrow self.next and return a mutable
reference to the inner pointer simultaneously.

If there's no next element, this
item is the tail; just return self.

We have Box within Option, so we
need to unwrap the Option from a
mutable reference and return a
mutable reference from within.

This method provides a convenient reference to T.

```rust
impl<T> SinglyLinkedList<T> {
    fn new(data: T) -> Self {
        SinglyLinkedList {
            head: ListItem::new(data),
        }
    }
    fn append(&mut self, data: T) {
        let mut tail = self.head.mut_tail();
        tail.next = Some(Box::new(ListItem::new(data)));
    }
    fn head(&self) -> &ListItem<T> {
        &self.head
    }
}
```

We require a first element for a new
list; to permit an empty list, the head
element would need to be optional.

We can assume the
tail's next is None when
appending a new item.

We add our new
element to the tail
item's next pointer,
and the new element
becomes the new tail.

For convenience, we provide direct access
to the head element via a method.

There's a lot to unpack in the linked list example. For someone new to Rust, implementing a linked list is one of the best ways to learn about Rust's unique features. The preceding example provides some nice features, and it's safe. The list will never be empty or invalid or contain null pointers. This is a really powerful feature of Rust, and it's only possible thanks to Rust's rules about object ownership.

We can test the linked list we just created using the following code:

```
fn main() {
    let mut list = SinglyLinkedList::new("head");       Creates a new linked list of strings,
    list.append("middle");                              with a head element, and then we
    list.append("tail");                                add a middle and tail element.
    let mut item = list.head();     ⟵——— Gets a reference to the head of the list
    loop {                                      ⟵
        println!("item: {}", item.data());   │ Loops until we've visited every item in the list
        if let Some(next_item) = item.next() {   ⟵——┐
            item = next_item;                          Fetches the next item in the list
        } else {                                       using an if let statement, which
            break;   ⟵——┐                              unwraps the Option
        }            We terminate the loop with a
    }                break when we've reached the
}                    end of the list, which we know
                     when the next item is None.
```

Prints the value of each item (label pointing to `println!("item: {}", item.data());`)

Running the preceding code produces the following output:

```
item: head
item: middle
item: tail
```

Before moving on to the next sections, I suggest you take some time to understand the singly linked list in Rust. Try implementing it yourself from scratch, and refer to the example provided as needed. In the next section, we'll do a more advanced version of the linked list. If you care to read on anyway, it may be worth revisiting this exercise if you want to get a better handle on Rust's memory management once you have a good understanding of the overall language.

Finally, in practice, you'll likely never need to implement your own linked list in Rust. Rust's core library provides std::collections::LinkedList in case you really want a linked list. For most cases, however, just use a Vec. Additionally, the example provided here is not optimized.

5.6 Reference counting

In the previous section, we talked about Box, which is a useful—but very limited—smart pointer and something you'll encounter often. Notably, a Box cannot be shared. That is to say, you can't have two separate boxes pointing to the same data in a Rust program; Box owns its data and doesn't allow more than one borrow at a time. This is, for the most part, a feature (or antifeature) worth being excited about. However, there are cases in which you do want to share data: perhaps, across threads of execution or by storing the same data in multiple structures to address it differently (such as a `Vec` and a `HashMap`).

In cases where `Box` doesn't cut it, what you're probably looking for are *reference-counted* smart pointers. Reference counting is a common technique in memory management to avoid keeping track of how many copies of a pointer exist, and when there are no more copies, the memory is released. The implementation usually relies on keeping a static counter of the number of copies of a given pointer and incrementing the counter every time a new copy is made. When a copy is destroyed, the counter is decremented. If the counter ever reaches zero, the memory can be released because that means there are no more copies of the pointer, and thus, the memory is no longer in use or accessible.

> **TIP** Implementing a reference-counted smart pointer is a fun exercise to do on your own; however, it's a bit tricky in Rust and requires the use of raw (i.e., unsafe) pointers. If you find the linked list exercise too easy, try making your own reference-counted smart pointer.

Rust provides two different reference-counted pointers:

- `Rc`—A single-threaded, reference-counted smart pointer, which enables shared ownership of an object
- `Arc`—A multithreaded, reference-counted smart pointer, which enables shared ownership of objects across threads

Single- vs. multithreaded objects in Rust

Many programming languages distinguish between functions or objects that can be used across threads as thread *safe* versus *unsafe*. In Rust, this distinction doesn't quite map directly, as everything is safe by default. Instead, some objects can be moved or synchronized across threads, and others can't. This behavior comes from whether an object implements the `Send` and `Sync` traits, which we discuss in greater detail in chapter 6.

In the case of `Rc` and `Arc`, `Rc` doesn't provide `Send` or `Sync` (in fact, `Rc` explicitly marks these traits as not implemented), so `Rc` can only be used in a single thread. `Arc`, on the other hand, implements both `Send` and `Sync`; thus, it can be used in multithreaded code.

`Arc`, in particular, uses *atomic* counters, which are platform dependent and usually implemented at the operating system or CPU level. Atomic operations are more costly than regular arithmetic, so only use `Arc` when you need atomicity.

It's important to note that so long as you aren't using the `unsafe` keyword to bypass language rules, Rust code is always safe. Getting it to compile, on the other hand, can be quite a challenge when you don't understand Rust's unique patterns and jargon.

To use reference-counted pointers effectively, we also need to introduce another concept in Rust called *interior mutability*. Interior mutability is something you may need when Rust's borrow checker doesn't provide enough flexibility with mutable references. If this sounds like an escape hatch, then pat yourself on the back for being an astute reader because it *is* an escape hatch. But worry not, it doesn't break Rust's safety contracts and still allows you to write safe code.

To enable interior mutability, we need to introduce two special types in Rust: `Cell` and `RefCell`. If you're new to Rust, you probably haven't encountered these yet, and it's unlikely you would bump into them under normal circumstances. In most cases, you'll want to use `RefCell` rather than `Cell`, as `RefCell` allows us to borrow references, whereas `Cell` moves values in and out of itself (which is probably not the behavior you want most of the time).

Another way to think about `RefCell` and `Cell` is that they allow you to provide the Rust compiler with more information about how you want to borrow data. The compiler is quite good, but it's limited in terms of flexibility, and there are some cases in which perfectly safe code won't compile because the compiler doesn't understand what you're trying to do (regardless of how correct it might be).

You shouldn't need `RefCell` or `Cell` very often; if you find yourself trying to use these to get around the borrow checker, you might need to rethink what you're doing. They are mainly needed for specific cases, such as containers and data structures that hold data that needs to be accessed mutably.

One limitation of `Cell` and `RefCell` is that they're only for single-threaded applications. In the case where you require safety across threads of execution, you can use `Mutex` or `RwLock`, which provide the same feature to enable interior mutability but can be used across threads. These would typically be paired with `Arc` rather than `Rc` (we'll explore concurrency in greater detail in chapter 10).

Let's update the linked list example from the previous section to use `Rc` and `RefCell` instead of `Box`, which gives us more flexibility. Notably, we can now make our singly linked list a *doubly* linked list, as shown in the following listing. This isn't possible using `Box` because it doesn't allow shared ownership.

Listing 5.6 Code of a doubly linked list using `Rc`, `RefCell`, and `Box`

```
use std::cell::RefCell;
use std::rc::Rc;

struct ListItem<T> {
    prev: Option<ItemRef<T>>,        ◁──── We've added a pointer to the
    data: Box<T>,                    ◁──    previous item in the list.
    next: Option<ItemRef<T>>,
}
                                        The data is still kept in a Box; we don't need to use an
                                        Rc here because we're not sharing ownership of the
                                        data, only the pointers to nodes in the list.

type ItemRef<T> = Rc<RefCell<ListItem<T>>>;   ◁──┐
                                                  This type alias helps
struct DoublyLinkedList<T> {                      keep the code clean.
    head: ItemRef<T>,
}
```

```
impl<T> ListItem<T> {
    fn new(data: T) -> Self {
        ListItem {
            prev: None,
            data: Box::new(data),    <──── Data is moved into a Box here.
            next: None,
        }
    }
    fn data(&self) -> &T {
        self.data.as_ref()
    }
}

impl<T> DoublyLinkedList<T> {
    fn new(data: T) -> Self {
        DoublyLinkedList {
            head: Rc::new(RefCell::new(ListItem::new(data))),
        }
    }
    fn append(&mut self, data: T) {
        let tail = Self::find_tail(self.head.clone());
        let new_item = Rc::new(RefCell::new(ListItem::new(data)));
        new_item.borrow_mut().prev = Some(tail.clone());
        tail.borrow_mut().next = Some(new_item);
    }
    fn head(&self) -> ItemRef<T> {
        self.head.clone()
    }
    fn tail(&self) -> ItemRef<T> {
        Self::find_tail(self.head())
    }
    fn find_tail(item: ItemRef<T>) -> ItemRef<T> {
        if let Some(next) = &item.borrow().next {
            Self::find_tail(next.clone())
        } else {
            item.clone()
        }
    }
}
```

Creates a pointer for the new item we're about to append.

First, we need to find the pointer to the tail item in the list.

We'll update the prev pointer in the new item to point to the previous tail.

Update the next pointer of the previous tail to point to the new tail, which is the newly inserted item.

Checks if the next pointer is empty and continues searching recursively if not.

We clone the next pointer and return it, continuing the search.

If the next pointer is empty, we're at the end (or tail) of the list. It returns the current item pointer after cloning it.

This version of the linked list looks quite different from the previous version. Introducing Rc and RefCell adds some complexity but provides us with a lot more flexibility. We'll revisit this example again later in the book as we explore more language features. To summarize, Rc and Arc provide reference-counted pointers, but to access inner data mutably, you'll need to use an object such as RefCell or Cell (and for multi-threaded applications, Mutex or RwLock).

5.7   *Clone on write*

Earlier in this chapter, we discussed avoiding copies. However, there are cases in which you prefer making copies of data, rather than ever mutating data in place. This pattern has some very nice features, especially if you prefer functional programming patterns.

You may not have heard of *clone on write* before, but you're probably familiar with *copy on write*.

Copy on write is a design pattern in which data is never mutated in place, but rather, any time data needs to be changed, it's copied to a new location and mutated, and then a reference to the new copy of data is returned. Some programming languages enforce this pattern as a matter of principle, such as in Scala, where data structures are classified as either mutable or immutable, and all the immutable structures implement copy on write. A very popular JavaScript library, Immutable.js, is based entirely on this pattern, with all data structure mutations resulting in a new copy of the data. Building data structures based on this pattern makes it much easier to reason about how data is handled within programs.

For example, with a copy-on-write list or array, the append operation would return a new list with all the old elements, plus the new element appended, while leaving the original list of items intact. The programmer assumes the compiler can handle optimizations and cleanup of old data.

In Rust, this pattern is referred to as clone on write, as it depends on the Clone trait. Clone has a cousin, the Copy trait, and they differ in that Copy denotes a *bitwise* copy (i.e., literally copying the bytes of an object to a new memory location), whereas Clone is an *explicit* copy. In the case of Clone, we call the clone() method on an object to clone it, but Copy occurs implicitly via assignment (i.e., let x = y;). The Clone trait is normally implemented automatically using #[derive(Clone)], but it can be implemented manually for special cases.

Rust provides three smart pointers to help implement clone on write:

- Cow—An enum-based smart pointer that provides convenient semantics
- Rc and Arc—Both reference-counted smart pointers provide clone-on-write semantics with the make_mut() method. Rc is the single-threaded version, and Arc is the multithreaded version.

Let's look at the type signature for Cow in the following listing.

Listing 5.7 Snippet of Cow definition from the Rust standard library

```
pub enum Cow<'a, B> where
    B: 'a + ToOwned + ?Sized,  {
    Borrowed(&'a B),
    Owned(<B as ToOwned>::Owned),
}
```

Cow is an enum that can contain either a borrowed variant or an owned variant. For the owned variant, it behaves a lot like Box, except that with Cow, the data is not necessarily allocated on the heap. If you want heap-allocated data with Cow, you'll need to use a Box within Cow, or use Rc or Arc instead. Rust's clone-on-write feature is also not a language-level feature—you need to explicitly use the Cow trait.

To demonstrate the use of Cow, let's update the singly linked list example so that the data structure becomes immutable. First, let's examine the following listing, which, aside from adding #[derive(Clone)], isn't too different from the previous version.

Listing 5.8   Code listing of `ListItem` for a singly linked list using `Cow`

```
#[derive(Clone)]
struct ListItem<T>                  ◁───   We derive the Clone trait for
where                                      both structs. Cow depends on
    T: Clone,                              the behavior of the Clone trait.
{
    data: Box<T>,
    next: Option<Box<ListItem<T>>>,
}

impl<T> ListItem<T>
where
    T: Clone,
{
    fn new(data: T) -> Self {
        ListItem {
            data: Box::new(data),
            next: None,
        }
    }
    fn next(&self) -> Option<&Self> {
        if let Some(next) = &self.next {
            Some(&*next)
        } else {
            None
        }
    }
    fn mut_tail(&mut self) -> &mut Self {
        if self.next.is_some() {
            self.next.as_mut().unwrap().mut_tail()
        } else {
            self
        }
    }
    fn data(&self) -> &T {
        self.data.as_ref()
    }
}
```

Next, let's look at the following listing, which shows the usage of Cow in our list.

Listing 5.9   Code listing of `SinglyLinkedList` for singly linked list using `Cow`

```
#[derive(Clone)]
struct SinglyLinkedList<'a, T>
where
    T: Clone,
```

```
{
    head: Cow<'a, ListItem<T>>,
}

impl<T> ListItem<T>
where
    T: Clone,
{
    fn new(data: T) -> Self {
        ListItem {
            data: Box::new(data),
            next: None,
        }
    }
    fn next(&self) -> Option<&Self> {
        if let Some(next) = &self.next {
            Some(&*next)
        } else {
            None
        }
    }
    fn mut_tail(&mut self) -> &mut Self {
        if self.next.is_some() {
            self.next.as_mut().unwrap().mut_tail()
        } else {
            self
        }
    }
    fn data(&self) -> &T {
        self.data.as_ref()
    }
}

impl<'a, T> SinglyLinkedList<'a, T>
where
    T: Clone,
{
    fn new(data: T) -> Self {
        SinglyLinkedList {
            head: Cow::Owned(ListItem::new(data)),
        }
    }
    fn append(&self, data: T) -> Self {
        let mut new_list = self.clone();
        let mut tail = new_list.head.to_mut().mut_tail();
        tail.next = Some(Box::new(ListItem::new(data)));
        new_list
    }
    fn head(&self) -> &ListItem<T> {
        &self.head
    }
}
```

The head pointer is stored within a Cow. We must include a lifetime specifier for the struct, so the compiler knows that the struct and the head parameter have the same lifetime.

Here, we initialize the list with the head pointer.

The append signature has changed such that it no longer requires a mutable self, and instead, it returns an entirely new linked list.

The call to_mut() triggers the clone on write, which happens recursively, by obtaining a mutable reference to the head.

5.8   *Custom allocators*

In some cases, you may find yourself needing to customize memory allocation behavior. The following are some example cases:

- Embedded systems, which are highly memory constrained or lack an operating system.
- Performance-critical applications that required optimized memory allocation, including custom heap managers, such as jemalloc (http://jemalloc.net/) or TCMalloc (https://github.com/google/tcmalloc).
- Applications with strict security or safety requirements, where you may want to protect memory pages using the `mprotect()` and `mlock()` system calls, for example
- Some library or plugin interfaces may require special allocators when handing off data to avoid memory leaks; this is quite common when working across language boundaries (i.e., integrating between Rust and a garbage collected language).
- Implementing custom heap management, such as memory usage tracking from within your application.

By default, Rust will use the standard system implementation for memory allocation, which on most systems is the `malloc()` and `free()` functions provided by the system's C library. This behavior is implemented by Rust's *global allocator*. The global allocator can be overridden for an entire Rust program using the `GlobalAlloc` API, and individual data structures can be overridden using custom allocators with the `Allocator` API.

> **NOTE**   The `Allocator` API in Rust is a nightly-only feature, as of the time of writing. For more details on the status of this feature, refer to https://github.com/rust-lang/rust/issues/32838. You can still use the `GlobalAlloc` API in stable Rust.

Even if you never need to write your own allocator (most people are unlikely to need a custom allocator), it's worth getting a feel for the allocator interface to have a better understanding of Rust's memory management. In practice, you're unlikely to ever need to worry about allocators except in special circumstances such as those mentioned.

5.8.1   *Writing a custom allocator*

Let's explore writing a custom `Allocator`, which we'll use with a `Vec`. Our allocator will simply call the `malloc()` and `free()` functions. To start, let's examine the `Allocator` trait as defined in the Rust standard library at http://mng.bz/g7ze. The trait is shown in the following listing.

Listing 5.10   Code listing for `Allocator` trait, from the Rust standard library

```
pub unsafe trait Allocator {
    fn allocate(&self, layout: Layout)
      -> Result<NonNull<[u8]>, AllocError>;          Required
    unsafe fn deallocate(&self, ptr: NonNull<u8>, layout: Layout);   methods
```

```
fn allocate_zeroed(
    &self,
    layout: Layout
) -> Result<NonNull<[u8]>, AllocError> { ... }
unsafe fn grow(
    &self,
    ptr: NonNull<u8>,
    old_layout: Layout,
    new_layout: Layout
) -> Result<NonNull<[u8]>, AllocError> { ... }
unsafe fn grow_zeroed(
    &self,
    ptr: NonNull<u8>,
    old_layout: Layout,
    new_layout: Layout
) -> Result<NonNull<[u8]>, AllocError> { ... }
unsafe fn shrink(
    &self,
    ptr: NonNull<u8>,
    old_layout: Layout,
    new_layout: Layout
) -> Result<NonNull<[u8]>, AllocError> { ... }
fn by_ref(&self) -> &Self { ... }
}
```

Optional methods, with default implementations provided

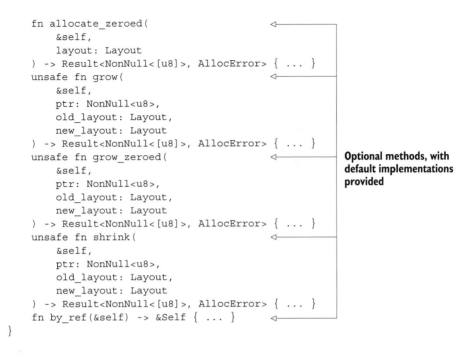

To implement an allocator, we only need to provide two methods: `allocate()` and `deallocate()`. These are analogous to `malloc()` and `free()`. The other methods are provided for cases when you wish to optimize allocation further. The C-equivalent call for `allocated_zeroed()` would be `calloc()`, whereas for the grow and shrink functions, you'd use `realloc()`.

NOTE You may notice the `unsafe` keyword on some of the `Allocator` trait's methods. Allocating and deallocating memory nearly always involves unsafe operations in Rust, which is why these methods are marked as unsafe.

Rust provides default implementations for the optional methods in the `Allocator` trait. In the case of growing and shrinking, the default implementation will simply allocate new memory, copy all the data, and then deallocate old memory. For allocating zeroed data, the default implementation calls `allocate()` and writes zeroes to all the memory locations. Let's begin by writing an allocator that passes through to the global allocator.

Listing 5.11   Code for a pass-through allocator

```
#![feature(allocator_api)]

use std::alloc::{AllocError, Allocator, Global, Layout};
use std::ptr::NonNull;
```

```
pub struct PassThruAllocator;

unsafe impl Allocator for PassThruAllocator {
  fn allocate(&self, layout: Layout) -> Result<NonNull<[u8]>, AllocError> {
      Global.allocate(layout)
  }
  unsafe fn deallocate(&self, ptr: NonNull<u8>, layout: Layout) {
      Global.deallocate(ptr, layout)
  }
}
```

NOTE The code samples for the allocator API are nightly only, and to compile or run them, you need to either use `cargo +nightly …` or override the toolchain within the project directory with `rustup override set nightly`.

The preceding code creates a pass-through allocator, which simply calls the underlying global allocator implementation, with the minimum required code. Run the following to test our allocator:

```
fn main() {
    let mut custom_alloc_vec: Vec<i32, _> =
        Vec::with_capacity_in(10, BasicAllocator);    ⬅──  Creates a Vec using
    for i in 0..10 {                                         our custom allocator,
        custom_alloc_vec.push(i as i32 + 1);                 initializing the vector
    }                                                        with a capacity of 10
    println!("custom_alloc_vec={:?}", custom_alloc_vec);     items
}
```

Running this code provides the following output, as expected:

```
custom_alloc_vec=[1, 2, 3, 4, 5, 6, 7, 8, 9, 10]
```

Now, let's change the allocator to call the `malloc()` and `free()` functions directly from the C library instead. The `Layout` struct provides us with the details needed to determine how much memory to allocate using the `size()` method.

Listing 5.12 Code for a basic custom allocator using `malloc()` and `free()`

```
#![feature(allocator_api)]

use std::alloc::{AllocError, Allocator, Layout};
use std::ptr::NonNull;

use libc::{free, malloc};

pub struct BasicAllocator;

unsafe impl Allocator for BasicAllocator {    ⬅──
    fn allocate(
```

The allocate() method in the Allocator trait does not include the unsafe keyword, but we still need to make unsafe calls. Thus, this code block is wrapped in an unsafe {} block.

```
        &self,
        layout: Layout,
    ) -> Result<NonNull<[u8]>, AllocError> {
        unsafe {
            let ptr = malloc(layout.size() as libc::size_t);
            let slice = std::slice::from_raw_parts_mut(
                ptr as *mut u8,
                layout.size(),
            );
            Ok(NonNull::new_unchecked(slice))
        }
    }
    unsafe fn deallocate(&self, ptr: NonNull<u8>, _layout: Layout) {
        free(ptr.as_ptr() as *mut libc::c_void);
    }
}
```

We're calling the C library's malloc(), and we assume normal standard alignment from the Layout struct.

The block of memory is returned as a slice, so first we convert the raw C pointer into a Rust slice.

Finally, create and return the final pointer to the slice of bytes.

deallocate() is essentially the reverse of allocate(), but this method is already marked as unsafe for us. The pointer must be converted from its raw Rust representation to a C pointer.

NOTE The `Layout` struct contains `size` and `align` properties, both of which should be handled for portability. The `size` property specifies the minimum number of bytes to allocate, and the `align` property is the minimum byte alignment for a block in powers of two. For details, refer to the Rust documentation on `Layout` at http://mng.bz/eEY9.

Pay attention to the use of the preceding `unsafe` keyword; the `deallocate()` method includes `unsafe` as part of the function signature itself, and `allocate()` requires the use of `unsafe` within the method. In both cases, `unsafe` is required and cannot be avoided because we're handling raw pointers and memory. `deallocate()` is marked as unsafe because if the method is called with invalid data (e.g., a bad pointer or incorrect layout), the behavior is undefined and, therefore, considered unsafe. In the event you need to write a custom allocator, the preceding code provides a starting point for you, regardless of your allocation needs.

5.8.2 Creating a custom allocator for protected memory

Let's quickly explore a more advanced example of a custom memory allocator to shed light on a scenario in which you'd want to utilize Rust's allocator API. For this example, the allocator can be applied piecewise to individual data structures, rather than to the program as a whole, which allows fine tuning for performance purposes.

In the `dryoc` crate, which I use for example purposes throughout this book, I make use of the `Allocator` trait to implement the protected memory feature of `dryoc`. Modern operating systems provide several memory-protection features for developers who are writing safety- or security-critical systems, and to utilize those features in a Rust program, you would need to write your own memory allocation code. Specifically, the `dryoc` crate uses the `mprotect()` and `mlock()` system calls on UNIX-like systems and the `VirtualProtect()` and `VirtualLock()` system calls on Windows. These system calls provide the ability to lock and control access to specific regions of memory within a process, both to code inside and outside the process. This is an important feature for code that manages sensitive data, such as secret keys.

As part of the implementation of memory-locking and -protection features, memory must be allocated by special platform-dependent memory functions (posix_memalign() on UNIX and VirtualAlloc() on Windows), such that it's aligned to platform-specific memory pages. Additionally, in the following code, two extra memory blocks are allocated before and after the target memory region, and those blocks are locked, which provides additional protection against certain types of memory attacks. These regions can be thought of as bumpers, like those you would find on an automobile.

When our custom allocator is used, memory will be allocated on the heap, as shown in figure 5.2. The active region is a subset of the total memory allocated, and a subset that excludes the first and last pages is returned as a slice by the allocator.

Let's examine a partial code sample of this allocator (the full code listing is included with the book's code). First, we'll examine the following listing.

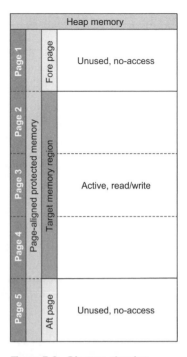

Figure 5.2 Diagram showing protected memory layout, with fore and aft regions.

Listing 5.13 Partial code listing for `allocate()` from page-aligned allocator

```
fn allocate(&self, layout: Layout,
) -> Result<ptr::NonNull<[u8]>, AllocError> {
    let pagesize = *PAGESIZE;
    let size = _page_round(layout.size(), pagesize) + 2 * pagesize;
    #[cfg(unix)]
    let out = {
        let mut out = ptr::null_mut();
        let ret = unsafe {
            libc::posix_memalign(&mut out, pagesize as usize, size)
        };
        if ret != 0 {
            return Err(AllocError);
        }
        out
    };
    #[cfg(windows)]
    let out = {
        use winapi::um::winnt::{MEM_COMMIT, MEM_RESERVE, PAGE_READWRITE};
        unsafe {
            winapi::um::memoryapi::VirtualAlloc(
                ptr::null_mut(), size, MEM_COMMIT | MEM_RESERVE,
```

Rounds the size of the memory region to the nearest page length, adding two additional pages before and after the memory region

Allocates page-aligned memory on POSIX-based systems

Allocates page-aligned memory on Windows-based systems

```
                    PAGE_READWRITE,
            )
        }
    };
    let fore_protected_region = unsafe {
        std::slice::from_raw_parts_mut(out as *mut u8, pagesize)
    };
    mprotect_noaccess(fore_protected_region)
        .map_err(|err| {
            eprintln!("mprotect error = {:?}, in allocator", err)
        })
        .ok();
    let aft_protected_region_offset =
        pagesize + _page_round(layout.size(), pagesize);
    let aft_protected_region = unsafe {
        std::slice::from_raw_parts_mut(
            out.add(aft_protected_region_offset) as *mut u8,
            pagesize,
        )
    };
    mprotect_noaccess(aft_protected_region)
        .map_err(|err| {
            eprintln!("mprotect error = {:?}, in allocator", err)
        })
        .ok();
    let slice = unsafe {
        std::slice::from_raw_parts_mut(
            out.add(pagesize) as *mut u8,
            layout.size(),
        )
    };
    mprotect_readwrite(slice)
        .map_err(|err| {
            eprintln!("mprotect error = {:?}, in allocator", err)
        })
        .ok();
    unsafe { Ok(ptr::NonNull::new_unchecked(slice)) }
}
```

Marks the memory page in front of the new region as no-access to prevent scanning

Marks the memory page after the new region as no access to prevent scanning

Marks the new region of memory as read/write

Returns the new pointer as a slice consisting of the memory location and size

Next, let's look at the implementation for `deallocate()` in the following listing.

Listing 5.14   Partial code for `deallocate()` from page-aligned allocator

```
unsafe fn deallocate(&self, ptr: ptr::NonNull<u8>, layout: Layout) {
    let pagesize = *PAGESIZE;
    let ptr = ptr.as_ptr().offset(-(pagesize as isize));
    // unlock the fore protected region
    let fore_protected_region =
        std::slice::from_raw_parts_mut(ptr as *mut u8, pagesize);
    mprotect_readwrite(fore_protected_region)
        .map_err(|err| eprintln!("mprotect error = {:?}", err))
        .ok();
    // unlock the aft protected region
    let aft_protected_region_offset =
```

Returns the fore memory page to read/write, the default state

```
        pagesize + _page_round(layout.size(), pagesize);
    let aft_protected_region = std::slice::from_raw_parts_mut(
        ptr.add(aft_protected_region_offset) as *mut u8,          Returns the aft
        pagesize,                                                 memory page to
    );                                                            read/write, the
    mprotect_readwrite(aft_protected_region)                      default state
        .map_err(|err| eprintln!("mprotect error = {:?}", err))
        .ok();
    #[cfg(unix)]
    {                                                      Releases the page-aligned
        libc::free(ptr as *mut libc::c_void);              memory on POSIX-based systems
    }
    #[cfg(windows)]
    {
        use winapi::shared::minwindef::LPVOID;
        use winapi::um::memoryapi::VirtualFree;           Releases the page-aligned
        use winapi::um::winnt::MEM_RELEASE;               memory on Windows-based
        VirtualFree(ptr as LPVOID, 0, MEM_RELEASE);       systems
    }
}
```

This code listing is based on code from the `dryoc` crate. You can find the full code listing on GitHub at http://mng.bz/p1R5, which may include future improvements. .

Using the cfg and cfg_attr attributes, and the cfg macro for conditional compilation

We've talked about attributes throughout the book, but it's a good time to take a moment to discuss `cfg` in more depth, as seen in the custom allocator example.

If you're coming from a language like C or C++, you're likely familiar with using macros to enable or disable code at compile time (e.g., `#ifdef FLAG { … } #endif`). Enabling and disabling features at compile time is a common pattern, especially for compiled languages that need access to OS-specific features (as in the custom allocator example). Rust's equivalent features look similar to, but behave differently from, what you may have seen in C and C++.

Rust provides three built-in tools for handling conditional code compilation:

- The `cfg` attribute, which conditionally includes the attached code (i.e., the item on the following line of code, whether it be a block or statement)
- The `cfg_attr` attribute, which behaves like `cfg` except that it allows you to set new compiler attributes based on the existing ones
- The `cfg` macro, which returns `true` or `false` at compile time

To illustrate its use, consider the following example:

```
#[cfg(target_family = "unix")]
fn get_platform() -> String {
    "UNIX".into()
}
```

```
#[cfg(target_family = "windows")]
fn get_platform() -> String {
    "Windows".into()
}

fn main() {
    println!("This code is running on a {} family OS", get_platform());
    if cfg!(target_feature = "avx2") {
        println!("avx2 is enabled");
    } else {
        println!("avx2 is not enabled");
    }
    if cfg!(not(any(target_arch = "x86", target_arch = "x86_64"))) {
        println!("This code is running on a non-Intel CPU");
    }
}
```

In the preceding example, the `cfg` attribute applies to the entire function block for `get_platform()`—hence, it appears twice. We use the `cfg` macro to test whether the `avx2` target feature is enabled and whether we're using a non-Intel architecture.

Shorthand configuration predicates are defined by the compiler, such as `unix` and `windows`, as shown in the custom allocator example. In other words, rather than writing `#[cfg(target_family = "unix")]`, you can use `#[cfg(unix)]`. A full list of the configuration values for your target CPU can be obtained by running `rustc --print=cfg -C target-cpu=native`.

Predicates may also be combined using `all()`, `any()`, and `not()`. `all()` and `any()` accept a list of predicates, whereas `not()` accepts one predicate. For example, you can use `#[cfg(not(any(target_arch = "x86", target_arch = "x86_64")`. The full listing of the compile-time configuration options can be found at http://mng.bz/OP7K.

5.9 *Smart pointers summarized*

In table 5.2, I have summarized the core smart pointer and memory container types to guide you when you are deciding which to use. You can refer to it as you learn more about Rust and start experimenting with more advanced memory management.

Table 5.2 Summarizing Rust's smart pointers and containers

Type	Kind	Description	When to use	Single- or multithreaded
`Box`	Pointer	Heap-allocated smart pointer	Any time you need to store a single object on the heap (and not in a container such as a `Vec`)	Single
`Cow`	Pointer	Smart pointer with clone-on-write, which can be used with owned *or* borrowed data	When you need heap-allocated data with clone-on-write functionality	Single

Table 5.2   Summarizing Rust's smart pointers and containers *(continued)*

Type	Kind	Description	When to use	Single- or multithreaded
Rc	Pointer	Reference-counted, heap-allocated smart pointer that enables shared ownership	When you need shared ownership of heap-allocated data	Single
Arc	Pointer	Atomically reference-counted, heap-allocated smart pointer that enables shared ownership	When you need shared ownership of heap-allocated data across threads	Multi
Cell	Container	Memory container that enables interior mutability using *move*	When you need to enable interior mutability of data within a smart pointer using *move*	Single
RefCell	Container	Memory container that enables interior mutability using *references*	When you need to enable interior mutability using *references*	Single
Mutex	Container	Mutual exclusion primitive that also enables interior mutability with a reference	When you need to synchronize data sharing across threads	Multi
RwLock	Container	Mutual exclusion primitive that provides distinction between readers and writers, and enables interior mutability with a reference	When you need reader/writer locking across threads	Multi

Summary

- Box and Vec provide methods to allocate memory on the heap. Vec should be preferred when you need a list of items; otherwise, use Box for a single item.
- The Clone trait can be used to provide deep copying of data structures in Rust.
- Rc and Arc provide reference-counted smart pointers for shared ownership.
- Cell and RefCell provide an escape hatch for the interior mutability problem when you need to mutate data inside an immutable structure but only for single-threaded applications.
- Mutex and RwLock provide synchronization primitives, which can be used with Arc to enable internal mutability.
- The Allocator and GlobalAlloc APIs provide a way to customize memory allocation behavior in Rust.

Part 3

Correctness

Writing good software is hard, and it's hard in many dimensions. We often hear about the importance of simplicity, but we tend to hear less about simplicity's sibling: correctness. Writing simple code is an admirable goal, but without correctness, even the world's most beautiful and simple code can still be wrong. We tend to hide complexity behind abstractions, but complexity is everywhere, always, even when hidden, so we must ensure we retain correctness.

Correctness is both qualitative and quantitative. Whether code is correct depends on how well the API is specified and whether the API's definition and implementations match. For example, I can write an adder function that accepts two parameters and returns their sum, but it should also correctly handle edge cases, such as overflows, signedness, bad inputs, and so on. For our adder to correctly handle those cases, they need to be specified. Unspecified behavior is the enemy of correctness.

In the upcoming chapters, we'll discuss testing strategies for guaranteeing correctness in your code. By writing tests for your code, you can also reveal weaknesses in specifications by finding ambiguities, in addition to verifying the correctness of your implementations.

Unit testing

Unit testing is one way to improve code quality, as it can catch regressions and ensure code meets requirements before shipping. Rust includes a built-in unit testing framework to make your life easier. In this chapter, we'll review some of the features Rust provides and discuss some of the shortfalls of Rust's unit testing framework—and how to overcome them.

6.1   *How testing is different in Rust*

Before we jump into the details of Rust's unit testing features, we should talk about the differences between Rust and other languages and how they relate to unit testing. For those coming from languages like Haskell or Scala, you may find Rust has similar properties when it comes to testing. Compared to most languages, however, Rust varies greatly, in that the kinds of unit tests you might see in other languages aren't necessary in Rust.

To elaborate, there are many cases in Rust in which, so long as the code compiles, the code must be correct. In other words, the Rust compiler can be thought of as an automatic test suite that's always applied to code. This only remains true for certain types of tests, and there are a variety of ways to break this contract in Rust.

The two most commons ways to undo some of Rust's safety guarantees are

- Using the `unsafe` keyword
- Converting compile-time errors into run-time errors

The latter can happen in a variety of ways, but the most common is by using `Option` or `Result` without properly dealing with both result cases. In particular, this error can be made by calling `unwrap()` on these types without handling the failure case. In some cases, this is the desired behavior, but it's also a mistake people often make simply because they don't want to spend time handling errors. To avoid these problems, the simple solution is to handle all cases and avoid calling functions that panic at run time (such as `unwrap()`). Rust *does not* provide a way to verify that code is panic free.

In the case of Rust's standard library, functions and methods that panic on failures are generally noted as such in the documentation. As a general rule, for any kind of programming, any functions that perform I/O or nondeterministic operations may fail (or panic) at any time, and those failure cases should be handled appropriately (unless, of course, the correct way to handle the failure is to panic).

> **NOTE**   In Rust, the term *panic* means to raise an error and abort the program. If you want to force a panic yourself, the `panic!()` macro can be used. Additionally, you can use the `compile_error!()` macro to induce a compile-time error.

Often, the Rust compiler can catch errors before code ships, without the help of unit tests. What the Rust compiler cannot do, however, is catch logic errors. For example, the Rust compiler can detect certain cases of divide-by-zero errors, but it can't tell you when you mistakenly used division instead of multiplication.

As a rule, the best way to write software that's both easy to test and unlikely to be wrong is accomplished by breaking down code into small units of computation (functions) that generally satisfy the following properties:

1 Functions should be stateless when possible.
2 Functions should be idempotent in cases where they must be stateful.

3   Functions should be deterministic whenever possible; the result of a function should always be the same for any given set of inputs.

4   Functions that might fail should return a `Result`.

5   Functions that may return no value (i.e., null) should return an `Option`.

Following points 4 and 5 allows you to make heavy use of the `?` operator in Rust (`?` is shorthand for returning early with an error result if the result is not `Ok`), which can save you from typing a lot of code. In chapter 4, we discussed using `Result` with the `From` trait, which greatly simplifies error handling in your code. For any given function you write that returns a `Result`, you only need to write the necessary `From` trait implementation for any possible errors within the function, and then you can handle those errors appropriately with the `?` operator. Keep in mind this only works in generic situations and may not be appropriate in cases where the error handling is specific to the function in question.

> **TIP** If you want to panic on an unexpected result, use the `expect()` function. `expect()` takes a message as an argument explaining why the program panicked. `expect()` is a safer alternative to `unwrap()` and can be thought of as behaving similarly to `assert()`.

By convention, Rust unit tests are stored in the same source file as the code being tested. That is to say, for any given struct, function, or method, its corresponding unit test would generally be within the same source file. Tests are typically located near the bottom of the file. This has the nice side effect of helping you keep code relatively small and as separate concerns. If you try to pack too much logic into one file, it can grow quite large, especially if you have complicated tests. Once you pass the 1,000-line mark, you may need to think about refactoring.

Finally, most of this advice is not necessarily Rust specific—it applies to all programming languages. For Rust specifically, your code should always handle return values and avoid the use of `unwrap()`, except when necessary.

6.2   *Review of built-in testing features*

Rust provides several basic testing features (table 6.1), although you may find the built-in features lacking compared to more mature testing frameworks. One notable difference between Rust and other languages is that the core Rust tooling and language includes testing features without the use of additional libraries or frameworks. In many languages, testing is an afterthought and requires additional tooling and libraries bolted on to properly test code. Features not provided by Rust can usually be

found in crates; however, you may also find that Rust makes testing much easier overall, thanks to the strict language guarantees.

Table 6.1 Summary of Rust's testing features

Feature	Description
Unit testing	Rust and Cargo provide unit testing directly without the use of additional libraries, using the `tests` mod within source files. The `tests` mod must be marked with `#[cfg(test)]`, and test functions must be marked with the `#[test]` attribute.
Integration testing	Rust and Cargo provide integration testing, which allows testing of libraries and applications from their public interfaces. Tests are typically constructed as their own individual applications, separate from the main source code.
Documentation testing	Code samples in source code documentation using `rustdoc` are treated as unit tests, which cleverly improve the overall quality of documentation *and* testing, simultaneously.
Cargo integration	Unit, integration, and documentation tests work with Cargo automatically and don't require additional work beyond defining the tests themselves. The `cargo test` command handles filtering, displaying assertion errors, and even parallelizing tests for you.
Assertion macros	Rust provides assertion macros, such as `assert!()` and `assert_eq!()`, although these are not exclusive to tests (they can be used anywhere because they're normal Rust macros). Cargo, however, will properly handle assertion failures when running unit tests and provide helpful output messages.

Let's examine the anatomy of a simple library with a unit test to demonstrate Rust's
testing features. Consider the following example, which provides a generic adder.

Listing 6.1 Code for a basic unit test in Rust

This is an addition function that takes two parameters of
the same type and returns the result of the same type. The
type T needs to have the std::ops::Add trait implemented
for the same output type.

```
pub fn add<T: std::ops::Add<Output = T>>(a: T, b: T) -> T {
    a + b
}

#[cfg(test)]
mod tests {
    use super::*;

    #[test]
    fn test_add() {
        assert_eq!(add(2, 2), 4);
    }
}
```

Our mod tests contains our tests, and
the #[cfg(test)] attribute tells the
compiler this is our unit test mod.

This is a convenient shorthand to include
everything from the outer scope of this mod.
You'll often see this used in tests.

The #[test] attribute tells the
compiler this function is a unit test.

This test passes, which is great. If you run `cargo test`, the output looks like the code in the following listing.

Listing 6.2   Successful test run

```
$ cargo test
   Compiling unit-tests v0.1.0
   (/Users/brenden/dev/code-like-a-pro-in-rust/code/c6/6.2/unit-tests)
    Finished test [unoptimized + debuginfo] target(s) in 0.95s
     Running unittests (target/debug/deps/unit_tests-c06c761997d04f8f)

running 1 test
test tests::test_add ... ok

test result: ok. 1 passed; 0 failed; 0 ignored; 0 measured; 0 filtered out;
finished in 0.00s

   Doc-tests unit-tests

running 0 tests

test result: ok. 0 passed; 0 failed; 0 ignored; 0 measured; 0 filtered out;
finished in 0.00s
```

6.3   *Testing frameworks*

Rust's unit testing doesn't include the helpers, fixtures, harnesses, or parameterized testing features, like you may find in other unit testing frameworks. For those, you'll either need to code your own or try some libraries.

For basic parameterized testing, the `parameterized` (https://crates.io/crates/parameterized) crate provides a nice interface to create tests. The `test-case` (https://crates.io/crates/test-case) crate provides another implementation of parameterized testing that's simple, concise, and easy to use. For fixtures, you can try the `rstest` (https://crates.io/crates/rstest) crate. The `assert2` (https://crates.io/crates/assert2) crate provides assertions inspired by the popular C++ Catch2 library.

One library worth mentioning in detail is the proptest (https://lib.rs/crates/proptest) crate, which provides a Rust implementation of QuickCheck (https://github.com/nick8325/quickcheck), a Haskell library originally released in 1999, and one which you may have already encountered. Proptest isn't a 1:1 port of QuickCheck to Rust, but rather, it provides equivalent functionality with some Rust-specific differences, which are documented at http://mng.bz/YRno.

Property testing can save you a lot of time by generating random test data, verifying results, and reporting back with the minimum test case required to create an error. This is a huge time saver, although it's not necessarily a replacement for testing well-known values (e.g., when verifying spec compliance).

NOTE There's no free lunch with property testing; it comes with the tradeoff of possibly having to spend more CPU cycles testing random values, as opposed to hand-picked or well-known values. You can tune the number of random values to test, but for data with a large set of possible values, it's often not practical to test every outcome.

Let's revisit our adder example from the previous section, but this time, we'll try it with proptest, which will provide the test data for our test function.

Listing 6.3   Code listing of adder with proptest

```
pub fn add<T: std::ops::Add<Output = T>>(a: T, b: T) -> T {
    a + b
}

#[cfg(test)]
mod tests {
    use super::*;
    use proptest::prelude::*;          Here, we include the proptest library,
    proptest! {                        which includes the proptest! macro.
        #[test]
        fn test_add(a: i64, b: i64) {  Our test function's parameters,
            assert_eq!(add(a, b), a + b);   a and b, will be provided by the
        }                              proptest! macro.
    }
}                                      We assert that our adder does,
                                       indeed, return the result of a + b.
```

Now, let's run this test again with proptest:

```
cargo test
   Compiling proptest v0.1.0
   (/Users/brenden/dev/code-like-a-pro-in-rust/code/c6/6.2/proptest)
    Finished test [unoptimized + debuginfo] target(s) in 0.59s
      Running unittests (target/debug/deps/proptest-db846addc2c2f40d)

running 1 test
test tests::test_add ... FAILED

failures:

----- tests::test_add stdout -----
# ... snip ...
thread 'tests::test_add' panicked at 'Test failed: attempt to add with
overflow; minimal failing input: a = -2452998745726535882,
b = -6770373291128239927
    successes: 1
    local rejects: 0
    global rejects: 0
', src/lib.rs:9:5

failures:
    tests::test_add
```

```
test result: FAILED. 0 passed; 1 failed; 0 ignored; 0 measured; 0 filtered
out; finished in 0.00s

error: test failed, to rerun pass '--lib'
```

Uh oh! It looks like our adder wasn't so great after all. It turns out it can "blow up" under certain circumstances (in this case, the addition operation overflowed because we're adding two signed integers of finite length). We weren't expecting this kind of failure and probably wouldn't have caught it unless we were manually generating random data for a and b.

Arithmetic overflow in Rust

Arithmetic operations in Rust may trip people up at first, especially when testing. There's a simple reason for this: in Rust, code compiled in debug mode (e.g., tests) uses *checked* arithmetic by default. When the same code is compiled in release mode, it will use *unchecked* arithmetic. Thus, you can have code that fails when run in debug mode but works fine (i.e., does not produce an error or crash the program) in production.

Rust's approach can be a bit confusing because of how the behavior is different depending on how code is compiled. The rationale in Rust is that test code should be stricter to catch more bugs, but for compatibility, the code should behave the way most other programs behave at run time.

Developers sometimes take arithmetic overflow for granted because most languages either emulate the behavior of languages like C (which is usually referred to as *wrapped* arithmetic; i.e., when the integer overflows it just wraps around). Rust provides a number of alternative arithmetic functions for primitive types, which are documented in the standard library for each type. For example, i32 provides checked_add(), unchecked_add(), carrying_add(), wrapping_add(), overflowing_add(), and saturating_add().

To emulate the C behavior, you can use the Wrapping struct (documented at http://mng.bz/G97M) or call the corresponding method for each type and operation. This behavior is document in RFC 560 (http://mng.bz/z01w).

We have a few options for fixing the previous test, but the easiest one is to just explicitly wrap overflows (i.e., follow the C behavior of integer overflow). Let's update our code to look like this:

We're relying on the num_traits crate, which provides the WrappingAdd trait.

```
extern crate num_traits;              ◁
use num_traits::ops::wrapping::WrappingAdd;

pub fn add<T: WrappingAdd<Output = T>>(a: T, b: T) -> T {     ◁── The trait bound is
    a.wrapping_add(&b)                                             switched from Add
}                                                                 to WrappingAdd.

#[cfg(test)]
mod tests {
    use super::*;
```

```
use proptest::prelude::*;
proptest! {
    #[test]
    fn test_add(a: i64, b: i64) {
        assert_eq!(add(a, b), a.wrapping_add(b));
    }
}
}
```

The test needs to be updated so that it is also using wrapping_add().

We've added the `num_traits` crate, a small library that provides the `WrappingAdd` trait, to the preceding code. The Rust standard library doesn't have an equivalent trait, and it's difficult to create a generic function this way without one (we'll explore traits in greater depth in chapters 8 and 9).

If we run our code now, it passes as expected:

```
cargo test
    Compiling wrapping-adder v0.1.0
    (/Users/brenden/dev/code-like-a-pro-in-rust/code/c6/6.2/wrapping-adder)
     Finished test [unoptimized + debuginfo] target(s) in 0.65s
      Running unittests (target/debug/deps/wrapping_adder-5330c09f59045f6a)

running 1 test
test tests::test_add ... ok

test result: ok. 1 passed; 0 failed; 0 ignored; 0 measured; 0 filtered out;
finished in 0.01s

    Running unittests (target/debug/deps/wrapping_adder-a198d5a6a64245d9)

running 0 tests

test result: ok. 0 passed; 0 failed; 0 ignored; 0 measured; 0 filtered out;
finished in 0.00s

   Doc-tests wrapping-adder

running 0 tests

test result: ok. 0 passed; 0 failed; 0 ignored; 0 measured; 0 filtered out;
finished in 0.00s
```

6.4 *What not to test: Why the compiler knows better than you*

Rust is a statically typed language, which brings with it some major advantages, especially when it comes to testing. One way to think about statically typed languages, as opposed to dynamically typed languages, is that the compiler does the work of limiting the set of possible inputs and outputs to any given statement or block of code by analyzing the source code before it runs. The possible set of inputs and outputs are constrained by type specifications. That is to say, a string can't be an integer, and vice versa. The compiler verifies that the types match what's expected and references are valid. You don't need to worry about mixing up strings and integers at run time because the compiler doesn't let it happen; this frees you (the developer) from having to worry about a host of problems, provided you use types correctly.

In dynamically typed languages, type errors are one of the most common types of problems. In interpreted languages, the combination of invalid syntax and type errors creates a potent opportunity for run-time errors that can be difficult to catch before code is shipped. Many dynamic languages have been retrofitted with static analyzer tools, but they're not always adequately strict or thorough to catch common errors.

When it comes to testing, we never need to test anything the compiler or borrow checker tests for us. For example, we don't need to check whether an integer is an integer or a string is a string. We don't need to check that references are valid or whether data is being mutated by two different threads (a race condition).

Let's be clear that this doesn't mean you don't need to test—it just means most of what you test in Rust is logic, rather than type validation or memory use. It's true that you still need to perform type conversions, which might fail, but handling these is a matter of logic. Rust's ergonomics make it hard to handle things that might fail improperly.

Testing properly in Rust begins with effectively using Rust's type system. Overuse of `Option`, `unwrap()`, or unsafe code can lead to harder-to-find bugs, especially if you use these features as a way to avoid handling edge cases. Stateful operations and I/O need to be checked and handled appropriately (as a good habit, functions or methods performing I/O should probably return a `Result`).

6.5 *Handling parallel test special cases and global state*

When Cargo runs unit tests, it does so in parallel. Rust uses threads to execute multiple tests simultaneously, to speed up testing. Most of the time, this works transparently, and you don't need to worry about it. However, we sometimes find ourselves needing to create global state or fixtures for tests, and doing so may require shared state.

Rust provides a couple of facilities for handling this problem: one is to create your own `main()` function for testing (by, effectively, overriding Rust's *libtest*, which is the built-in testing library in Rust and not something you typically interact with directly). That option, however, is probably more trouble than it's worth, so instead, I'll direct you to an alternative: the handy `lazy_static` (https://crates.io/crates/lazy_static) crate.

> **TIP** If you *do* want to provide your own `main()` for testing, you can do so by disabling Rust's built in harness libtest with `harness = false` in the target settings.

Some details on how to do this can be found in the `rustc` (https://doc.rust-lang .org/rustc/tests/index.html) and libtest (https://doc.rust-lang.org/test/index.html) documentation.

If, by some chance, you haven't already encountered `lazy_static` at this point, then you'll be pleased to learn about it now. The `lazy_static` crate makes the creation of static variables in Rust much easier. Creating global shared state in Rust is somewhat tricky because you sometimes need to initialize static structures at run time. To accomplish this, you can create a static reference and update that reference when it's first accessed, which is what `lazy_static` does.

To illustrate the problem with global state, consider the following code listing.

Listing 6.4   Unit test with global count

```
#[cfg(test)]
mod tests {
    static mut COUNT: i32 = 0;          ⊲——┐ Defines a static mutable
                                              counter variable
    #[test]
    fn test_count() {                   ┌— Increments the counter
        COUNT += 1;                     ⊲—┘ within our test
    }
}
```

This code fails to compile, with the following error:

```
error[E0133]: use of mutable static is unsafe and requires unsafe function
or block
  --> src/lib.rs:7:9
   |
7  |          COUNT += 1;
   |          ^^^^^^^^^^^ use of mutable static
   |
   = note: mutable statics can be mutated by multiple threads: aliasing
   violations or data races will cause undefined behavior
```

The compiler is correctly catching the error here. If you wrote equivalent code in C, it would compile and run without complaint (and it will probably work most of the time … until it doesn't).

We've got a couple of options to fix the code. In this case, we've just got a simple count, so we can simply use an atomic integer instead (which is thread safe). Seems easy enough, right? Let's try the following:

```
#[cfg(test)]
mod tests {                                                    Uses an Atomic integer
    use std::sync::atomic::{AtomicI32, Ordering};             provided by Rust's
    static mut COUNT: AtomicI32 = AtomicI32::new(0);  ⊲—      standard library

    #[test]                                      Performs a fetch and add operation,
    fn test_count() {                            which increments the atomic integer;
        COUNT.fetch_add(1, Ordering::SeqCst);  ⊲— Ordering::SeqCst tells the compiler
    }                                            how to synchronize operations,
}                                                documented at http://mng.bz/0lRp.
```

If we try compiling our updated test, it prints the exact same error (`use of mutable static`). So what gives? `rustc` is being *very* strict: it's complaining about the *ownership* of the `COUNT` variable, which, itself, doesn't implement the `Send` trait. We'll have to introduce `Arc` to implement `Send` as well.

> **Rust's Send and Sync traits**
>
> Rust provides two important traits for handling shared state across threads: `Send` and `Sync`. These traits are what the compiler uses to provide Rust's thread safety guarantees, and you'll need to understand them when working with multithreaded Rust code and shared state.
>
> These traits are defined as such:
>
> - `Send` marks objects that can be safely *moved* between threads.
> - `Sync` marks objects that can be safely *shared* between threads.
>
> For example, if you want to move a variable from one thread to another, it needs to be wrapped in something that implements `Send`. If you want to have shared references to the same variable across threads, you'll need to wrap it in something that implements `Sync`.
>
> These traits are automatically derived by the compiler where appropriate. You don't need to implement them directly, but rather, you can use combinations of `Arc`, `Mutex`, and `RwLock` (discussed in chapter 5) to achieve thread safety.

Let's update our code again, now that we've realized we need to use `Arc`:

```
#[cfg(test)]
mod tests {
    use std::sync::atomic::{AtomicI32, Ordering};
    use std::sync::Arc;

    static COUNT: Arc<AtomicI32> = Arc::new(AtomicI32::new(0));

    #[test]
    fn test_count() {
        let count = Arc::clone(&COUNT);
        count.fetch_add(1, Ordering::SeqCst);
    }
}
```

We need to clone the Arc before we can use it to obtain a reference in this thread context.

If we try to compile this, we're going to be disappointed again with a new error:

```
error[E0015]: calls in statics are limited to constant functions, tuple
structs and tuple variants
 --> src/lib.rs:6:38
  |
6 |     static COUNT: Arc<AtomicI32> = Arc::new(AtomicI32::new(0));
  |                                    ^^^^^^^^^^^^^^^^^^^^^^^^^^^^^
```

If you reached this point on your own, you may feel like giving up here. However, the solution is pretty simple: `lazy_static`. The compiler doesn't let us create globals that aren't constants, so we need to either write custom code to do the initialization at run time, or we can just use `lazy_static`. Let's update the test one more time:

```
#[cfg(test)]
mod tests {
    use lazy_static::lazy_static;
    use std::sync::atomic::{AtomicI32, Ordering};
    use std::sync::Arc;
    lazy_static! {
        static ref COUNT: Arc<AtomicI32> = Arc::new(AtomicI32::new(0));
    }

    #[test]
    fn test_count() {
        let count = Arc::clone(&COUNT);
        count.fetch_add(1, Ordering::SeqCst);
    }
}
```

The lazy_static! macro is used to wrap our static variable definitions.

When initializing with lazy_static!, you supply a code block returning the initialized object. In this case, it all fits on one line, so the braces ({ ... }) are omitted.

Presto! Now, our code compiles and runs safely. The `lazy_static!` macro takes care of the details of initializing the data at run time. When the variable is first accessed, it's initialized automatically, and we can use it globally. To understand what `lazy_static` does, let's view the code generated by the macro with `cargo expand` (introduced in chapter 3):

```
#[allow(missing_copy_implementations)]
#[allow(non_camel_case_types)]
#[allow(dead_code)]
struct COUNT {
    __private_field: (),
}
#[doc(hidden)]
static COUNT: COUNT = COUNT {
    __private_field: (),
};
impl ::lazy_static::__Deref for COUNT {
    type Target = Arc<AtomicI32>;
    fn deref(&self) -> &Arc<AtomicI32> {
        #[inline(always)]
        fn __static_ref_initialize() -> Arc<AtomicI32> {
            Arc::new(AtomicI32::new(0))
        }
        #[inline(always)]
        fn __stability() -> &'static Arc<AtomicI32> {
            static LAZY: ::lazy_static::lazy::Lazy<Arc<AtomicI32>> =
                ::lazy_static::lazy::Lazy::INIT;
            LAZY.get(__static_ref_initialize)
        }
        __stability()
    }
}
impl ::lazy_static::LazyStatic for COUNT {
    fn initialize(lazy: &Self) {
        let _ = &**lazy;
    }
}
```

lazy_static implements the Deref trait (within its code, __Deref is aliased to the core library Deref).

This block will be replaced with the initialization code supplied by us (in our case, a single line).

lazy_static uses the std::sync::Once primitive internally, from the Rust core library, which is initialized at this point.

Examining `lazy_static`'s source code, we can see it is based on the `std::sync::Once` primitive (provided by the standard library). We can drop the superfluous `Arc` that we added in the previous step because `lazy_static` provides `Send`. The final result when using lazy_static looks like this:

```
#[cfg(test)]
mod tests {
    use lazy_static::lazy_static;
    use std::sync::atomic::{AtomicI32, Ordering};
    lazy_static! {
        static ref COUNT: AtomicI32 = AtomicI32::new(0);
    }

    #[test]
    fn test_count() {
        COUNT.fetch_add(1, Ordering::SeqCst);
    }
}
```

And while `lazy_static` helps us solve the problem of sharing global state, it doesn't help us with synchronizing the tests themselves. For example, if you want to ensure your tests execute one at a time, you'll have to either implement your own `main()` to run your tests; instruct libtest to run the tests with only one thread; or synchronize your tests using a mutex, as shown in the following code:

```
#[cfg(test)]
mod tests {
    use lazy_static::lazy_static;
    use std::sync::Mutex;
    lazy_static! {
        static ref MUTEX: Mutex<i32> = Mutex::new(0);
    }
    #[test]
    fn first_test() {
        let _guard = MUTEX.lock().expect("couldn't acquire lock");
        println!("first test is running");
    }
    #[test]
    fn second_test() {
        let _guard = MUTEX.lock().expect("couldn't acquire lock");
        println!("second test is running");
    }
}
```

If you run this code repeatedly with `cargo test --nocapture`, you may notice that the output doesn't always print in the same order. That's because we can't guarantee the order of execution (libtest is still trying to run these tests in parallel). If you need tests to run in a particular order, you need to either use a barrier or condition variable or implement your own `main()` function to run your tests.

As a final note, let it be said that unit tests shouldn't require synchronization or shared state. If you find yourself doing this, you may need to consider whether your design needs to be refactored.

6.6   *Thinking about refactoring*

One value proposition of unit testing is catching regressions—code changes that break existing features or behaviors—before software ships. Indeed, if your unit tests cover the software's specification in its entirety, any change to that software that does not conform to the specification will result in test failures.

Code refactoring—which I'll define here as code changes that don't affect the behavior of public interfaces to the software—is common practice and carries with it advantages as well as risks. The main risk of refactoring is the introduction of regressions. The benefits of refactoring can be some combination of improved code quality, faster compilation, and better performance.

We can employ various strategies when writing tests to improve the quality of our software. One strategy is to test public interfaces in addition to private or internal interfaces. This works especially well if you can achieve near 100% coverage (and we'll discuss code coverage later in this chapter).

In practical software development, unit tests break frequently and can often consume a great deal of development time to debug, fix, and maintain. For that reason, only testing what needs to be tested can, perhaps counterintuitively, save you time and provide equivalent or better software quality. Determining what needs to be tested can be accomplished by analyzing test coverage, determining what's required by the specifications, and removing anything that doesn't need to be there (provided it's not a breaking change).

With good testing, we can refactor mercilessly with confidence. Too much testing makes our software inflexible, and we spin our wheels managing tests. Combining automated testing tools, such as property-based testing, fuzz testing (discussed in the next chapter), and code coverage analysis, gives us a great deal of quality and flexibility without requiring superpowers.

6.7   *Refactoring tools*

So now you have some wonderful tests and a clean API, and you want to start improving the internals of your software by cleaning things up. Some refactorings are harder than others, but there are a few tools we can use to make things smoother.

Before we discuss which tools to use, we need to break down the process of refactoring into types of refactorings. Some examples of common refactoring tasks include the following:

- *Reformatting*—Adjusting whitespace and rearranging symbols for readability
- *Renaming*—Changing the names of variables, symbols, constants
- *Relocating*—Moving code from one location to another within the source tree, possibly into different crates
- *Rewriting*—Completely rewriting sections of code or algorithms

6.7.1 Reformatting

For code formatting, the preferred tool is rustfmt (introduced in chapter 3). You will rarely need to manually reformat Rust code; rustfmt can be configured according to your preferences. Review the rustfmt section in chapter 3 for details on how to adjust the rustfmt settings to your preferences. Using rustfmt is as simple as running `cargo fmt` as needed, or it can be integrated directly into your editor or IDE using `rust-analyzer`.

6.7.2 Renaming

Let's discuss renaming, which can be a tricky task in certain complex situations. Most code editors include some type of find-and-replace tool to apply code changes (or you can do this from the command line using `sed` or some other command), but that's not always the best way to do big refactorings. Regular expressions are very powerful, but sometimes, we need something more contextually aware.

The `rust-analyzer` tool can intelligently rename symbols, and it also provides a structural search-and-replace tool (documented at http://mng.bz/K97P). You can use both of these directly from your IDE or code editor. In VS Code, rename a symbol by selecting it with the cursor and pressing F2 or use the context menu to select Rename Symbol.

Using the structural search-and-replace feature of `rust-analyzer` can be accomplished either through the command palette or by adding a comment with the replacement string. The replacement is applied to the entire workspace by default, which makes refactoring a snap. `rust-analyzer` will parse the syntax tree to find matches and perform replacements on expressions, types, paths, or items, in a way that doesn't introduce syntax errors. A substitution is only applied if the result is valid. For example, using the `Mutex` guard example from earlier in this chapter, we can use the `$m.lock() => Mutex::lock(&$m)` substitution, as shown in figure 6.1.

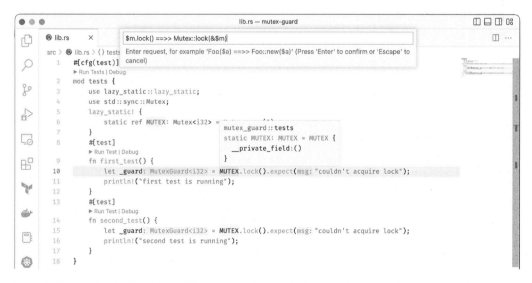

Figure 6.1 Structural substitution with `rust-analyzer`, before applying

After applying the substitution, we get the result shown in figure 6.2. In this example, calling `MUTEX.lock()` and `Mutex::lock(&MUTEX)` are equivalent, but some might prefer the latter form. The structural search and replace is contextual, as you can see in the preceding example, where I only specify `Mutex::lock()` instead of `std::sync::Mutex::lock()`. `rust-analyzer` knows I'm asking for `std::sync::Mutex::lock()` because of the use `std::sync::Mutex` statement on line 4.

Figure 6.2   Structural substitution with `rust-analyzer`, after applying

6.7.3   *Relocating*

At the time of writing, `rust-analyzer` doesn't have any features for relocating or moving code. For example, if you want to move a struct and its methods to a different file or module, you'll need to do this process manually.

I wouldn't normally recommend noncommunity projects, but I feel it's worth mentioning that the IntelliJ IDE Rust plugin *does* provide a move feature for relocating code (as well as many other features comparable to `rust-analyzer`), documented at http://mng.bz/9QJx. This plugin is specific to IntelliJ and (to the best of my knowledge) can't be used with other editors, though it is open source.

6.7.4   *Rewriting*

If you find yourself needing to rewrite large swaths of code or individual algorithms, a great way to test whether the new code works just like the old code is to use the prop-test crate, which we discussed earlier in this chapter. Consider the following implementation of the FizzBuzz algorithm and corresponding test.

Listing 6.5   FizzBuzz with unit test

```
fn fizzbuzz(n: i32) -> Vec<String> {
    let mut result = Vec::new();

    for i in 1..(n + 1) {
        if i % 3 == 0 && i % 5 == 0 {
            result.push("FizzBuzz".into());
        } else if i % 3 == 0 {
            result.push("Fizz".into());
        } else if i % 5 == 0 {
            result.push("Buzz".into());
        } else {
            result.push(i.to_string());
        }
    }

    result
}

#[cfg(test)]
mod tests {
    use super::*;
    #[test]
    fn test_fizzbuzz() {
        assert_eq!(fizzbuzz(3), vec!["1", "2", "Fizz"]);
        assert_eq!(fizzbuzz(5), vec!["1", "2", "Fizz", "4", "Buzz"]);
        assert_eq!(
            fizzbuzz(15),
            vec![
                "1", "2", "Fizz", "4", "Buzz", "Fizz", "7", "8", "Fizz",
                "Buzz", "11", "Fizz",
                "13", "14", "FizzBuzz"
            ]
        )
    }
}
```

We're pretty confident this algorithm works, but we want to write a different version of the code. So we write our new implementation like so, using a `HashMap` (with the same unit test):

```
fn better_fizzbuzz(n: i32) -> Vec<String> {
    use std::collections::HashMap;
    let mappings = HashMap::from([(3, "Fizz"), (5, "Buzz")]);
```

```
    let mut result = vec![String::new(); n as usize];
    let mut keys: Vec<&i32> = mappings.keys().collect();
    keys.sort();
    for i in 0..n {
        for key in keys.iter() {
            if (i + 1) % *key == 0 {
                result[i as usize].push_str(mappings.get(key)
                    .expect("couldn't fetch mapping"));
            }
        }
        if result[i as usize].is_empty() {
            result[i as usize] = (i + 1).to_string();
        }
    }

    result
}
```

Our new implementation is a little more complicated, and while it passes all the test cases, we aren't as confident that it works. Here's where proptest comes in: we can just generate test cases using proptest and compare them to the original implementation:

```
use proptest::prelude::*;
proptest! {
    #[test]
    fn test_better_fizzbuzz_proptest(n in 1i32..10000) {
        assert_eq!(fizzbuzz(n), better_fizzbuzz(n))
    }
}
```

We limit the range of values from 1 to 10,000 for this test, so it doesn't run too long.

Here, we just compare the result of our old and new algorithms, which we expect to always be the same.

6.8 *Code coverage*

Code coverage analysis is an important tool in assessing the quality and effectiveness of your tests and code. We can automatically generate code coverage reports using a crate called Tarpaulin (https://crates.io/crates/cargo-tarpaulin), which is provided as a Cargo command. Once installed with `cargo install cargo-tarpaulin`, you can start generating coverage reports.

Using the code from the previous section, we can generate a local HTML coverage report using `cargo tarpaulin --out Html`, the result of which is shown in figures 6.3 and 6.4. Our report shows 100% coverage for lib.rs, which means every line of code has been tested by our unit tests.

/Users/brenden/dev/code-like-a-pro-in-rust-book/c06/rewriting-fizzbuzz/src	Covered: 24 of 24 (100.00%)
Path	**Coverage**
 lib.rs	24 / 24 (100.00%)

Figure 6.3 Summary of coverage report

| Back   /Users/brenden/dev/code-like-a-pro-in-rust-book/c06/rewriting-fizzbuzz/src/lib.rs   Covered: 24 of 24 (100.00%) |

```
fn fizzbuzz(n: i32) -> Vec<String> {
    let mut result = Vec::new();

    for i in 1..(n + 1) {
        if i % 3 == 0 && i % 5 == 0 {
            result.push("FizzBuzz".into());
        } else if i % 3 == 0 {
            result.push("Fizz".into());
        } else if i % 5 == 0 {
            result.push("Buzz".into());
        } else {
            result.push(i.to_string());
        }
    }

    result
}

fn better_fizzbuzz(n: i32) -> Vec<String> {
    use std::collections::HashMap;
    let mappings = HashMap::from([(3, "Fizz"), (5, "Buzz")]);
    let mut result = vec![String::new(); n as usize];
    let mut keys: Vec<&i32> = mappings.keys().collect();
    keys.sort();
    for i in 0..n {
        for key in keys.iter() {
            if (i + 1) % *key == 0 {
                result[i as usize].push_str(
                    mappings.get(key).expect("couldn't fetch mapping"),
                );
            }
        }
        if result[i as usize].is_empty() {
            result[i as usize] = (i + 1).to_string();
```

Figure 6.4   Coverage report for lib.rs detail

These reports can either be examined locally or integrated with a CI/CD system to track code coverage over time. Services like Codecov (https://about.codecov.io/) and Coveralls (https://coveralls.io/) offer a free tier for open source projects. The `dryoc` crate, for example, uses Codecov, which can be viewed at https://app.codecov.io/gh/brndnmtthws/dryoc/. These services track coverage changes over time, integrate with GitHub pull requests, and make it easy to measure progress.

A final note on code coverage: achieving 100% coverage shouldn't be your end goal. In fact, sometimes, it can be nearly impossible to test every line of code. Coverage data can be used to see if you're improving over time, or at least not getting worse, but the number itself is an arbitrary metric that doesn't have qualitative substance. As Voltaire said, "Perfect is the enemy of good."

6.9   *Dealing with a changing ecosystem*

Rust is continuously improving and being updated, both in terms of the language itself and its core libraries, as well as all the crates available in the Rust ecosystem. While it's great to be on the cutting edge, this brings with it some challenges. In particular, maintaining backward and forward compatibility can be tricky.

Unit testing plays an important role in continuous maintenance, especially when dealing with moving targets. You may be tempted to simply pin dependency versions and avoid updates, but this will do more harm than good in the long run, especially as dependencies can intertwine. Even a few tests go a long way in helping detect regressions, especially from third-party library updates or even language changes you weren't expecting.

Summary

- Rust's strong, static typing, strict compiler, and borrow checker lessen the burden of unit testing, as runtime type errors don't need to be tested, like they do in other languages.
- The built-in testing features are minimal, but several crates exist to augment and automate unit testing.
- Rust's libtest runs unit tests in parallel, which provides a nice speedup for normal situations, but code that's sensitive to timing or requires synchronization needs to be handled accordingly.
- Property testing can greatly limit the amount of time and effort spent maintaining unit tests and provide a higher level of assurance.
- Measuring and analyzing code coverage over time allows you to quantify the effectiveness of unit tests.
- Unit tests help ensure third-party libraries and crates function as expected after upgrades.

Integration testing

This chapter covers

- Understanding the differences between unit testing and integration testing
- Using integration testing effectively
- Comparing Rust's built-in integration testing to external testing
- Exploring libraries and tools for integration testing
- Fuzzing your tests

In chapter 6, we discussed unit testing in Rust. In this chapter, we'll discuss how to use integration testing in Rust, and how it compares to unit testing. Both unit testing and integration testing are powerful strategies to improve the quality of your software. They are often used together with slightly different goals.

Integration testing can sometimes be a little more difficult because it may require more work to create harnesses and test cases, depending on the type of software being tested. It's more common to find unit tests than integration tests, but Rust provides the basic tools you need to write effective integration tests without spending too much time on boilerplate and harnesses. We'll also explore some libraries that can help turbocharge your integration testing without requiring much additional work.

7.1   *Comparing integration and unit testing*

Integration testing is the testing of individual modules or groups from their public interfaces. This is in contrast to *unit testing*, which is the testing of the smallest testable components within software, sometimes including private interfaces. *Public interfaces* are those which are exposed to external consumers of software, such as the public library interfaces or the CLI commands, in the case of a command line application.

In Rust, integration tests share very little with unit tests. Unlike unit tests, integration tests are located outside of the main source tree. Rust treats integration tests as a separate crate; thus, they only have access to the publicly exported functions and structures.

Let's write a quick, generic implementation of the quicksort algorithm (https://en.wikipedia.org/wiki/Quicksort), which many of us know and love from our computer science studies, as shown in the following listing.

> **Listing 7.1   Quicksort implemented in Rust**

```
pub fn quicksort<T: std::cmp::PartialOrd + Clone>(slice: &mut [T]) {      ◁─────┐
    if slice.len() < 2 {                              This is our public quicksort()
        return;                                       function, denoted as such by
    }                                                           the pub keyword.
    let (left, right) = partition(slice);
    quicksort(left);
    quicksort(right);
}

fn partition<T: std::cmp::PartialOrd + Clone>(              Our private partition()
    slice: &mut [T]                                         function is not accessible
) -> (&mut [T], &mut [T]) {                         ◁─────  outside of the local scope.
    let pivot_value = slice[slice.len() - 1].clone();
    let mut pivot_index = 0;
    for i in 0..slice.len() {
        if slice[i] <= pivot_value {
            slice.swap(i, pivot_index);
            pivot_index += 1;
        }
    }
    if pivot_index < slice.len() - 1 {
        slice.swap(pivot_index, slice.len() - 1);
    }

    slice.split_at_mut(pivot_index - 1)
}
```

Integration tests are located within the tests directory, at the top level of the source tree. These tests are automatically discovered by Cargo. An example directory structure for a small library (in src/lib.rs) and a single integration test would look like this:

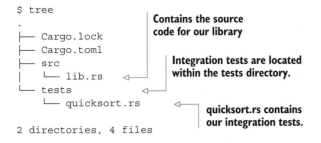

```
$ tree
.
├── Cargo.lock
├── Cargo.toml
├── src
│   └── lib.rs          ◁─
└── tests               ◁─
    └── quicksort.rs    ◁─

2 directories, 4 files
```

Contains the source code for our library

Integration tests are located within the tests directory.

quicksort.rs contains our integration tests.

Test functions are marked with the `#[test]` attribute, which will be run by Cargo automatically. You can either use the automatically provided `main()` function from libtest or supply your own, as with unit tests. Cargo handles these integration tests as separate crates. You can have multiple separate sets of crates by creating directories within the tests directory, each containing their own separate integration tests.

As with unit tests, we typically use the assertion macros (`assert!()` and `assert_eq!()`) to verify results. The integration is shown in practice in the following listing.

Listing 7.2   Code sample of the integration test for quicksort implementation

```rust
use quicksort::quicksort;

#[test]
fn test_quicksort() {
    let mut values = vec![12, 1, 5, 0, 6, 2];
    quicksort(&mut values);
    assert_eq!(values, vec![0, 1, 2, 5, 6, 12]);

    let mut values = vec![1, 13, 5, 10, 6, 2, 0];
    quicksort(&mut values);
    assert_eq!(values, vec![0, 1, 2, 5, 6, 10, 13]);
}
```

This looks a lot like unit tests, yes? The difference in an example like this is almost entirely semantics—in fact, this code sample includes unit tests, which look nearly the same in the following listing.

Listing 7.3   Code sample of unit tests for quicksort implementation

```rust
#[cfg(test)]
mod tests {
    use crate::{partition, quicksort};

    #[test]
    fn test_partition() {
        let mut values = vec![0, 1, 2, 3];
        assert_eq!(
            partition(&mut values),
```

```
            (vec![0, 1, 2].as_mut_slice(), vec![3].as_mut_slice())
        );

        let mut values = vec![0, 1, 2, 4, 3];
        assert_eq!(
            partition(&mut values),
            (vec![0, 1, 2].as_mut_slice(), vec![3, 4].as_mut_slice())
        );
    }

    #[test]
    fn test_quicksort() {
        let mut values = vec![1, 5, 0, 6, 2];
        quicksort(&mut values);
        assert_eq!(values, vec![0, 1, 2, 5, 6]);

        let mut values = vec![1, 5, 10, 6, 2, 0];
        quicksort(&mut values);
        assert_eq!(values, vec![0, 1, 2, 5, 6, 10]);
    }
}
```

The only real difference with this code is that in the unit tests, we're also testing the `partition()` function, which is nonpublic. Is this a case where we *shouldn't* bother writing integration tests? No. Why? Because we're creating a library with a public interface, and we should test the library, as it's intended to be used *externally*. Integration tests live *outside* the library (or application) we're testing; thus, they only have visibility to public (and external) interfaces. This forces us to write tests the same way that downstream users of our library or application would use the software. Integration testing helps us make sure the public API works as intended from the perspective of external users.

7.2   *Integration testing strategies*

It wasn't too long ago that *test driven development* (TDD) was all the rage. TDD is based on the idea that you write your tests *before* writing software. The theory of TDD is that writing tests first helps you build quality code faster. TDD seems to have fallen out of favor, but it does provide us with some insights, especially regarding integration testing.

One thing we can learn from TDD is that designing APIs is just as important as the testing itself. The ergonomics of your software matters, whether you're building libraries; command line applications; or web, desktop, or mobile apps. The end user experience (UX) is surfaced when writing integration tests; these tests force you to think about how your software is used from the perspective of the person using it.

Integration testing and unit testing aren't mutually exclusive; they should be used to complement each other where appropriate. Integration tests shouldn't be written the same way as unit tests because we're testing different things. When we think about writing integration tests, we need to consider more than just the correctness of an algorithm or the logic it implements.

We should think about integration tests not only as a way of verifying our code works but also as a way of testing the UX of our software. There are plenty of examples of good and bad software design, and the process of writing integration tests for your own software forces you to sample a taste of *your* design. It's easy to get tunnel vision and lose sight of the big picture when writing software, and integration tests are, by definition, a holistic perspective of your code.

I've personally experienced this tunnel vision problem many times. For example, when writing the dryoc crate, I got a little carried away with some of the optional features, and it wasn't until I tried to write integration tests that I realized I'd done a poor job of designing the interface at the time. I had to refactor my design substantially to make the library easier to use.

Regarding TDD, should you write integration tests *before* writing your library or application? This is not a practice that I follow, but I don't believe it's necessarily bad, so I recommend testing and determining whether it works for you. I do think, however, that you should write integration tests to empathize with your end users. Which order you write the tests in is up to you. In any case, you should be flexible in your design and refactor mercilessly.

The words of a prolific architect and inventor come to mind:

> *When I am working on a problem, I never think about beauty but when I have finished, if the solution is not beautiful, I know it is wrong.*

—R. Buckminster Fuller

The previous quicksort example provides is an illustration of how we can improve our interface, which becomes apparent when writing tests for this library. Currently, we have a standalone `quicksort()` function, which accepts a slice as input. This is fine, but we can make our code more Rustaceous by creating a trait (traits are discussed in greater detail in chapter 8) and providing an implementation, as shown in the following listing.

Listing 7.4 Code for Quicksort trait

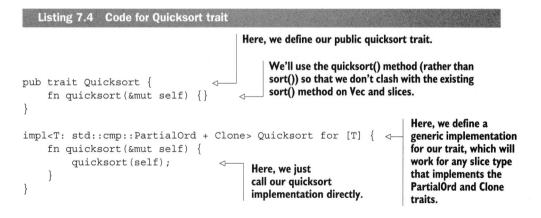

Here, we define our public quicksort trait.

We'll use the quicksort() method (rather than sort()) so that we don't clash with the existing sort() method on Vec and slices.

```
pub trait Quicksort {
    fn quicksort(&mut self) {}
}

impl<T: std::cmp::PartialOrd + Clone> Quicksort for [T] {
    fn quicksort(&mut self) {
        quicksort(self);
    }
}
```

Here, we define a generic implementation for our trait, which will work for any slice type that implements the PartialOrd and Clone traits.

Here, we just call our quicksort implementation directly.

Now, we can update our tests, as shown in the following listing.

Listing 7.5 Code for integration test with the quicksort trait

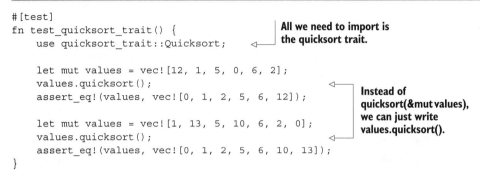

```
#[test]
fn test_quicksort_trait() {
    use quicksort_trait::Quicksort;        ←┐  All we need to import is
                                              the quicksort trait.
    let mut values = vec![12, 1, 5, 0, 6, 2];
    values.quicksort();
    assert_eq!(values, vec![0, 1, 2, 5, 6, 12]);        ←┐  Instead of
                                                           quicksort(&mut values),
    let mut values = vec![1, 13, 5, 10, 6, 2, 0];          we can just write
    values.quicksort();                        ←┘          values.quicksort().
    assert_eq!(values, vec![0, 1, 2, 5, 6, 10, 13]);
}
```

This code doesn't look substantially different, and for the most part, we're just using a bit of syntax sugar to clean things up. Calling `arr.quicksort()` instead of `quicksort(&mut arr)` looks nicer and requires typing four fewer characters, as we don't need to specify the explicit mutable borrow with `&mut`.

7.3 *Built-in integration testing vs. external integration testing*

Rust's built-in integration testing will serve most people well, but it's not a panacea. You may benefit from external integration testing tools, from time to time. For example, testing an HTTP service in Rust could be best served with simple (and nearly ubiquitous) tools like curl (https://curl.se/) or HTTPie (https://github.com/httpie/httpie). These tools aren't related to Rust specifically; they are generic tools that operate at the system level, rather than the language level.

A quick web search will show there are many, many existing software test tools, especially for HTTP services. Unless you're trying to create your own testing framework, it's almost always better to use existing tools than reinvent the wheel.

For command line applications written in Rust, writing the integration tests in Rust isn't always the best approach. Rust is designed for safety and performance—test harnesses don't usually need to be safe or fast, just correct. In many cases, it'll be much easier to write integration tests as Bash, Ruby, or Python script rather than a Rust program.

While it's great to do everything in Rust, you'll need to weigh the value of spending the time required to build your integration tests in Rust, depending on the complexity involved. Dynamic scripting languages offer many advantages for noncritical applications, as you can usually make things happen quickly with little effort, even if you're an expert in Rust.

However, there is one big advantage to *only* using Rust for integration tests: you'll be able to run your tests on any platform supported by Rust, with no need for external tooling aside from the Rust toolchain. This can have some advantages, especially in constrained environments. Additionally, if you find Rust to be your most productive language, then there's no reason not to use it.

7.4 Integration testing libraries and tooling

Most of the tools and libraries used for unit testing also apply for integration tests. There are, however, a few crates that can make life much easier for integration testing, which we'll explore in this section.

7.4.1 Using assert_cmd to test CLI applications

For testing command line applications, let's look at the `assert_cmd` crate (https://crates.io/crates/assert_cmd), which makes it easy to run commands and check their result. To demonstrate, we'll create a command line interface for our quicksort implementation, which sorts integers from CLI arguments, shown in the following listing.

> **Listing 7.6 CLI application using quicksort**

```
use std::env;

fn main() {
    use quicksort_proptest::Quicksort;

    let mut values: Vec<i64> = env::args()
        .skip(1)
        .map(|s| s.parse::<i64>().expect(&format!("{s}: bad input: ")))
        .collect();

    values.quicksort();

    println!("{values:?}");
}
```

Reads the command line arguments, skipping the first argument, which is always the program name

Parses each value (a string) into an i64

Collects the values into a Vec

We can test this by running `cargo run 5 4 3 2 1`, which will print `[1, 2, 3, 4, 5]`.

Now, let's write some tests using `assert_cmd` in the following listing.

> **Listing 7.7 Quicksort CLI integration tests using `assert_cmd`**

```
use assert_cmd::Command;

#[test]
fn test_no_args() -> Result<(), Box
    <dyn std::error::Error>> {
    let mut cmd = Command::cargo_bin("quicksort-cli")?;
    cmd.assert().success().stdout("[]\n");

    Ok(())
}
#[test]
```

Our test functions return a Result, which lets us use the ? operator.

At the end of the test, we just return Ok(()). () is the special unit type, which can be used as a placeholder and has no value. It can be thought of as equivalent to a tuple with zero elements.

```
fn test_cli_well_known() -> Result<(), Box
➡ <dyn std::error::Error>> {
    let mut cmd = Command::cargo_bin("quicksort-cli")?;
    cmd.args(&["14", "52", "1", "-195", "1582"])
        .assert()
        .success()
        .stdout("[-195, 1, 14, 52, 1582]\n");

    Ok(())
}
```

Our test functions return a Result, which lets us use the ? operator.

At the end of the test, we just return Ok(()). () is the special unit type, which can be used as a placeholder and has no value. It can be thought of as equivalent to a tuple with zero elements.

These tests are fine, but for testing against well-known values, we can do a little better. Rather than hardcoding into the source code, we can create some simple file-based fixtures to test against well-known values in a programmatic way.

First, we'll create a simple directory structure on the filesystem to store our test fixtures. The structure consists of numbered folders, with a file for the arguments (args) and the expected result (expected):

```
$ tree tests/fixtures
tests/fixtures
├── 1
│   ├── args
│   └── expected
├── 2
│   ├── args
│   └── expected
└── 3
    ├── args
    └── expected

3 directories, 6 files
```

Next, we'll create a test that iterates over each directory within the tree and reads the arguments and expected result; then runs our test; and, finally, checks the result, as shown in the following listing.

Listing 7.8   Quicksort CLI integration tests with file-based fixtures

```
#[test]
fn test_cli_fixtures() -> Result<(), Box<dyn std::error::Error>> {
    use std::fs;
    let paths = fs::read_dir("tests/fixtures")?;

    for fixture in paths {
        let mut path = fixture?.path();
        path.push("args");
        let args: Vec<String> = fs::read_to_string
        (&path)?
            .trim()
            .split(' ')
            .map(str::to_owned)
            .collect();
```

Performs a directory listing within tests/fixtures within our crate

Pushes the args name into our path buffer

Iterates over each listing within the directory

Reads the contents of the args file into a string and parses the string into a Vec— the trim() method removes the trailing newline from the args file; split(' ') will split the contents on spaces; map(str::to_owned) will convert a &str into an owned String; and, finally, collect() will collect the results into a Vec.

Pops args off of the path buffer

```
path.pop();
path.push("expected");
let expected = fs::read_to_string(&path)?;

let mut cmd = Command::cargo_bin
    ("quicksort-cli")?;
cmd.args(args).assert().success().stdout
    (expected);
}

    Ok(())
}
```

Pushes expected onto the path buffer

Reads the expected values from the file into a string

Runs the quicksort CLI, passes the arguments, and checks the expected results

7.4.2   Using proptest with integration tests

Next, to make our tests even more robust, we can add the proptest crate (which we discussed in the previous chapter) to our quicksort implementation within an integration test in the following listing.

Listing 7.9   Proptest-based integration test with quicksort

```
use proptest::prelude::*;

proptest! {
    #[test]
    fn test_quicksort_proptest(
        vec in prop::collection::vec(prop::num::i64::ANY, 0..1000)
    ) {
        use quicksort_proptest::Quicksort;

        let mut vec_sorted = vec.clone();
        vec_sorted.sort();

        let mut vec_quicksorted = vec.clone();
        vec_quicksorted.quicksort();

        assert_eq!(vec_quicksorted, vec_sorted);
    }
}
```

prop::collection::vec provides us with a Vec of random integers, with a length up to 1,000.

Here, we clone then sort (using the built-in sorting method) the random values to use as our control.

Here, we clone and sort the random values using our quicksort implementation.

It's worth noting that testing with tools that automatically generate test data—such as proptest—can have unintended consequences, should your tests have external side effects, such as making network requests or writing to an external database. You should try to design your tests to account for this, either by setting up and tearing down the whole environment before and after each test or providing some other way to return to a known good state before and after the tests run. You may discover some surprising edge cases when using random data.

> **NOTE** The proptest crate prints the following warning when running as an integration test: proptest: FileFailurePersistence::SourceParallel set, but failed to find lib.rs or main.rs. This warning can be ignored; refer to the GitHub issue at https://github.com/AltSysrq/proptest/issues/233 for more information.

7.4.3 *Other integration testing tools*

The following are some more crates worth mentioning to turbocharge your integration tests:

- rexpect—Automates and tests interactive CLI applications (https://crates.io/crates/rexpect).
- assert_fs—Offers filesystem fixtures for applications that consume or produce files (https://crates.io/crates/assert_fs).

7.5 *Fuzz testing*

Fuzz testing is similar to property testing, which we've already discussed in this chapter. The difference between the two, however, is that with fuzz testing, you test your code with randomly generated data that isn't necessarily valid. When we do property testing, we generally restrict the set of inputs to values we consider valid. With property testing, we do this because it often doesn't makes sense to test all possible inputs, and we also don't have infinite time to test all possible input combinations.

Fuzz testing, on the other hand, does away with the notion of valid and invalid and simply feeds random bytes into your code, so you can see what happens. Fuzz testing is especially popular in security-sensitive contexts, where you want to understand what happens when code is misused.

A common example of this is public-facing data sources, such as web forms. Web forms can be filled with data from any source that needs to be parsed, validated, and processed. Since these forms are out in the wild, there's nothing stopping someone from filling web forms with random data. For example, imagine a login form with a username and password, where someone (or something) could try every combination of username and password, or a list of the most common combinations, to gain access to the system, either by guessing the correct combination or injecting some "magic" set of bytes that causes an internal code failure and bypasses the authentication system. These types of vulnerabilities are surprisingly common, and fuzz testing is one strategy to mitigate them.

The main problem with fuzz testing is that it can take an unfeasible amount of time to test every set of possible inputs, but in practice, you don't necessarily need to test *every* combination of input bits to find bugs. You may be quite surprised how quickly a fuzz test can find bugs in code you may have thought was bulletproof.

To fuzz test, we're going to use a library called libFuzzer (https://llvm.org/docs/LibFuzzer.html), which is part of the LLVM project. You could use libFuzzer directly with FFI (we explored FFI in chapter 4), but instead, we'll use a crate called cargo-fuzz, which takes care of providing a Rust API for libFuzzer and generates boilerplate for us.

Before we dive into a code sample, let's talk about how libFuzzer works at a high level: the library will populate a structure (which you provide) with random data that contains function arguments, and it calls your code's function repeatedly. If the data triggers an error, this is detected by the library, and a test case is constructed to trigger the bug.

Once we've installed the `cargo-fuzz` crate with `cargo install cargo-fuzz`, we can write a test. In the following listing, I've constructed a relatively simple function that looks like it works, but in fact, it contains a subtle bug that will trigger under specific conditions.

> **Listing 7.10 String-parsing function with a bug**

```
pub fn parse_integer(s: &str) -> Option<i32> {     ⟵  Checks if string contains _only_
    use regex::Regex;                                   digits using a regular expression,
                                                        including negative numbers
    let re = Regex::new(r"^-?\d{1,10}$").expect("Parsing regex failed");   ⟵
    if re.is_match(s) {                             Will match a string with
        Some(s.parse().expect("Parsing failed"))    1–10 digits, prefixed by
    } else {                                        an option "-"
        None
    }
}
```

This function will accept a string as input and parse the string into an `i32` integer, provided it's between 1 and 10 digits in length and, optionally, prefixed by a - (minus) symbol. If the input doesn't match the pattern, `None` is returned. The function shouldn't cause our program to crash on invalid input. This seems innocuous enough, but there's a major bug.

These kinds of bugs are surprisingly common and something we have all probably written at some point. Edge case bugs like this can lead to undefined behavior, which—in a security context—can lead to bad things happening.

Next, let's create a small fuzz test using `cargo-fuzz`. First, we need to initialize the boilerplate code by running `cargo fuzz init`. This will create the following structure within our project:

```
$ tree .
.
├── Cargo.lock
├── Cargo.toml
├── fuzz
│   ├── Cargo.lock
│   ├── Cargo.toml
│   └── fuzz_targets
│       └── fuzz_target_1.rs
└── src
    └── lib.rs

3 directories, 6 files
```

Here, we can see that `cargo-fuzz` created a new project in the `fuzz` subdirectory, and there's a test in `fuzz_target_1`. We can list the fuzz targets (or tests) with `cargo fuzz list`, which will print `fuzz_target_1`.

Next, we need to write the fuzz test. To test our function, we're just going to call it with a random string, which is supplied by the fuzzing library. We'll use the `Arbitrary` (https://crates.io/crates/arbitrary) crate to derive data in the form we need. The fuzz test is shown in the following listing.

Listing 7.11   Fuzz test

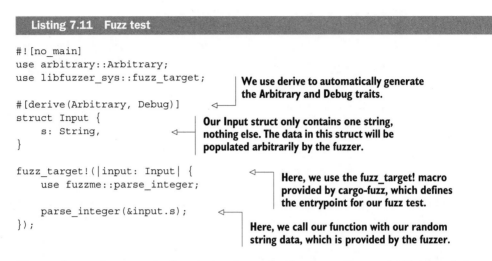

```
#![no_main]
use arbitrary::Arbitrary;
use libfuzzer_sys::fuzz_target;              We use derive to automatically generate
                                             the Arbitrary and Debug traits.
#[derive(Arbitrary, Debug)]
struct Input {
    s: String,                               Our Input struct only contains one string,
}                                            nothing else. The data in this struct will be
                                             populated arbitrarily by the fuzzer.

fuzz_target!(|input: Input| {
    use fuzzme::parse_integer;               Here, we use the fuzz_target! macro
                                             provided by cargo-fuzz, which defines
                                             the entrypoint for our fuzz test.
    parse_integer(&input.s);
});                                          Here, we call our function with our random
                                             string data, which is provided by the fuzzer.
```

Now, we're ready to run the fuzz test and see what happens. You probably already know at this point that there's a bug, so we expect it to crash. When we run the fuzzer with `cargo fuzz run fuzz_target_1`, we'll see output that looks similar to the following listing (which has been shortened because the fuzzer generates a lot of logging output).

Listing 7.12   Output of `cargo fuzz run fuzz_target_1`

```
cargo fuzz run fuzz_target_1
   Compiling fuzzme-fuzz v0.0.0
   (/Users/brenden/dev/code-like-a-pro-in-rust/code/c7/7.5/fuzzme/fuzz)
    Finished release [optimized] target(s) in 1.07s
    Finished release [optimized] target(s) in 0.01s
     Running `fuzz/target/x86_64-apple-darwin/release/fuzz_target_1
     -artifact_prefix=/Users/brenden/dev/code-like-a-pro-in-rust/
     ➥ code/c7/7.5/fuzzme/fuzz/artifacts/fuzz_target_1/
/Users/brenden/dev/code-like-a-pro-in-rust/code/c7/7.5/fuzzme/
➥ fuzz/corpus/fuzz_target_1`
fuzz_target_1(14537,0x10d0a6600) malloc: nano zone abandoned due to
inability to preallocate reserved vm space.
INFO: Running with entropic power schedule (0xFF, 100).
... snip ...

Failing input:

    fuzz/artifacts/fuzz_target_1/
    crash-105eb7135ad863be4e095db6ffe64dc1b9a1a466

Output of `std::fmt::Debug`:
```

```
    Input {
        s: "8884844484",
    }
```

Reproduce with:

```
    cargo fuzz run fuzz_target_1 fuzz/artifacts/fuzz_target_1/
    crash-105eb7135ad863be4e095db6ffe64dc1b9a1a466
```

Minimize test case with:

```
    cargo fuzz tmin fuzz_target_1 fuzz/artifacts/fuzz_target_1/
    crash-105eb7135ad863be4e095db6ffe64dc1b9a1a466
```

> **NOTE** Running the fuzzer can take quite some time, even on fast machines. While this example should trigger fairly quickly (within 60 seconds, in most cases), more complex tests may take much longer. For unbounded data (e.g., a string with no limit in length), the fuzzer can take an infinite amount of time.

Near the bottom of the output, `cargo-fuzz` prints information about the input that caused the crash. Additionally, it creates a test case for us, which we can use to make sure this bug isn't triggered again in the future. For the preceding example, we can simply run `cargo fuzz run fuzz_target_1 fuzz/artifacts/fuzz_target_1/crash-105eb7135ad863be4e095db6ffe64dc1b9a1a466` to test our code again with the same input, which will make it easy to test a fix for this bug without having to rerun the fuzzer from scratch. It can take a long time to find test cases that trigger a crash, so this is helpful in limiting the amount of time we need to spend running the fuzzer.

As an exercise, try modifying the function so that it no longer crashes. There are a few different ways to solve this problem, and I'll provide a hint: the `parse()` method already returns a `Result` for us. For more details on using `cargo-fuzz`, consult the documentation at https://rust-fuzz.github.io/book/.

Summary

- Integration tests complement unit tests, but they differ in one major way: integration tests apply only to public interfaces.
- We can use integration tests as a way to test our API design and make sure it's appropriate and well designed for the end user.
- Rust's built-in integration testing framework provides minimal features, but it's more than adequate for most purposes.
- Like unit tests, Rust's integration tests use the libtest library, which is part of core Rust.
- Crates like proptest, `assert_cmd`, `assert_fs`, and rexpect can be used to further enhance our integration tests.
- The `cargo-fuzz` crate provides libFuzzer integration and Cargo commands to set up and run fuzz tests.

Part 4

Asynchronous Rust

Y ou won't get far in programming without encountering situations in which you need to utilize concurrency and parallelization techniques to accomplish a task. Sometimes, we can get away with avoiding these, which is often the best course of action because it allows us to avoid complexity, but modern computers are highly parallelized, and any sufficiently complex system will require some degree of concurrency.

Asynchronous programming, often combined with parallelism, is a popular technique for handling concurrency. Async programming is, in many ways, just syntactic sugar that allows us to write code without having to exercise as many brain cells. We hide the complexity behind abstractions that free our thinking capacity for high-level problems, which, in turn, provides leverage to our skills.

To use async Rust effectively in a systems programming context, you need to understand what's going on beneath the abstractions. But fear not, once you learn the definitions, abstractions, and jargon used in async Rust, you'll find it a joy to use, warts and all.

Async Rust

8

Concurrency is an important concept in computing, and it's one of the greatest force multipliers of computers. Concurrency allows us to process inputs and outputs—such as data, network connections, or peripherals—faster than we might be able to without concurrency. And it's not always about speed but also latency, overhead, and system complexity. We can run thousands or millions of tasks concurrently, as illustrated in figure 8.1, because concurrent tasks tend to be relatively lightweight. We can create, destroy, and manage many concurrent tasks with very little overhead.

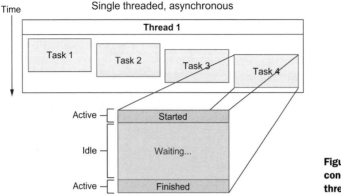

Figure 8.1 Tasks executing concurrently within the same thread

Asynchronous programming uses concurrency to take advantage of idle processing time between tasks. Some kinds of tasks, such as I/O, are much slower than ordinary CPU instructions, and after a slow task is started, we can set it aside to work on other tasks while waiting for the slow task to be completed.

Concurrency shouldn't be confused with *parallelism* (which I'll define here as the ability to execute multiple tasks simultaneously). Concurrency differs from parallelism in that tasks may be executed concurrently without necessarily being executed in parallel. With parallelism, it's possible to execute program code while simultaneously sharing the same region of memory on the host machine, either across multiple CPUs or using context switching at the OS level (a detailed discussion of which is beyond the scope of this book). Figure 8.2 illustrates two threads executing in parallel, simultaneously.

To think about this analogously, consider how humans operate consciously: we can't do most tasks in parallel, but we can do a lot of things concurrently. For example, try having a conversation with two or more people at the same time—it's much harder than it sounds. It's possible to talk to many people at the same time, but you have to context switch between them and pause when switching from one person to another. Humans do concurrency reasonably well, but we suck at parallelism.

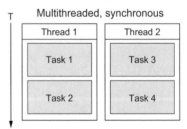

Figure 8.2 Synchronous tasks executing in parallel across two threads

In this chapter, we're going to discuss Rust's asynchronous concurrency system, which provides *both* concurrency and parallelism, depending on what your needs are. It's relatively easy to implement parallelism without async (using threads), but it's quite difficult to implement concurrency without async. Async is a vast topic, so we're really only going to cover the basics in this chapter. However, if you're already familiar with asynchronous programming, you'll find everything you need to be effective with async in Rust.

8.1   Runtimes

Rust's async is similar to what you may have encountered in other languages, though it has its own unique features in addition to borrowing much of what works well from other languages. If you're familiar with async from JavaScript, Python, or even C++'s `std::async`, you should have no problem adjusting to Rust's async. Rust does have one big difference: the language itself does not provide or prescribe an asynchronous runtime implementation. Rust *only* provides the `Future` trait, the `async` keyword, and the `.await` statement; implementation details are largely left to third-party libraries. At the time of writing, there are three widely used async runtime implementations, outlined in table 8.1.

Table 8.1   Summary of async runtimes

Name	Downloads[a]	Description
Tokio	144,128,598	Full-featured async runtime
async-std	18,874,366	Rust standard library implementation with async
Smol	3,604,871	A lightweight runtime, intended to compete with Tokio

[a]The number of downloads for each crate is accurate as of December 26, 2023.

Both `async-std` and smol provide compatibility with the Tokio runtime; however, it is not practical to mix competing async runtimes within the same context in Rust. While separate runtimes do implement the same async API, you will likely require runtime-specific features for most use cases. As such, the recommendation is to use Tokio for most purposes, as it is the most mature and widely used runtime. It may become easier to swap or interchange runtimes in the future, but for the time being, this is not worth the headache.

Crates that provide async features could, theoretically, use any runtime, but in practice, this is uncommon, as they typically work best with one particular runtime. As such, some bifurcation exists in the Rust async ecosystem, where most crates are designed to work with Tokio, but some are specific to smol or `async-std`. For these reasons, this book will focus on the Tokio async runtime as the preferred async runtime.

8.2   Thinking asynchronously

When we talk about *asynchronous programming*, we are usually referring to a way of handling control flow for any operation that involves waiting for a task to complete, which is often I/O. Examples of this include interacting with the filesystem or a socket, but it could also be slow operations, such as computing a hash or waiting for a timer to finish. Most people are familiar with synchronous I/O, which (with the exception of certain languages like JavaScript) is the default mode of handling I/O. The main advantages of using asynchronous programming (as opposed to synchronous) are as follows:

- I/O tends to be very fast with async because there is no need to perform a context switch between threads to support concurrency. Context switching, which often involves synchronization or locking with mutexes, can create a surprising amount of overhead.
- It's often much easier to reason about software that's written asynchronously because we can avoid many kinds of race conditions.
- Asynchronous tasks are very lightweight; thus, we can easily handle thousands or millions of asynchronous tasks simultaneously.

When it comes to I/O operations in particular, the amount of time waiting for operations to complete is often far greater than the amount of time spent processing the result of the I/O operation. Because of this, we can do other work while we're waiting for tasks to finish, rather than executing every task sequentially. In other words, with async programming, we are effectively breaking up and interleaving our function calls between the gaps created by time spent waiting for an I/O operation to finish.

In figure 8.3, I've illustrated the difference with respect to T (time) of blocking versus nonblocking I/O operations. Async I/O is nonblocking, whereas synchronous I/O is blocking. If we assume the time to process the result of an I/O operation is much less than the time spent waiting for I/O to complete, asynchronous I/O will often be faster. It should also be noted that you *can* use multi-threaded programming with async, but often, it's faster to simply use a single thread.

There's no free lunch here; however, if the time to process data from I/O operations becomes greater than the time spent waiting for I/O to complete, we'd see worse performance (assuming single-threaded async). As such, async isn't necessarily ideal for every use case. The good news is that Tokio provides quite a bit of flexibility in choosing how to execute async tasks, such as how many worker threads to use.

You can also mix parallelism with async, so comparing async directly to synchronous programming is not always meaningful. Async code can run concurrently in parallel across several threads, which acts like a performance multiplier that synchronous code can't really compete with.

Once you adjust to the mental model required for thinking about async programming, it's much less complex than synchronous programming, especially compared to multithreaded synchronous programming.

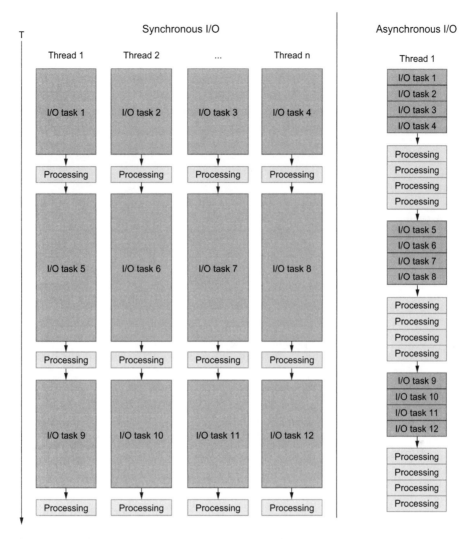

Figure 8.3 Comparing synchronous to asynchronous I/O

8.3 *Futures: Handling async task results*

Most async libraries and languages are based on *futures*, which is a design pattern for handling tasks that return a result in the future (hence the name). When we perform an asynchronous operation, the result of that operation is a future, as opposed to directly returning the value of the operation itself (as we'd see in synchronous programming or an ordinary function call). While futures are a convenient abstraction, they do require a little more work on the part of the programmer to handle correctly.

To better understand futures, let's consider how a timer works: we can create (or start) an async timer, which returns a future to signal the completion of the timer. Merely creating the timer is not enough; we also need to tell the executor (which is part of the async runtime) to execute the task. In synchronous code, when we want to sleep for 1 second, we can just call the `sleep()` function.

> **NOTE** It's true that you could call `sleep()` within async code, but you should never do this. An important rule of asynchronous programming is to never block the main thread. While calling `sleep()` won't cause your program to crash, it will effectively defeat the purpose of async programming, and it is considered an anti-pattern.

To compare an async timer to a synchronous one, let's look at what it takes to write a tiny Rust program that sleeps for 1 second and prints `"Hello, world!"`. First, let's look at the synchronous code:

```
fn main() {
    use std::{thread, time};

    let duration = time::Duration::from_secs(1);

    thread::sleep(duration);

    println!("Hello, world!");
}
```

The synchronous code looks nice and simple. Next, let's examine the async version:

```
fn main() {
    use std::time;

    let duration = time::Duration::from_secs(1);

    tokio::runtime::Builder::new_current_thread()
        .enable_time()                              ◁─── The runtime supports time
        .build()                                         or I/O, which can be enabled
        .unwrap()                                        individually or entirely with
        .block_on(async {                           ◁─── enable_all().
            tokio::time::sleep(duration).await;
            println!("Hello, world!");                   We create an async block, which
        });                                              waits on the future returned by
}                                                        tokio::time::sleep() and then
                                                         prints "Hello, world!".
```

Yikes! That's much more complicated. Why do we need all this complexity? In short, async programming requires special control flow, which is mostly managed by the runtime but still requires a different style of programming. The runtime's scheduler decides what to run when, but we need to yield to the scheduler to allow an opportunity for it to switch between tasks. The runtime will manage most of the details, but we still need to be aware of this to use async effectively. Yielding to the scheduler (in most cases) is as simple as using `.await`, which we'll discuss in greater depth in the next section.

What does it mean to block the main thread?

As I've mentioned, the trick to writing good async code is to avoid blocking the main thread. When we say *block the main thread*, we really mean that the runtime should not be prevented from switching tasks for long periods of time. We typically consider I/O to be a blocking operation because the amount of time an I/O operation takes to complete depends on several factors outside the context of our program and its control. However, you could also have strictly CPU-bound tasks that are considered blocking, provided they take long enough to complete.

We can prevent blocking the main thread for too long by introducing yield points. A *yield point* is any code that passes control back to the scheduler. Joining or waiting on a future creates a yield point by passing control up through the chain to the runtime.

The question of what constitutes a *long period of time* is largely context dependent, so I can't provide hard guidelines. We can, however, estimate what constitutes fast versus slow operations by looking at how long CPU-bound and I/O-bound operations typically take. To gauge the difference between fast and slow, we can compare a typical function call (which is a fast operation) to how long a simple I/O operation takes (a slow operation).

Let's estimate the time it takes for a typical function to execute. We can calculate the time of one clock cycle by taking the inverse of the CPU frequency (assuming one instruction per clock cycle).

For example, for a 2 GHz CPU, the time per instruction is 0.5 ns. For an operation that requires 50 instructions (which would approximate a typical function call), we can assume about 25 ns to execute.

By comparison, a small I/O operation, such as reading 1,024 bytes from a file, can take significantly longer. Running a small test on my laptop, we can demonstrate this:

```
$ dd if=/dev/random of=testfile bs=1k count=1      ⟵      Writes l,000 random bytes
1+0 records in                                             from /dev/random to testfile.
1+0 records out
1024 bytes (1.0 kB, 1.0 KiB) copied, 0.000296943 s, 3.4 MB/s
$ dd if=testfile of=/dev/null          ⟵        Reads the contents of testfile
2+0 records in                                  and writes them to /dev/null.
2+0 records out
1024 bytes (1.0 kB, 1.0 KiB) copied, 0.000261919 s, 3.9 MB/s
```

In the preceding test, reading from a small file takes on the order of 262 μs, which is about 5,240 times longer than 50 ns. Network operations are likely to be another one to two orders of magnitude slower, depending on several factors.

For non-I/O operations you think might take a relatively long time to complete, you should either treat them as blocking using `tokio::task::spawn_blocking()` or break them up by introducing `.await` as needed, allowing the scheduler an opportunity to give other tasks time to run. If unsure, you should benchmark your code to decide whether you would benefit from such optimizations.

8.3.1   *Defining a runtime with #[tokio::main]*

Tokio provides a macro for wrapping our `main()` function, so we can simplify the preceding timer code into the following form if we want:

```
#[tokio::main]
async fn main() {
    use std::time;

    let duration = time::Duration::from_secs(1);

    tokio::time::sleep(duration).await;
    println!("Hello, world!");
}
```

With the help of some syntax sugar, our code now looks just like the synchronous version. We've turned `main()` into an async function with the `async` keyword, and the `#[tokio::main]` handles the boilerplate needed to start the Tokio runtime and create the async context we need.

Remember that the result of any async task is a future, but we need to execute that future on the runtime before anything actually happens. In Rust, this is normally done with the `.await` statement, which we will discuss in the next section.

8.4   *The async and .await keywords: When and where to use them*

The `async` and `.await` keywords are quite new in Rust. It's possible to use futures directly without these, but you're better off just using `async` and `.await` when possible because they handle much of the boilerplate without sacrificing functionality. A function or block of code marked as `async` will return a future, and `.await` tells the runtime we want to wait for a result. The syntax of `async` and `.await` allows us to write async code that looks like synchronous code but without much of the complexity that comes with working with futures. You can use `async` with functions, closures, and code blocks. `async` blocks don't execute until they're polled, which you can do with `.await`.

Under the hood, using `.await` on a future uses the runtime to call the `poll()` method from the `Future` trait and waits for the future's result. If you never call `.await` (or explicitly poll a future), the future will never execute.

To use `.await`, we need to be within an async context. We can create an async context by creating a block of code marked with `async` and executing that code on the async runtime. You don't *have* to use `async` and `.await`, but it's much easier to do things this way, and the Tokio runtime (along with many other async crates) has been designed to be used this way.

For example, consider the following program, which includes a fire-and-forget async code block spawned with `tokio::task::spawn()`:

```
#[tokio::main]
async fn main() {
    async {
        println!("This line prints first");
```

```
    }
    .await;
    let _future = async {
        println!("This line never prints");
    };
    tokio::task::spawn(async {
        println!(
            "This line prints sometimes, depending on how quick it runs"
        )
    });

    println!("This line always prints, but it may or may not be last");
}
```

If you run this code repeatedly, it will (confusingly) print either two or three lines. The first `println!()` will always print before the others because of the `.await` statement, which awaits the result of the first future. The second `println!()` never prints because we didn't execute the future by calling `.await` or spawning it on the runtime. The third `println!()` is spawned onto the Tokio runtime, but we don't wait for it to complete, so it's not guaranteed to run, and we don't know if it will run before or after the last `println!()`, which will always print.

Why does the third `println!()` not print consistently? It's possible that the program will exit before the Tokio runtime's scheduler gets a chance to execute the code. If we want to guarantee that the code runs before exiting, we need to wait for the future returned by `tokio::task::spawn()` to complete.

The `tokio::task::spawn()` function has another important feature: it allows us to launch an async task on the async runtime from outside an async context. It also returns a future (`tokio::task::JoinHandle`, specifically), which we can pass around like any other object. Tokio's join handles also allow us to abort tasks if we want. Let's look at the example in the following listing.

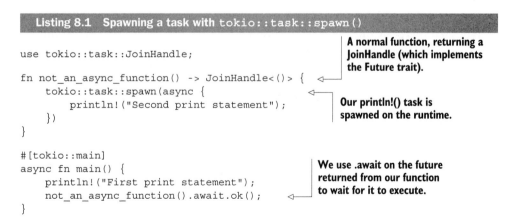

Listing 8.1 Spawning a task with `tokio::task::spawn()`

```
use tokio::task::JoinHandle;

fn not_an_async_function() -> JoinHandle<()> {
    tokio::task::spawn(async {
        println!("Second print statement");
    })
}

#[tokio::main]
async fn main() {
    println!("First print statement");
    not_an_async_function().await.ok();
}
```

A normal function, returning a JoinHandle (which implements the Future trait).

Our println!() task is spawned on the runtime.

We use .await on the future returned from our function to wait for it to execute.

In the preceding code listing, we've created a normal function that returns a `JoinHandle` (which is just a type of future). `tokio::task::spawn()` returns a `JoinHandle`, which allows us to join the task (i.e., retrieve the result of our code block, which is just a unit in this example).

What happens if you want to use `.await` *outside* of an async context? Well, in short, you can't. You can, however, block on the result of a future to await its result using the `tokio::runtime::Handle::block_on()` method. To do so, you'll need to obtain a *handle* for the runtime, and move that runtime handle into the thread where you want to block. Handles can be cloned and shared, providing access to the async runtime from outside an async context, as shown in the following listing.

Listing 8.2   Using a Tokio `Handle` to spawn tasks

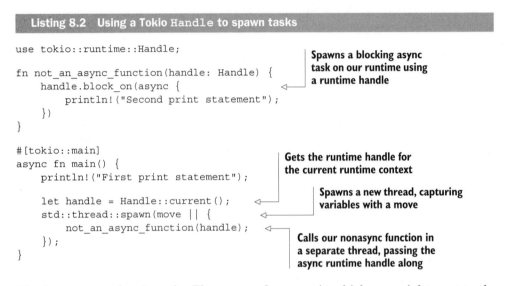

```
use tokio::runtime::Handle;

fn not_an_async_function(handle: Handle) {
    handle.block_on(async {
        println!("Second print statement");
    })
}

#[tokio::main]
async fn main() {
    println!("First print statement");

    let handle = Handle::current();
    std::thread::spawn(move || {
        not_an_async_function(handle);
    });
}
```

Spawns a blocking async task on our runtime using a runtime handle

Gets the runtime handle for the current runtime context

Spawns a new thread, capturing variables with a move

Calls our nonasync function in a separate thread, passing the async runtime handle along

That's not pretty, but it works. There are a few cases in which you might want to do things like this, which we'll discuss in the next section, but for the most part, you should try to use `async` and `.await` when possible.

In short, wrap code blocks (including functions and closures) with `async` when you want to perform async tasks or return a future, and use `.await` when you need to wait for an async task. Creating an async block does not execute the future; it still needs to be executed (or spawned with `tokio::task::spawn()`) on the runtime.

8.5 *Concurrency and parallelism with async*

At the beginning of the chapter, I discussed the differences between concurrency and parallelism. With async, we don't get either concurrency or parallelism for free. We still have to think about how to structure our code to take advantage of these features.

With Tokio, there's no explicit control over parallelism (aside from launching a blocking task with `tokio::task::spawn_blocking()`, which always runs in a separate thread). We do have explicit control over concurrency, but we can't control the parallelism of individual tasks, as those details are left up to the runtime. What Tokio does allow us to configure is the number of worker threads, but the runtime will decide which threads to use for each task.

Introducing concurrency into our code can be accomplished in one of three ways:

- Spawning tasks with `tokio::task::spawn()`
- Joining multiple futures with `tokio::join!(...)` or `futures::future::join_all()`
- Using the `tokio::select! { ... }` macro, which allows us to wait on multiple concurrent code branches (modeled after the UNIX `select()` system call)

To introduce *parallelism*, we have to use `tokio::task::spawn()`, but we don't get explicit parallelism this way. Instead, when we spawn a task, we're telling Tokio that this task can be executed on any thread, but Tokio still decides which thread to use. If we launch our Tokio runtime with only one worker thread, for example, all tasks will execute in one thread, even when we use `tokio::task::spawn()`. We can demonstrate the behavior with some sample code.

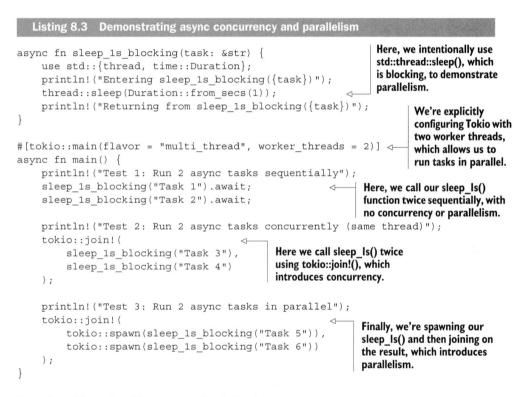

Listing 8.3 Demonstrating async concurrency and parallelism

```
async fn sleep_1s_blocking(task: &str) {
    use std::{thread, time::Duration};
    println!("Entering sleep_1s_blocking({task})");
    thread::sleep(Duration::from_secs(1));            ◄── Here, we intentionally use
    println!("Returning from sleep_1s_blocking({task})");   std::thread::sleep(), which
}                                                            is blocking, to demonstrate
                                                            parallelism.

#[tokio::main(flavor = "multi_thread", worker_threads = 2)]  ◄── We're explicitly
async fn main() {                                                configuring Tokio with
    println!("Test 1: Run 2 async tasks sequentially");         two worker threads,
    sleep_1s_blocking("Task 1").await;          ◄──             which allows us to
    sleep_1s_blocking("Task 2").await;                          run tasks in parallel.

                                                    Here, we call our sleep_1s()
    println!("Test 2: Run 2 async tasks concurrently (same thread)");  function twice sequentially, with
    tokio::join!(                                   no concurrency or parallelism.
        sleep_1s_blocking("Task 3"),       ◄──
        sleep_1s_blocking("Task 4")            Here we call sleep_1s() twice
    );                                         using tokio::join!(), which
                                               introduces concurrency.

    println!("Test 3: Run 2 async tasks in parallel");
    tokio::join!(                              ◄──
        tokio::spawn(sleep_1s_blocking("Task 5")),   Finally, we're spawning our
        tokio::spawn(sleep_1s_blocking("Task 6"))    sleep_1s() and then joining on
    );                                               the result, which introduces
}                                                    parallelism.
```

Running this code will generate the following output:

```
Test 1: Run 2 async tasks sequentially
Entering sleep_1s_blocking(Task 1)
Returning from sleep_1s_blocking(Task 1)
Entering sleep_1s_blocking(Task 2)
Returning from sleep_1s_blocking(Task 2)
Test 2: Run 2 async tasks concurrently (same thread)
Entering sleep_1s_blocking(Task 3)
Returning from sleep_1s_blocking(Task 3)
```

```
Entering sleep_1s_blocking(Task 4)
Returning from sleep_1s_blocking(Task 4)
Test 3: Run 2 async tasks in parallel
Entering sleep_1s_blocking(Task 5)
Entering sleep_1s_blocking(Task 6)
Returning from sleep_1s_blocking(Task 5)
Returning from sleep_1s_blocking(Task 6)
```

> In the third test, we can see our sleep_1s() function is running in parallel because both functions are entered before returning.

We can see from this output that only in the third test, where we launch each task with `tokio::spawn()` (which is equivalent to `tokio::task::spawn()`), does the code execute in parallel. We can tell it's executing in parallel because we see both of the `Entering …` statements *before* the `Returning …` statements. An illustration of the sequence of events is shown in figure 8.4.

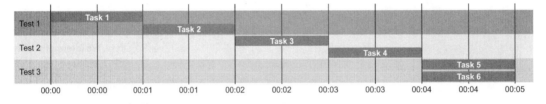

Figure 8.4   Diagram showing the sequence of events in blocking sleep

Note that, while the second test is, indeed, running concurrently, it is not running in parallel; thus, the tasks execute sequentially because we used a blocking sleep in listing 8.3. Let's update the code to add nonblocking sleep as follows:

```
async fn sleep_1s_nonblocking(task: &str) {
    use tokio::time::{sleep, Duration};
    println!("Entering sleep_1s_nonblocking({task})");
    sleep(Duration::from_secs(1)).await;
    println!("Returning from sleep_1s_nonblocking({task})");
}
```

After updating our `main()` to add three tests with the nonblocking sleep, we get the following output:

```
Test 4: Run 2 async tasks sequentially (non-blocking)
Entering sleep_1s_nonblocking(Task 7)
Returning from sleep_1s_nonblocking(Task 7)
Entering sleep_1s_nonblocking(Task 8)
Returning from sleep_1s_nonblocking(Task 8)
Test 5: Run 2 async tasks concurrently (same thread, non-blocking)
Entering sleep_1s_nonblocking(Task 9)
Entering sleep_1s_nonblocking(Task 10)
Returning from sleep_1s_nonblocking(Task 10)
Returning from sleep_1s_nonblocking(Task 9)
Test 6: Run 2 async tasks in parallel (non-blocking)
Entering sleep_1s_nonblocking(Task 11)
```

> We can see here that our sleep happens concurrently now that we changed the sleep function to nonblocking.

```
Entering sleep_1s_nonblocking(Task 12)
Returning from sleep_1s_nonblocking(Task 12)
Returning from sleep_1s_nonblocking(Task 11)
```

Figure 8.5 illustrates how both tests 5 and 6 appear to execute in parallel, although only test 6 is actually running in parallel, whereas test 5 is running concurrently. If you again update your Tokio settings and change `worker_threads = 1` and then rerun the test, you will see in the blocking sleep version all of the tasks run sequentially, but in the concurrent nonblocking version, they still run concurrently, even with one thread.

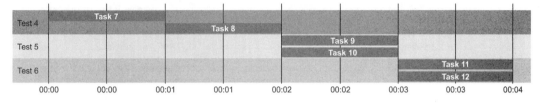

Figure 8.5   Diagram showing the sequence of events in nonblocking sleep

It may take some time to wrap your head around concurrency and parallelism with async Rust, so don't worry if this seems confusing at first. I recommend trying this sample yourself and experimenting with different parameters to get a better understanding of what's going on.

8.6   Implementing an async observer

Let's look at implementing the observer pattern in async Rust. This pattern happens to be incredibly useful in async programming, so we'll see what it takes to make it work with async.

> **NOTE**   Async traits are expected to be added to Rust in an upcoming release, though at the time of writing, they are not yet available.

At the time of writing, there is one big limitation to Rust's async support: we can't use traits with async methods. For example, the following code is invalid:

```
trait MyAsyncTrait {
    async fn do_thing();
}
```

Because of this, implementing the observer pattern with async is somewhat tricky. There are a few ways to work around this problem, but I will present a solution that also provides some insight into how Rust implements the `async fn` syntax sugar.

As mentioned earlier in this chapter, the `async` and `.await` features are just convenient syntax for working with futures. When we declare an `async` function or code block, the compiler is wrapping that code with a future for us. Thus, we can still create the equivalent of an `async` function with traits, but we have to do it explicitly (without the syntax sugar).

The observer trait looks as follows:

```
pub trait Observer {
    type Subject;
    fn observe(&self, subject: &Self::Subject);
}
```

To convert the `observe()` method into an async function, the first step is to make it return a `Future`. We can try something like this as a first step:

```
pub trait Observer {
    type Subject;
    type Output: Future<Output = ()>;        ◁───
    fn observe(&self, subject: &Self::Subject) -> Self::Output;   ◁───┐
}
```

> Here, we define an associated type with the Future trait bound, returning ().

> Now, our observe() method returns the Output associated type.

At first glance, this seems like it should work, and the code compiles. However, as soon as we try to implement the trait, we'll run into a few problems. For one, because `Future` is just a trait (not a concrete type), we don't know what type to specify for `Output`. Thus, we can't use an associated type this way. Instead, we need to use a trait object. To do this, we need to return our future within a `Box`. We'll update the trait like so:

```
pub trait Observer {
    type Subject;
    type Output;        ◁───
    fn observe(
        &self,
        subject: &Self::Subject,
    ) -> Box<dyn Future<Output = Self::Output>>;    ◁───┐
}
```

> We kept the associated type for the return type here, which adds some flexibility.

> Now, we return a Box <dyn Future> instead.

Let's try to put it together by implementing our new async observer for `MyObserver`:

```
struct Subject;
struct MyObserver;

impl Observer for MyObserver {
    type Subject = Subject;
    type Output = ();
    fn observe(
        &self,
        _subject: &Self::Subject,
    ) -> Box<dyn Future<Output = Self::Output>> {      ◁───┐
        Box::new(async {
            // do some async stuff here!
            use tokio::time::{sleep, Duration};
            sleep(Duration::from_millis(100)).await;
        })
    }
}
```

> Note that we have to box the future we're returning.

So far, so good! The compiler is happy too. Now, what happens if we try to test it? Let's write a quick test:

```
#[tokio::main]
async fn main() {
    let subject = Subject;
    let observer = MyObserver;
    observer.observe(&subject).await;
}
```

And now we hit our next snag. Trying to compile this will generate the following error:

```
error[E0277]: `dyn Future<Output = ()>` cannot be unpinned
  --> src/main.rs:29:31
   |
29 |       observer.observe(&subject).await;
   |                                  ^^^^^^ the trait `Unpin` is not
   implemented for `dyn Future<Output = ()>`
   |
   = note: consider using `Box::pin`
   = note: required because of the requirements on the impl of `Future` for
   `Box<dyn Future<Output = ()>>`
   = note: required because of the requirements on the impl of `IntoFuture`
   for `Box<dyn Future<Output = ()>>`
help: remove the `.await`
   |
29 -       observer.observe(&subject).await;
29 +       observer.observe(&subject);
   |

For more information about this error, try `rustc --explain E0277`.
```

What's happening here? To understand, we need to look at the `Future` trait from the Rust standard library:

```
pub trait Future {
    type Output;
    fn poll(self: Pin<&mut Self>, cx: &mut Context<'_>) -
    > Poll<Self::Output>;
}
```

Notice that, the `poll()` method takes its `self` parameter as the type `Pin<&mut Self>`. In other words, before we can poll a future (which is what `.await` does), it needs to be *pinned*. A pinned pointer is a special kind of pointer in Rust that can't be moved (until it's unpinned). Lucky for us, obtaining a pinned pointer is easy; we just need to update our `Observer` trait again as follows:

```
pub trait Observer {
    type Subject;
    type Output;
```

```
fn observe(
    &self,
    subject: &Self::Subject,
) -> Pin<Box<dyn Future<Output = Self::Output>>>;
}
```

Now, we wrap our Box in Pin, which gives us a pinned box.

Next, we'll update our implementation like so:

```
impl Observer for MyObserver {
    type Subject = Subject;
    type Output = ();
    fn observe(
        &self,
        _subject: &Self::Subject,
    ) -> Pin<Box<dyn Future<Output = Self::Output>>> {
        Box::pin(async {
            // do some async stuff here!
            use tokio::time::{sleep, Duration};
            sleep(Duration::from_millis(100)).await;
        })
    }
}
```

Now, we return Pin<Box<...>>.

Box::pin() conveniently returns a pinned box for us.

At this point, our code will compile, and it works. You might think we're out of the woods, but unfortunately, we are not. The implementation for the Observable trait is even more complicated. Let's take a look at the Observable trait:

```
pub trait Observable {
    type Observer;
    fn update(&self);
    fn attach(&mut self, observer: Self::Observer);
    fn detach(&mut self, observer: Self::Observer);
}
```

We need to make the update() method from Observable async, but it's more complicated because, inside update(), we pass self to each of the observers. Passing a self reference inside an async method won't work without specifying a lifetime for that reference. Additionally, we need each Observer instance to implement both Send and Sync because we want to observe updates concurrently, which requires that our observers can move across threads. The final form of our Observer trait is shown in the following listing.

Listing 8.4   Implementing the async `Observer` trait

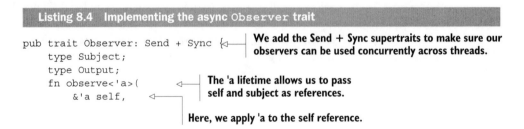

```
pub trait Observer: Send + Sync {
    type Subject;
    type Output;
    fn observe<'a>(
        &'a self,
```

We add the Send + Sync supertraits to make sure our observers can be used concurrently across threads.

The 'a lifetime allows us to pass self and subject as references.

Here, we apply 'a to the self reference.

```
        subject: &'a Self::Subject,        ⭠──── Here, we apply 'a to the subject reference.
    ) -> Pin<Box<dyn Future<Output = Self::Output> + 'a + Send>>;   ⭠──┐
}
```

We add 'a + Send to the trait bounds to allow moving across threads and ensure the return future doesn't outlive any captured references for 'a.

Our updated `Observable` trait is shown in the following listing.

Listing 8.5 Implementing the async `Observable` trait

```
pub trait Observable {          │ As with Observer, we
    type Observer;              │ need to add a lifetime
    fn update<'a>(       ⭠──────┘ for our references.
        &'a self,
    ) -> Pin<Box<dyn Future<Output = ()> + 'a + Send>>;
    fn attach(&mut self, observer: Self::Observer);
    fn detach(&mut self, observer: Self::Observer);
}
```

Now, we'll implement `Observable` for our `Subject`.

Listing 8.6 Implementing the async `Observable` trait for `Subject`

```
pub struct Subject {
    observers:
        Vec<Weak<dyn Observer<Subject = Self, Output = ()>>>,
    state: String,
}

impl Subject {
    pub fn new(state: &str) -> Self {
        Self {
            observers: vec![],
            state: state.into(),
        }
    }

    pub fn state(&self) -> &str {
        self.state.as_ref()
    }
}
```

We generate the list of observers to notify outside the async context and collect this into a new Vec.

```
impl Observable for Subject {
    type Observer =
        Arc<dyn Observer<Subject = Self, Output = ()>>;
    fn update<'a>(&'a self) -> Pin<Box<dyn Future<Output = ()> + 'a + Send>>
    {
        let observers: Vec<_> =
            self.observers.iter().flat_map(|o| o.upgrade()).collect();   ⭠────

        Box::pin(async move {        ⭠──┐
            futures::future::join_all(
```

Using join_all() here introduces concurrency across our observers.

We use a move on our async block to move the captured observers list into the async block.

```
                observers.iter().map(|o| o.observe(self)),  ◄─┐
        )
    )                                                          │
    .await;    ◄─┐                                             │
})              │                                              │
}               │                                              │
fn attach(&mut self, observer: Self::Observer) {
    self.observers.push(Arc::downgrade(&observer));
}
fn detach(&mut self, observer: Self::Observer) {
    self.observers
        .retain(|f| !f.ptr_eq(&Arc::downgrade(&observer)));
}
}
```

Each observer's observe function is called with the same self reference.

Finally, we .await on the join operation within our async block.

Now, we can finally test our async observer pattern.

Listing 8.7 Testing our async observer pattern

```
#[tokio::main]
async fn main() {
    let mut subject = Subject::new("some subject state");

    let observer1 = MyObserver::new("observer1");
    let observer2 = MyObserver::new("observer2");

    subject.attach(observer1.clone());
    subject.attach(observer2.clone());

    // ... do something here ...

    subject.update().await;
}
```

Running the preceding code will produce the following output:

```
observed subject with state="some subject state" in observer1
observed subject with state="some subject state" in observer2
```

8.7 *Mixing sync and async*

The Rust async ecosystem is growing fast, and many libraries have support for `async` and `.await`. However, in spite of this, there are cases where you may need to deal with synchronous and asynchronous code together. We already demonstrated two such examples in the previous section, but let's elaborate more on that.

> **TIP** As a general rule, you should avoid mixing sync and async. In some cases, it may be worth the effort to add async support when it's missing or upgrade code that's using older versions of Tokio that don't work with the new `async` and `.await` syntax.

The most common scenario in which you'll have to mix sync and async is when you're using a crate which doesn't support async, such as a database driver or networking library. For example, if you want to write an HTTP service using the Rocket crate (https://crates.io/crates/rocket) with async, you may need to read or write to a database that doesn't yet have async support. Adding async support to sufficiently complex libraries might not be the best use of your time, even when it's a noble cause.

To call synchronous code from within an async context, the preferred way is to use the `tokio::task::spawn_blocking()` function, which accepts a function and returns a future. When a call to `spawn_blocking()` is placed, it will execute the function provided on a thread queue managed by Tokio (which can be configured). You can then use `.await` on the future returned by `spawn_blocking()`, like you normally would with any async code.

Let's look at an example of `spawn_blocking()` in action, by creating code that writes a file asynchronously and then reads it back synchronously:

```
use tokio::io::{self, AsyncWriteExt};

async fn write_file(filename: &str) -> io::Result<()> {        ⟵   Writes "Hello,
    let mut f = tokio::fs::File::create(filename).await?;          file!" to our file
    f.write(b"Hello, file!").await?;                               asynchronously
    f.flush().await?;

    Ok(())
}

fn read_file(filename: &str) -> io::Result<String> {    ⟵   Reads the contents of
    std::fs::read_to_string(filename)                       our file into a string,
}                                                           returning the string
                                                            synchronously
#[tokio::main]
async fn main() -> io::Result<()> {
    let filename = "mixed-sync-async.txt";
    write_file(filename).await?;

    let contents =
        tokio::task::spawn_blocking(|| read_file(filename)).await??;    ⟵

    println!("File contents: {}", contents);           Note the double ?? because
                                                       both spawn_blocking() and
    tokio::fs::remove_file(filename).await?;           read_file() return a Result.

    Ok(())
}
```

In the preceding code, we perform our synchronous I/O within the function called by `spawn_blocking()`. We can await the result just like any other ordinary async block, except that it's actually being executed on a separate blocking thread managed by Tokio. We don't have to worry about the implementation details, except that there needs to be an adequate number of threads allocated by Tokio. In the preceding example, we just use the default values, but you can change the number of blocking threads with the Tokio runtime builder (for which the full list of parameters can be found at http://mng.bz/j1WV).

> ### Synchronizing async code
>
> Sometimes, we need to synchronize async code, such as when we need to pass messages between different objects. Because our async code blocks may run across separate threads of execution, sharing data between them can be tricky, as we can introduce race conditions if we try to access data improperly (additionally, the Rust language won't allow it). An easy way to share data is to use shared state behind a mutex, but Tokio provides some better ways to share state.
>
> Within its `sync` module, Tokio provides several tools for synchronizing async code. Notably, you will likely want to learn about the multi-producer, single-consumer channel, which can be found within the `tokio::sync::mpsc` module. An `mpsc` channel lets you safely pass messages from several producers to a single consumer within an async context, without the need for explicit locking (i.e., introducing mutexes). Tokio provides other channels types, including `broadcast`, `oneshot`, and `watch`.
>
> With `mpsc` channels, you can build scalable, concurrent, message-passing interfaces in async Rust without explicit locking. An `mpsc` channel can be unbounded or bounded with a fixed length, providing backpressure to producers.
>
> Tokio's channels are similar to what you may find in other actor or event-processing frameworks, except they're relatively low level and fairly general purpose. They're more similar to socket programming than what you might find in higher-level actor libraries. For details on Tokio's synchronous tooling, refer to the `sync` module at https://docs.rs/tokio/latest/tokio/sync/index.html.

For the opposite case—using async code within synchronous code—it's possible to use the runtime handle with `block_on()`, as shown in the previous section. This, however, is probably not a common use case and is something to be avoided. For a more advanced discussion on this topic, please refer to the Tokio documentation at https://tokio.rs/tokio/topics/bridging.

8.8   *When to avoid using async*

Asynchronous programming is great for I/O-heavy applications, such as network services. This could be an HTTP server, some other custom network service, or even a program that initiates many network requests (as opposed to responding to requests). Async does bring with it some complexity that you generally don't need to worry about with synchronous programming, for the reasons outlined throughout this chapter.

It's reasonable to use async as a general rule but only in cases where concurrency is required. Many programming tasks don't require concurrency and are best served by synchronous programming. Some examples of this could be a simple CLI tool that reads or writes to a file or standard I/O or a simple HTTP client that makes a few sequential HTTP requests like curl. If you have a curl-like tool that needs to make thousands of concurrent HTTP requests, then, by all means, do use async.

It's worth noting that adding async after the fact is more difficult than building software with async support up front, so think carefully about whether your use case requires async. In terms of raw performance, there is practically no difference between using and not using async for simple sequential and nonconcurrent tasks; however, Tokio introduces some slight overhead, which may be measurable but is unlikely to be significant for most purposes.

8.9 *Tracing and debugging async code*

For any sufficiently complex networked application, it's critical to instrument your code to measure its performance and debug problems. The Tokio project provides a tracing crate (https://crates.io/crates/tracing) for this purpose. The tracing crate supports the OpenTelemetry (https://opentelemetry.io/) standard, which enables integration with a number of popular third-party tracing and telemetry tools, but it can also emit traces as logs.

Enabling tracing with Tokio also unlocks tokio-console (https://github.com/tokio-rs/console), which is a CLI tool similar to the top program you're likely familiar with from most UNIX systems. tokio-console allows you to analyze Tokio-based async Rust code in real time. Neat! While tokio-console is handy, in most environments, you'd likely emit traces to logs or with OpenTelemetry, as tokio-console is ephemeral and mainly useful as a debug tool. You also cannot attach tokio-console to a program that wasn't compiled for it ahead of time.

Enabling tracing requires configuring a subscriber to which the traces are emitted. Additionally, to use tracing effectively, you need to instrument functions at the points where you want to measure them. This can be done easily with the #[tracing::instrument] macro. Traces can be emitted at different levels and with a number of options, which are well documented in the tracing docs at https://docs.rs/tracing/latest/tracing/index.html.

Let's write a small program to demonstrate tracing with tokio-console, which requires some setup and boilerplate. Our program will have three different sleep functions, each instrumented, and they will run forever, concurrently, in a loop:

```
use tokio::time::{sleep, Duration};

#[tracing::instrument]
async fn sleep_1s() {
    sleep(Duration::from_secs(1)).await;
}

#[tracing::instrument]
async fn sleep_2s() {
    sleep(Duration::from_secs(2)).await;
}

#[tracing::instrument]
async fn sleep_3s() {
    sleep(Duration::from_secs(3)).await;
}
```

We'll use the instrument macro from the tracing crate to instrument our three sleep functions.

```
#[tokio::main]
async fn main() {
    console_subscriber::init();

    loop {
        tokio::spawn(sleep_1s());
        tokio::spawn(sleep_2s());
        sleep_3s().await;
    }
}
```

We have to initialize the console subscriber in our main function to emit the traces.

We'll fire and forget sleep 1 and sleep 2 and then block on sleep 3.

Here, we block on sleep 3 until 3 seconds have elapsed and then repeat the process forever.

We also need to add the following to our dependencies, specifically to enable the tracing feature in Tokio:

```
[dependencies]
tokio = { version = "1", features = ["full", "tracing"] }
tracing =  "0.1"
console-subscriber = "0.1"
```

The tracing feature in Tokio is not enabled by "full"; it must be explicitly enabled.

We'll install `tokio-console` with `cargo install tokio-console`, after which we can compile and run our program. However, we need to compile with `RUSTFLAGS="--cfg tokio_unstable"` to enable unstable tracing features in Tokio for `tokio-console`. We'll do this by running the program directly from Cargo with `RUSTFLAGS="--cfg tokio_unstable" cargo run`. With our program running, we can now run `tokio-console`, which will produce the output shown in figure 8.6. In addition to monitoring tasks, we can monitor resources, as shown in figure 8.7. We can also drill down into individual tasks and even see a histogram of poll times, as shown in figure 8.8.

```
● ● ●   ⌥⌘2                        tokio-console

connection: http://127.0.0.1:6669/ (CONNECTED)
views: t = tasks, r = resources
controls: ↔ or h, l = select column (sort), ↕ or k, j = scroll, ↵ = view details, i = invert sort
(highest/lowest), q = quit gg = scroll to top, G = scroll to bottom
┌Tasks (14) ► Running (0) ▯▮Idle (2)─────────────────────────────────────────────────────
Warn  ID  State  Name  Total✓      Busy        Idle       Polls  Target     Location        Fields
       5  ▯                2.0039s  497.2910µs  2.0034s    2      tokio::task src/main.rs:24:9  kind=task
       4  ▯                2.0035s  727.5410µs  2.0027s    2      tokio::task src/main.rs:24:9  kind=task
       7  ▯                2.0029s  557.2490µs  2.0023s    2      tokio::task src/main.rs:24:9  kind=task
       9  ▯                2.0024s  425.3740µs  2.0019s    2      tokio::task src/main.rs:24:9  kind=task
      12  ▯                2.0023s  494.2080µs  2.0018s    2      tokio::task src/main.rs:24:9  kind=task
       2  ▯                2.0022s  540.9580µs  2.0017s    2      tokio::task src/main.rs:24:9  kind=task
       1  ▯                1.0051s  1.6637ms    1.0034s    2      tokio::task src/main.rs:23:9  kind=task
       3  ▯                1.0036s  1.2935ms    1.0024s    2      tokio::task src/main.rs:23:9  kind=task
       6  ▯                1.0035s  507.4160µs  1.0030s    2      tokio::task src/main.rs:23:9  kind=task
       8  ▯                1.0027s  270.2910µs  1.0024s    2      tokio::task src/main.rs:23:9  kind=task
      11  ▯                1.0025s  618.1660µs  1.0019s    2      tokio::task src/main.rs:23:9  kind=task
      10  ▯                1.0021s  281.5830µs  1.0019s    2      tokio::task src/main.rs:23:9  kind=task
      13  ▮        989.1582ms  213.0000µs  988.9452ms  1      tokio::task src/main.rs:23:9  kind=task
      14  ▮        988.9660ms  123.1250µs  988.8429ms  1      tokio::task src/main.rs:24:9  kind=task
```

Figure 8.6 Running tasks, as shown in `tokio-console`

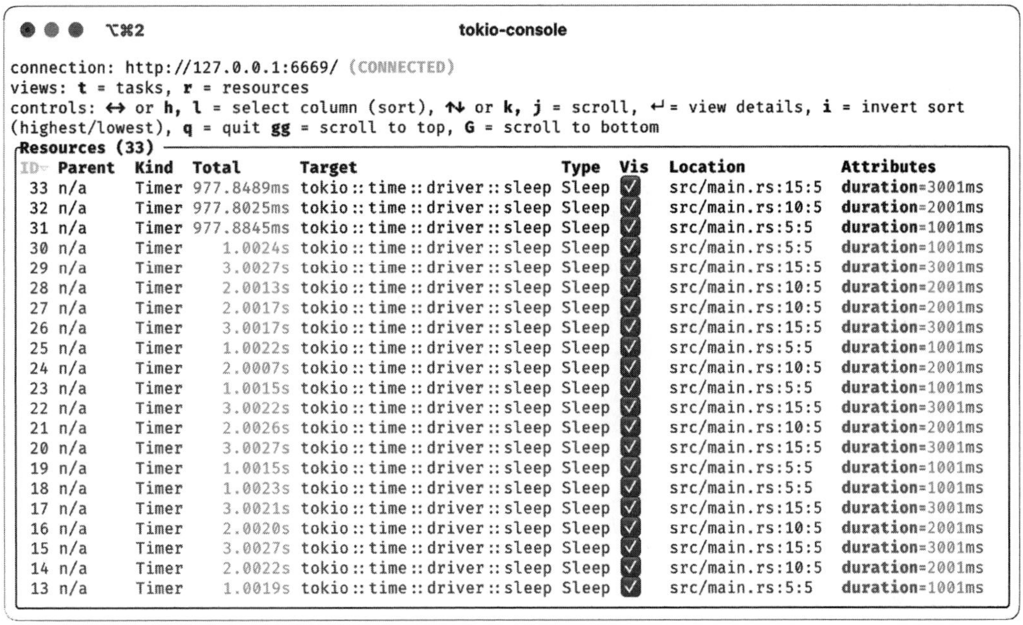

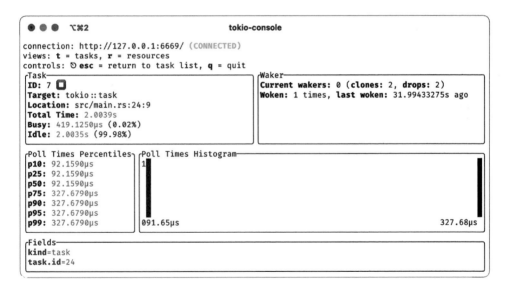

Figure 8.7   Resource usage, as shown in `tokio-console`

Figure 8.8   Individual task with poll time histogram

With `tokio-console`, we can see the state of tasks in real time, a variety of metrics associated with each one, additional metadata we may have included, as well as source file locations. `tokio-console` allows us to see both the tasks we've implemented and the

Tokio resources separately. All this data will also be made available in traces emitted to another sink, such as a log file or an OpenTelemetry collector.

8.10   *Dealing with async when testing*

The last thing we'll discuss in this chapter is testing async code. When it comes to writing unit or integration tests for async code, there are two strategies:

- Creating and destroying the async runtime for each separate test
- Reusing one or more async runtimes across separate tests

For most cases, it's preferable to create and destroy the runtime for each test, but there are exceptions to this rule, where reusing a runtime is more sensible. In particular, it's reasonable to reuse the runtime if you have many (i.e., hundreds or thousands) of tests.

To reuse a runtime across tests, we can use the `lazy_static` crate, which we discussed quite a bit in chapter 6. Rust's testing framework runs tests in parallel across threads, which must be handled correctly using `tokio::runtime::Handle`, as we demonstrated earlier in this chapter.

For most cases, you can simply use the `#[tokio::test]` macro, which works exactly like `#[test]`, except that it's for async functions. The Tokio test macro takes care of setting up the test runtime for you, so you can write your async unit or integration test like you normally would any other test. To demonstrate, consider the following function, which sleeps for 1 second:

```
async fn sleep_1s() {
    sleep(Duration::from_secs(1)).await;
}
```

We can write a test using the `#[tokio::test]` macro, which handles creating the runtime for us:

```
#[tokio::test]
async fn sleep_test() {
    let start_time = Instant::now();
    sleep(Duration::from_secs(1)).await;
    let end_time = Instant::now();
    let seconds = end_time
        .checked_duration_since(start_time)
        .unwrap()
        .as_secs();
    assert_eq!(seconds, 1);
}
```

This test runs normally like any other test, except it's running within an async context. You may certainly manage the runtime yourself if you wish, but as mentioned already, you must be mindful of the fact that Rust's tests will run in parallel.

Finally, Tokio provides the `tokio_test` crate, which can be enabled by adding the `"test-util"` feature (which is *not* enabled by the `"full"` feature flag). This includes some helper tools for mocking async tasks as well as some convenience macros for use with Tokio. The `tokio_test` crate is documented at https://docs.rs/tokio-test/latest/tokio_test/.

Summary

- Rust provides multiple async runtime implementations, but Tokio is appropriate for most purposes.
- Asynchronous programming requires special control flow, and our code must yield to the runtime's scheduler to allow it an opportunity to switch tasks. We can yield using `.await` or by spawning futures directly with `tokio::task::spawn()`.
- Asynchronous code blocks (e.g., functions) are denoted with the `async` keyword. Async code blocks always return futures.
- We can execute a future with the `.await` statement but only within an async context (i.e., an async code block).
- Async blocks are lazy and will not execute until we call `.await` or when they spawned explicitly. This differs from most other async implementations.
- Using `tokio::select! {}` or `tokio::join!()` allows us to introduce explicit concurrency.
- Spawning tasks with `tokio::task::spawn()` allows us to introduce concurrency and parallelism.
- If we want to perform blocking operations, we spawn them with `tokio::task::spawn_blocking()`.
- The `tracing` crate provides an easy way to instrument and emit telemetry to logs or OpenTelemetry collectors.
- We can use `tokio-console` with tracing to debug async programs.
- Tokio provides testing macros for unit and integration tests, which provide the necessary testing runtime environment. The `tokio_test` crate, which can be enabled with the `"test-util"` feature flag on Tokio, provides mocking and assertion tools for use with Tokio.

Building an HTTP
REST API service

In this chapter, we will put much of what we've learned in the previous chapters into practice by building a web service with async Rust. For completeness, we'll write an API client in chapter 10.

I'll focus mainly on the final code and spend less time discussing syntax, boiler-plate, and alternative implementations. I'm confident you will get the most value from a complete working example. Much of the "how to" content on the internet (and elsewhere) tends to omit many of the full-picture implementation details and gloss over many complexities, so I will do my best to point out what's missing from this example and where to go from here. I will not discuss the subjects of deploy-ment, load balancing, state management, cluster management, or high availability in depth because they are outside the scope of this book and not directly related to the Rust language.

At the end of this chapter, we'll have built a web API service that uses a database for state management to provide the critical features of nearly every web service in existence: creating, reading, updating, deleting, and listing items in a database. We'll model a "todo" CRUD app because this is a commonly used example for teaching purposes. Afterward, you can use this as a template or starter project for future development. Let's dive in!

9.1   *Choosing a web framework*

While writing this book, we've seen the async Rust landscape change quite a bit, especially with regard to the tools and libraries available for working with async Rust. The changes have largely been positive, and, in particular, I'm quite impressed with the progress of Tokio and its related projects.

For writing a web service, my recommendation is to use the axum framework, which is part of the larger Tokio project. The axum framework is somewhat minimal—as far as web frameworks go—but it packs a big punch, thanks to its flexible API and mostly macro-free implementation. It's relatively easy to integrate with other libraries and tools, and the simple API makes it quick and easy to get started. axum is based on Tower (https://github.com/tower-rs/tower), a library that provides abstractions for building networked services, and hyper (https://hyper.rs/), which provides an HTTP client and server implementation for both HTTP/1 and HTTP/2 (the book *HTTP/2 in Action* (Barry Pollard; https://www.manning.com/books/http2-in-action) provides a deep dive into the specifics of HTTP/2).

The best thing about axum is that it doesn't impose much on you in terms of patterns or practices. It does require that you learn the Tower library, if you wish to get into the nitty-gritty details, but for simple tasks, this is not necessary. A basic web service can be stood up quickly without needing to spend a great deal of time learning the web framework before writing a web service. For production services, axum includes support for tracing and metrics, which only require a small amount of configuration to enable.

> ### Honorable mentions
>
> The two other frameworks worth mentioning are Rocket (https://rocket.rs/), a web framework that aims to be a Ruby on Rails for Rust, and Actix (https://actix.rs/), one of the earliest Rust web frameworks.
>
> Both Rocket and Actix share the same flaw: they make significant use of macros to hide implementation details. axum, on the other hand, does not use macros for its core API, which (in my humble opinion) makes it much nicer to work with and easier to reason about.
>
> To their credit, both Rocket and Actix existed before Rust's stabilization of the Future trait and the async/await syntax—before which the use of macros was required. Additionally, both frameworks have made strides in reducing their reliance on macros in more recent versions.

9.2   *Creating an architecture*

For our web service, we'll follow a typical web tier architecture, which consists of at least three components: a
load balancer, the web service itself, and a stateful service
(i.e., a database). We're not going to implement a load
balancer (we'll assume one already exists or is provided),
and for the database, we'll use SQLite, but in practice,
you'd likely want to use a SQL database, such as PostgreSQL. The architecture is shown in figure 9.1.

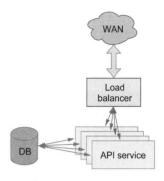

As shown in the diagram, our API service can scale
horizontally by simply adding more instances of the service. Each instance of our API service receives requests
from the load balancer and talks independently to the
database for storing and retrieving state.

**Figure 9.1   Web service
architecture**

Our application should accept its configuration from the environment, so we'll
pass configuration parameters using environment variables. We could use command-
line parsing or a config file instead, but environment variables are very convenient,
especially when deploying in contexts such as cluster orchestration systems. In our
case, we're only going to use a couple of configuration parameters: one to specify the
database and another to configure logging. We'll discuss these parameters later.

The configuration for each instance of our API service will be identical in most
cases, though there might be special circumstances in which you want to specify
parameters that are unique to each service instance, such as locality information or an
IP address to bind to. In practice, we typically bind to the 0.0.0.0 address, which binds
to all interfaces and effectively delegates the job of handling details to the OS networking stack (and can be configured as needed).

9.3   *API design*

For our service, we'll model a basic todo app. You may have encountered the todo app
before, and for this, we're only going to implement create, read, update, and delete
(CRUD) endpoints for the todos and a listing endpoint. We'll also add liveness and
readiness health check endpoints. We'll place our API routes under the /v1 path, as
shown in table 9.1.

Table 9.1   API service routes

Path	HTTP method	Action	Request body	Response
/v1/todos	GET	List	N/A	List of all todos
/v1/todos	POST	Create	New todo object	The newly created todo object
/v1/todos/:id	GET	Read	N/A	The newly created todo object

Table 9.1   API service routes *(continued)*

Path	HTTP method	Action	Request body	Response
/v1/todos/:id	PUT	Update	Updated todo object	The newly created todo object
/v1/todos/:id	DELETE	Delete	New todo object	The newly created todo object

For the read, update, and delete paths, we use a path parameter for the ID of each todo, which is denoted in the preceding paths with the :id token. We'll add liveness and readiness health check endpoints, as shown in table 9.2.

Table 9.2   API service health check endpoints

Path	HTTP method	Response
/alive	GET	Returns 200 with ok on success
/ready	GET	Returns 200 with ok on success

Now that we've described the API, let's look at the tools and libraries we'll use to build it in the next section.

9.4   *Libraries and tools*

We'll rely on existing crates to do much of the heavy lifting for our service. We don't need to write much code at all—most of what we'll do involves gluing existing components together to build our service. However, we have to pay close attention to how we combine the different components, but lucky for us, Rust's type system makes that easy by telling us when it's wrong, with compiler errors.

We can initialize the project with cargo new api-server, after which we can start adding the crates we need with cargo add .... The crates we need and their features are listed in table 9.3.

Table 9.3   API service dependencies

Name	Features	Description
axum	*Default*	Web framework
chrono	serde	Date/time library, with serde feature
serde	derive	Serialization/deserialization library, with #[derive(...)] feature
serde_json	*Default*	JSON serialization/deserialization for the serde crate
sqlx	runtime-tokio-rustls, sqlite, chrono, macros	Async SQL toolkit for SQLite, MySQL, and PostgreSQL
tokio	macros, rt-multi-thread	Async runtime, used with axum and sqlx

Table 9.3   API service dependencies (*continued*)

Name	Features	Description
`tower-http`	`trace,cors`	Provides HTTP middleware for `axum`, specifically, tracing and CORS
`tracing`	*default*	Async tracing library
`tracing-subscriber`	`env-filter`	Allows us to subscribe to tracing data within crates that use tracing

NOTE Dependency versions are not listed in table 9.3. These can be found in Cargo.toml from the source code listings for this book.

For dependencies with features, you can use the `--feature` flag with `cargo add`. For example, to add `axum` with the default features, we run `cargo add axum`, and for SQLx, we run `cargo add sqlx --features runtime-tokio-rustls,sqlite,chrono,macros`. You can also simply copy the Cargo.toml from the book's source code for this project.

You may also want to try the `sqlx-cli` (https://crates.io/crates/sqlx-cli) tool, which can be installed with `cargo install sqlx-cli`. This tool allows you to create databases, run migrations, and drop databases. Once installed, run `sqlx --help` for more information. This tool is not required to run the code, but it's useful if you want to do more with SQLx.

For your convenience, you can install everything from table 9.3 in a one-shot, "copy-pastable" command as follows:

```
cargo add axum
cargo add chrono --features serde
cargo add serde --features derive
cargo add serde_json
cargo add sqlx --features runtime-tokio-rustls,sqlite,chrono,macros
cargo add tokio --features macros,rt-multi-thread
cargo add tower-http --features trace,cors
cargo add tracing
cargo add tracing-subscriber --features env-filter
cargo install sqlx-cli
```

After running these commands, your Cargo.toml will look like the following listing.

Listing 9.1   API service Cargo.toml

```
[package]
name = "api-service"
version = "0.1.0"
edition = "2021"

# See more keys and their definitions at https://doc.rust-lang.org/cargo/
⇒ reference/manifest.html
```

```
[dependencies]
axum = "0.6.18"
chrono = { version = "0.4.26", features = ["serde"] }
serde = { version = "1.0.164", features = ["derive"] }
serde_json = "1.0.99"
sqlx = { version = "0.6.3", features = ["runtime-tokio-rustls", "sqlite",
➥ "chrono", "macros"] }
tokio = { version = "1.28.2", features = ["macros", "rt-multi-thread"] }
tower-http = { version = "0.4.1", features = ["trace", "cors"] }
tracing = "0.1.37"
tracing-subscriber = { version = "0.3.17", features = ["env-filter"] }
```

With our dependencies set up, we can dive into writing the code.

> **NOTE** In practice, you'd likely add and change the dependencies as you go, so don't take this as a suggestion that you need to set up all the dependencies ahead of time. As I like to say, *software is soft*, so never avoid modifying it to your taste (including the examples I provide).

9.5 Application scaffolding

Our application entry point in main.rs contains a small amount of boilerplate and the necessary setup for our application. Within it, we'll do the following:

- Declare our main entry point
- Initialize tracing and logging
- Create and initialize our database connection
- Run any necessary database migrations
- Define the routes for our API
- Start the service itself

9.5.1 main()

Let's start by taking a look at our main() function.

Listing 9.2 API service main() function from src/main.rs

```
#[tokio::main]
async fn main() {
    init_tracing();          ◄── Initializes the tracing and
                                 logging for our service and
                                 its dependencies

    let dbpool = init_dbpool().await
        .expect("couldn't initialize DB pool");   ◄── Initializes the DB pool

    let router = create_router(dbpool).await;    ◄── Creates the core application
                                                     service and its routes

    let bind_addr = std::env::var("BIND_ADDR")
        .unwrap_or_else(|_| "127.0.0.1:3000".to_string());   ◄── Fetches the binding
                                                                 address from the
                                                                 environment variable
                                                                 BIND_ADDR or uses
                                                                 the default value of
                                                                 127.0.0.1:3000

    axum::Server::bind(&bind_addr.parse().unwrap())   ◄── Parses the binding address
                                                          into a socket address
```

```
    .serve(router.into_make_service())   ◁───┐  Creates the service and
    .await                                    │  starts the HTTP server
    .expect("unable to start server")   ◁─────┘
}
```

Our `main()` doesn't contain much, and we have to dig deeper to understand what's going on. Before we do that, it should be noted that we're using Tokio's `tokio::main` macro to initialize the Tokio runtime, which hides a bit of complexity for us, such as setting the number of worker threads.

TIP   Tokio will read the `TOKIO_WORKER_THREADS` environment variable, and if provided, it will set the number of worker threads to the value defined.

For more complex scenarios, you may want to manually instantiate the Tokio runtime and configure it accordingly using `tokio::runtime::Builder`.

9.5.2   *init_tracing()*

Moving on, let's take a look at the tracing initialization in `init_tracing()`.

Listing 9.3   API service `init_tracing()` function in src/main.rs

```
fn init_tracing() {
    use tracing_subscriber::{
        filter::LevelFilter, fmt, prelude::*, EnvFilter        ◁─── Fetches the RUST_LOG
    };                                                              environment variable,
                                                                    providing a default
    let rust_log = std::env::var(EnvFilter::DEFAULT_ENV)   ◁───     value if it's not defined
        .unwrap_or_else(|_| "sqlx=info,tower_http=debug,info".to_string());
                                                       ◁───┐ Returns the default global registry
    tracing_subscriber::registry()    ◁────────────────────┘
        .with(fmt::layer())    ◁───┐ Adds a formatting layer, which provides
        .with(                     │ human-readable trace formatting
            EnvFilter::builder()                                      ◁────────────┐
                .with_default_directive(LevelFilter::INFO.into())                  │
                .parse_lossy(rust_log),                                            │
        )                                    Constructs an environment filter, with the
        .init();                             default log level set to info or using the value
}                                                        provided by RUST_LOG otherwise
```

Initializing the tracing is important if we want to see useful log messages. We probably don't want to turn on all tracing messages, just the traces that are useful, so we explicitly enable the debug level messages for `tower_http::*`, and info-level messages for `sqlx::*`. We could also add our own traces, but the ones included in the crates we're using are more than sufficient for our needs.

Determining which traces to enable can be a little tricky, but we can turn on all the traces by setting `RUST_LOG=trace`. This can generate a lot of logging output, so don't try this in production environments if you don't need to. `EnvFilter` is compatible with `env_logger`, which is used by many other Rust crates, so we can maintain compatibility and familiarity within the Rust ecosystem.

9.5.3 *init_dbpool()*

For our state management, we'll use a connection pool to obtain a connection to the database. The connection pool allows us to acquire and reuse connections to the database without needing to create a new connection for each request, which provides us a nice little optimization. The connection pool settings are database specific and can be configured as needed, but for this example, we'll stick with the default parameters. Additionally, the pooling is nice but not entirely necessary because we're using SQLite (as opposed to a network-connected database, like MySQL or PostgreSQL), which operates within the same process on background threads managed by the SQLite library. Let's look at init_dbpool() in the following listing.

Listing 9.4 API service `init_dbpool()` function in src/main.rs

```
async fn init_dbpool() -> Result<sqlx::Pool<sqlx::Sqlite>, sqlx::Error> {
    use sqlx::sqlite::{SqliteConnectOptions, SqlitePoolOptions};
    use std::str::FromStr;

    let db_connection_str =
        std::env::var("DATABASE_URL")
        .unwrap_or_else(|_| "sqlite:db.sqlite".to_string());

    let dbpool = SqlitePoolOptions::new()
        .connect_with(SqliteConnectOptions::from_str(&db_connection_str)?
        .create_if_missing(true))
        .await
        .expect("can't connect to database");

    sqlx::migrate!()
        .run(&dbpool)
        .await
        .expect("database migration failed");

    Ok(dbpool)
}
```

> We'll try to read the **DATABASE_URL** environment variable or default to sqlite:db.sqlite if not defined (which opens a file called db.sqlite in the current working directory).

> When we connect to the database, we ask the driver to create the database if it doesn't already exist.

> After we've connected to the DB, we run any necessary migrations.

> We can pass our newly created DB pool directly to SQLx, which will obtain a connection from the pool.

Databases are a complex topic and well outside the scope of this book, but I'll summarize what's happening in the preceding code listing:

- The connection string is pulled from the DATABASE_URL environment variable, defaulting to sqlite:db.sqlite, which opens the db.sqlite file in the current working directory. You could (theoretically) support multiple database drivers, but you would need to carefully adjust your SQL statements, depending on which driver is specified in DATABASE_URL. In practice, you should just pick one database and make sure your code works with that because each database has its quirks and differences, even if they are, technically speaking, the same language of SQL.

- We let the SQLite driver create the database upon connection by setting `create_if_missing(true)` on `SqliteConnectOptions`. SQLx will generate a `CREATE DATABASE IF NOT EXISTS` … for us, so we don't have to worry about creating the database. This is provided for convenience and should be relatively harmless, but you might not want to do this in all contexts.
- SQLx provides a migration API, which I won't go into too much detail about, but if you've used any other web frameworks, you've likely seen something similar. It's your responsibility to write the migrations, but SQLx can apply them for you. You need to make sure they're correct, idempotent, and (optionally) provide both the up (create) and down (destroy) migrations if you want to enable forward and backward migrations.
- Creating the database and running migrations are stateful and destructive operations. We're mutating the database, and if you make a mistake or typo, there is no magic undo button (unless you design that yourself). This is not something to be alarmed about—just something you should be aware of—because you never want to inadvertently apply a migration to a database you don't intend (like testing migrations against a production database before the code is ready for production). In the next section, we'll discuss the data model and how we interact with the database.

9.6 Data modeling

We're keeping this service simple by only modeling one kind of data: a todo item. Our todos only need two fields: a body (i.e., the todo item), which is just a text string, and a Boolean field to mark whether an item is completed. We could simply delete a todo once it's completed, but it might be nice to keep completed todos around if we want to look back at the old (completed) todos. We'll include a timestamp for the creation date and the time the todo was last updated. You might also want a third timestamp, the time at which an item is completed, but we'll keep this example simple.

9.6.1 SQL schema

Let's write the SQL schema for our todos table.

Listing 9.5 API service SQL schema from migrations/20230701202642_todos.sql

```
CREATE TABLE IF NOT EXISTS todos (
    id INTEGER PRIMARY KEY AUTOINCREMENT NOT NULL,
    body TEXT NOT NULL,
    completed BOOLEAN NOT NULL DEFAULT FALSE,
    created_at TIMESTAMP NOT NULL DEFAULT CURRENT_TIMESTAMP,
    updated_at TIMESTAMP NOT NULL DEFAULT CURRENT_TIMESTAMP
);
```

I won't go into too much detail, as the SQL itself is fairly self-explanatory. I want to note a couple of details, however:

- We rely on SQLite to provide a primary key for us and automatically increment the ID when a new record is created, such that we don't reuse any IDs. We could use something like a UUID instead, which would introduce another layer of complexity to validate that any UUID we create is actually unique. PostgreSQL supports UUID primary keys in recent versions, and some versions of MySQL-compatible DBs support them as well.

- We don't allow any field to be null or unspecified.

- We provide a default value for every column except the text body of the todo. This means we can create a new todo with only one piece of data: the text body of the todo.

- The `updated_at` column will be updated by our Rust code, as opposed to using a SQL trigger (or some other method). You may prefer to use a trigger here, and I'll leave that as an exercise for the reader. The main advantage of using a trigger is that you can always execute plain SQL queries, and the `updated_at` column will be updated accordingly.

Our CREATE TABLE … statement will be added as a migration, so when the database is first initialized and migrations are executed, the table will be created. We'll use the SQLx CLI to create the migration:

```
$ sqlx migrate add todos
# ...
```

This command creates a file called migrations/20230701202642_todos.sql, which we've populated with the SQL code from listing 9.5.

9.6.2   *Interfacing with our data*

We're now ready to write the Rust code to model our todos in Rust and interact with the database. We'll support five operations: create, read, update, delete, and list. These are the default table stakes CRUD operations that you generally get out of the box and that you will encounter many times over if you spend much time working with web frameworks.

Let's look at our Todo struct.

Listing 9.6   API service `Todo` struct from src/todo.rs

```rust
#[derive(Serialize, Clone, sqlx::FromRow)]
pub struct Todo {
    id: i64,
    body: String,
    completed: bool,
    created_at: NaiveDateTime,
    updated_at: NaiveDateTime,
}
```

We're deriving the Serialize trait from the serde crate and sqlx::FromRow, which allows us to get a Todo from a SQLx query.

We use the chrono::NaiveDateTime type to map SQL timestamps into Rust objects.

There isn't a lot to see for the `Todo` struct itself, so we'll jump into the `impl` blocks, which get more interesting. We'll first look at the listing and reading code.

Listing 9.7   API service `Todo` struct `impl` read block from src/todo.rs

```
impl Todo {
    pub async fn list(dbpool: SqlitePool) -> Result<Vec<Todo>, Error> {
        query_as("select * from todos")        ◁────┐ Selects all todos
            .fetch_all(&dbpool)                       │ from the todos table
            .await
            .map_err(Into::into)
    }
    pub async fn read(dbpool: SqlitePool, id: i64) -> Result<Todo, Error> {
        query_as("select * from todos where id = ?")   ◁──┐ Selects one todo from
            .bind(id)                                        │ the todos table with a
            .fetch_one(&dbpool)                              │ matching id field
            .await
            .map_err(Into::into)
    }
}
```

In this code, we have two methods: `list()` and `read()`. Each method applies the action you'd expect by executing a query against the database. The only real difference between `list()` and `read()` is the number of records returned and the fact that we need to select by ID when reading a single record. Now, let's look at the following listing, which shows the write `impl` block.

Listing 9.8   API service `Todo` struct `impl` write block from src/todo.rs

```
                                    We've added a new type here, CreateTodo, which we
                                    haven't defined yet. It contains the todo body, which
impl Todo {                         we need to create a todo.
    pub async fn create(
        dbpool: SqlitePool,
        new_todo: CreateTodo,  ◁──┘    We use the returning * SQL clause to retrieve the
    ) -> Result<Todo, Error> {                   record immediately after it's inserted.
        query_as("insert into todos (body) values (?) returning *")  ◁──┐
            .bind(new_todo.body())
            .fetch_one(&dbpool)      ◁──┐ We execute the query with fetch_one()
            .await                        │ because we expect this to return one row.
            .map_err(Into::into)
    }
    pub async fn update(                   We've added another new type here, UpdateTodo,
        dbpool: SqlitePool,                which contains the two fields we allow to be updated.
        id: i64,
        updated_todo: UpdateTodo,  ◁──┘       Once again, we're using the returning
    ) -> Result<Todo, Error> {                   * SQL clause to retrieve the updated
        query_as(                         record immediately. Notice how we set the
            "update todos set body = ?, completed = ?, \    updated_at field to the current date and time.
            updated_at = datetime('now') where id = ? returning *",   ◁───┘
```

```
        )
            .bind(updated_todo.body())        ◁──┐  Each value is bound in the order they're declared
            .bind(updated_todo.completed())   ◁──┘  within the SQL statement, using the ? token to
            .bind(id)                                bind values. This syntax varies, depending on the
            .fetch_one(&dbpool)    ◁──┐             SQL implementation.
            .await
                .map_err(Into::into)    We expect to fetch one row
    }                                    when this query is executed.
    pub async fn delete(dbpool: SqlitePool, id: i64) -> Result<(), Error> {
        query("delete from todos where id = ?")   ◁──┐
            .bind(id)                                   The delete is destructive; nothing
            .execute(&dbpool)    ◁──┐                  is left to return if it succeeds.
            .await?;
        Ok(())      ◁──┐           Here, we use execute() to execute the query, which
    }                              is used for queries that don't return records.
}
```

We return unit upon success (i.e., no previous errors).

The code for each action is quite similar, so let's discuss some of the shared behaviors:

- We assume any errors will result in the `sqlx::Error` being returned by the query execution, which we map to our own error type using the `From` trait—we apply this trait by using `.map_err(Into::into)`. The `From` and `Into` traits are reciprocal, so we can call the `Into::into` trait method on the error only by using `map_err()`.
- Every query except the delete action returns one or more records, and because we derived `sqlx::FromRow` for `Todo` (as previously noted), we can let SQLx map the type for us.
- We need to pass a handle to the database pool (we could also pass a connection directly) to execute each operation.
- When we use `bind()` to bind values to the SQL statement, we need to pay attention to the order of the values because they're bound in the order they're specified. Some SQL drivers let you use identifiers to bind values, but SQLite does not.

Let's take a quick look at the `CreateTodo` and `UpdateTodo` structs, which we introduced in listing 9.8. First, let's examine `CreateTodo`.

Listing 9.9 API service `CreateTodo` struct from src/todo.rs

```
#[derive(Deserialize)]
pub struct CreateTodo {
    body: String,
}

impl CreateTodo {
    pub fn body(&self) -> &str {
        self.body.as_ref()
    }
}
```

Notice how the only method we provide is an accessor for the `body` field. This is because we're relying on `Deserialize` to create the struct, which we derived at the top.

We don't need to construct a `CreateTodo`; we just need to deserialize it when we receive one in an API call.

Next, let's look at `UpdateTodo`.

Listing 9.10 API service `UpdateTodo` struct from src/todo.rs

```rust
#[derive(Deserialize)]
pub struct UpdateTodo {
    body: String,
    completed: bool,
}

impl UpdateTodo {
    pub fn body(&self) -> &str {
        self.body.as_ref()
    }

    pub fn completed(&self) -> bool {
        self.completed
    }
}
```

`UptadeTodo` is nearly the same as `CreateTodo`, except we have two fields: `body` and `completed`. Once again, we rely on the `serde` library to construct the object for us.

That's it for the data model. Now, we'll move on to defining the API routes in the next section.

9.7   *Declaring the API routes*

We've already designed our API, so all we need to do is declare the routes using `axum`'s `Router`. If you've used any other web frameworks, this code will look quite familiar, as it consists of the same components: a request path (with optional parameters), a request method, the request handler, the state we require for our handlers, and any additional layers for our service.

Let's go ahead and look at the code in the following listing from router.rs, which defines the service and its router.

Listing 9.11 API service router from src/router.rs

```rust
pub async fn create_router(
    dbpool: sqlx::Pool<sqlx::Sqlite>,         ◁──┐ The database pool is passed into
) -> axum::Router {                              │ the router, which takes ownership.
    use crate::api::{
        ping, todo_create, todo_delete, todo_list, todo_read, todo_update,
    };
    use axum::{routing::get, Router};
    use tower_http::cors::{Any, CorsLayer};
    use tower_http::trace::TraceLayer;

    Router::new()                                    Our liveness health check
        .route("/alive", get(|| async { "ok" }))  ◁── merely returns a 200
                                                     status with the body ok.
```

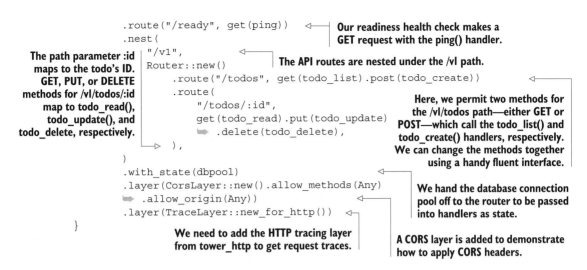

The path parameter :id maps to the todo's ID. GET, PUT, or DELETE methods for /v1/todos/:id map to todo_read(), todo_update(), and todo_delete, respectively.

Our readiness health check makes a GET request with the ping() handler.

The API routes are nested under the /v1 path.

Here, we permit two methods for the /v1/todos path—either GET or POST—which call the todo_list() and todo_create() handlers, respectively. We can change the methods together using a handy fluent interface.

We hand the database connection pool off to the router to be passed into handlers as state.

We need to add the HTTP tracing layer from tower_http to get request traces.

A CORS layer is added to demonstrate how to apply CORS headers.

`axum::Router` is the core abstraction of the `axum` web framework, which allows us to declare the routes and their handlers as well as mix in layers from other services, such as `tower_http`. Although this example is quite basic, you can get very far building upon what I've demonstrated here, as it will cover a significant portion of use cases. For practical purposes, you would need to consult the `axum` documentation at https://docs.rs/axum/ to go more in depth in the framework and its features. Let's move on to implementing the API route handlers.

9.8   *Implementing the API routes*

The final puzzle piece is the API route handlers, which we'll discuss now. Let's start by looking at the `ping()` handler for the readiness check because it's the most basic handler.

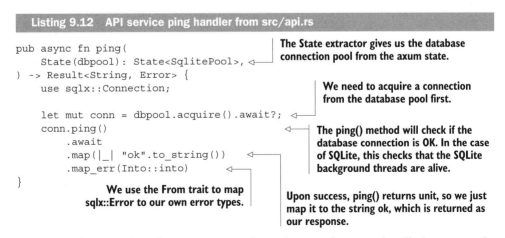

Listing 9.12   API service ping handler from src/api.rs

The State extractor gives us the database connection pool from the axum state.

We need to acquire a connection from the database pool first.

The ping() method will check if the database connection is OK. In the case of SQLite, this checks that the SQLite background threads are alive.

We use the From trait to map sqlx::Error to our own error types.

Upon success, ping() returns unit, so we just map it to the string ok, which is returned as our response.

In `ping()`, I've introduced a new concept from the `axum` framework called *extractors*. In short, an extractor is anything that implements the `axum::extract::FromRequest` or `axum::extract::FromRequestParts` traits, but we can also use one of the extractors that `axum` provides for use, which include the following:

- `axum::extract::State`—Extracts the global application state, which is supplied to the router with `.with_state()`, like we saw in listing 9.11 for the database pool.
- `axum::extract::Path`—Extracts path parameters, such as the `id` parameter we included in our routes.
- `axum::extract::Json`—Extracts the body of a request as a JSON object and deserializes it using the `serde` crate.

The `axum` framework provides several other extractors, and you can also create your own by implementing the extractor traits.

Moving on, let's get into the most import bits: the todo API route handlers.

Listing 9.13   API service todo handlers from src/api.rs

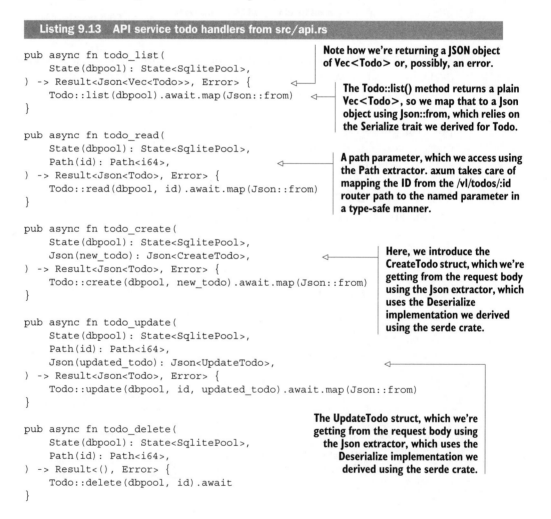

```
pub async fn todo_list(
    State(dbpool): State<SqlitePool>,
) -> Result<Json<Vec<Todo>>, Error> {
    Todo::list(dbpool).await.map(Json::from)
}

pub async fn todo_read(
    State(dbpool): State<SqlitePool>,
    Path(id): Path<i64>,
) -> Result<Json<Todo>, Error> {
    Todo::read(dbpool, id).await.map(Json::from)
}

pub async fn todo_create(
    State(dbpool): State<SqlitePool>,
    Json(new_todo): Json<CreateTodo>,
) -> Result<Json<Todo>, Error> {
    Todo::create(dbpool, new_todo).await.map(Json::from)
}

pub async fn todo_update(
    State(dbpool): State<SqlitePool>,
    Path(id): Path<i64>,
    Json(updated_todo): Json<UpdateTodo>,
) -> Result<Json<Todo>, Error> {
    Todo::update(dbpool, id, updated_todo).await.map(Json::from)
}

pub async fn todo_delete(
    State(dbpool): State<SqlitePool>,
    Path(id): Path<i64>,
) -> Result<(), Error> {
    Todo::delete(dbpool, id).await
}
```

Note how we're returning a JSON object of Vec<Todo> or, possibly, an error.

The Todo::list() method returns a plain Vec<Todo>, so we map that to a Json object using Json::from, which relies on the Serialize trait we derived for Todo.

A path parameter, which we access using the Path extractor. axum takes care of mapping the ID from the /v1/todos/:id router path to the named parameter in a type-safe manner.

Here, we introduce the CreateTodo struct, which we're getting from the request body using the Json extractor, which uses the Deserialize implementation we derived using the serde crate.

The UpdateTodo struct, which we're getting from the request body using the Json extractor, which uses the Deserialize implementation we derived using the serde crate.

The code for our API handlers is quite small. Because we've already done most of the hard work; at this point, it's just about defining the inputs and outputs for each of our handlers. axum will only match requests against handlers that have valid extractors for their given request path and method, and it does so in a way that's type safe, so we don't have to think too hard about whether our handlers will work once the code successfully compiles. This is the beauty of Rust and type safety.

> **NOTE**   To bring ourselves back down to earth, it should be noted that this API is designed in a way that's quite rigid. For example, you don't allow for optional fields in any of the endpoints—you can only provide exactly the fields required or else the service will return an error. In most cases, this is fine, but as an exercise for the reader, you may want to try making the completed field (for example) optional on PATCH or update requests. If you only need to modify one particular field, it seems reasonable that the API would gracefully handle only the fields that are specified—does it not?

We now have a fully functioning API service, with the main CRUD endpoints completed. We need to discuss one more topic—error handling—and then we can run some tests to see how this baby works.

Before I jump into error handling, let's quickly discuss how *responses* are handled in axum. Out of the box, axum will handle converting basic types (unit, String, Json, and axum::http::StatusCode) into HTTP responses. It does this by providing an implementation of the axum::response::IntoResponse trait for the most common response types. If you need to convert your type into a response, you must either transform it into something that implements IntoResponse or implement IntoResponse yourself, which we'll demonstrate in the next section.

9.9   Error handling

For error handling, I've kept things very simple. We'll define one enum called Error in error.rs.

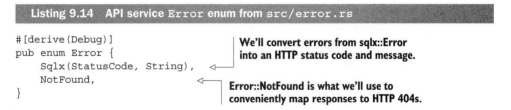

Listing 9.14   API service Error enum from src/error.rs

```
#[derive(Debug)]
pub enum Error {
    Sqlx(StatusCode, String),        ◁── We'll convert errors from sqlx::Error
    NotFound,                             into an HTTP status code and message.
}                                    ◁── Error::NotFound is what we'll use to
                                         conveniently map responses to HTTP 404s.
```

> **NOTE**   We're treating 404s (not found) as errors, but 404s are also a normal HTTP response that doesn't necessarily indicate an error. For convenience, we're treating anything that's not a 200 status code as an error.

There is not much to see with our error type. Next, we need to define the From trait for sqlx::Error, which converts SQLx errors to our error type.

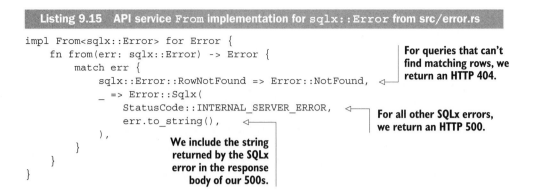

Listing 9.15 API service `From` implementation for `sqlx::Error` from src/error.rs

```
impl From<sqlx::Error> for Error {
    fn from(err: sqlx::Error) -> Error {
        match err {
            sqlx::Error::RowNotFound => Error::NotFound,        ◁── For queries that can't find matching rows, we return an HTTP 404.
            _ => Error::Sqlx(
                StatusCode::INTERNAL_SERVER_ERROR,              ◁── For all other SQLx errors, we return an HTTP 500.
                err.to_string(),                               ◁── We include the string returned by the SQLx error in the response body of our 500s.
            ),
        }
    }
}
```

Our `From<sqlx::Error>` for `Error` implementation is quite simple: we only handle one case as special, which is the `RowNotFound` case. For that, we map it to an HTTP 404, which is more helpful than returning a generic 500 error.

Next, we need to make it possible for `axum` to use our error type as a response, and for that, we'll implement `IntoResponse` for `Error`.

Listing 9.16 API service `From` implementation for `sqlx::Error` from src/error.rs

Pull the status code and response body out, and then call into_response() on a tuple of (StatusCode, String) because axum provides an implementation of IntoResponse for us.

```
impl IntoResponse for Error {
    fn into_response(self) -> Response {
        match self {
            Error::Sqlx(code, body) => (code, body).into_response(),      ◁──
            Error::NotFound => StatusCode::NOT_FOUND.into_response(),      ◁──
        }
    }
}
```

Call into_response() on StatusCode::NOT_FOUND, which gives us an empty HTTP 404 response.

You may notice in the preceding code that we don't even bother constructing a `Response`, as required by `IntoResponse`. Thanks to the implementations provided by `axum`, we merely delegate the response construction to `axum` using an existing implementation of `IntoResponse`. This is a neat trick that requires minimal effort on our part. The only case where you wouldn't want to do this is when the default implementation involves a costly conversion and you have enough information to optimize it better.

9.10 Running the service

Let's run our service and make sure it behaves as expected. When it's started with `cargo run`, we'll see output similar to what's shown in figure 9.2. The logging output we see in the figure shows the queries from SQLx at startup, which includes running the migrations. We aren't required to run the migrations automatically, but this is convenient for testing. In a production service, you would likely not run migrations automatically.

```
● ● ●  ⌥⌘2                                  cargo run
➜ api-service git:(main) ✗ cargo run
    Finished dev [unoptimized + debuginfo] target(s) in 0.08s
     Running `target/debug/api-service`
2023-08-11T17:39:33.802819Z  INFO sqlx::query: PRAGMA foreign_keys = ON; …; rows affected: 0, rows returned: 0, elapsed: 279.042µs

PRAGMA foreign_keys = ON;

2023-08-11T17:39:33.806712Z  INFO sqlx::query: CREATE TABLE IF NOT …; rows affected: 0, rows returned: 0, elapsed: 606.084µs

CREATE TABLE IF NOT EXISTS _sqlx_migrations (
  version BIGINT PRIMARY KEY,
  description TEXT NOT NULL,
  installed_on TIMESTAMP NOT NULL DEFAULT CURRENT_TIMESTAMP,
  success BOOLEAN NOT NULL,
  checksum BLOB NOT NULL,
  execution_time BIGINT NOT NULL
);

2023-08-11T17:39:33.807640Z  INFO sqlx::query: SELECT version FROM _sqlx_migrations …; rows affected: 0, rows returned: 0, elapsed: 76.833µs

SELECT
  version
FROM
  _sqlx_migrations
WHERE
  success = false
ORDER BY
  version
LIMIT
  1

2023-08-11T17:39:33.808293Z  INFO sqlx::query: SELECT version, checksum FROM …; rows affected: 0, rows returned: 1, elapsed: 89.458µs

SELECT
  version,
  checksum
FROM
  _sqlx_migrations
ORDER BY
  version
```

Figure 9.2 Running the API service

We need to test our API, but first, let's ensure the health check endpoints work as expected. For these tests, I will use the HTTPie (https://httpie.io/) tool, but you could just as easily use curl or another CLI HTTP client.

I'll run `http 127.0.0.1:3000/alive` followed by `http 127.0.0.1:3000/ready`, which will generate an HTTP `GET` request against each endpoint, with the result shown in figure 9.3. In the output shown in the figure, we see the logging output of our service on the left side and the output from HTTPie on the right side. So far, everything looks good; we can see the HTTP status code is 200 for each request, the request body is simply `ok`, and the CORS headers are present as expected.

Now, it's time to create a todo. For this, we'll make an HTTP `POST` request with `http post 127.0.0.1:3000/v1/todos body='wash the dishes'`, as shown in figure 9.4.

Now, let's test the HTTP `GET` methods for the read and list endpoints with `http 127.0.0.1:3000/v1/todos/1` (read) and `http 127.0.0.1:3000/v1/todos` (list), as shown in figure 9.5. Note how the first request (for a specific resource) returns just the todo object, and the second request (to list all resources) returns a list of objects. So far, so good. Next, let's test the `PUT` method to update our todo by marking it as completed with `http put 127.0.0.1:3000/v1/todos/1 body='wash the dishes' completed:=true`, as shown in figure 9.6.

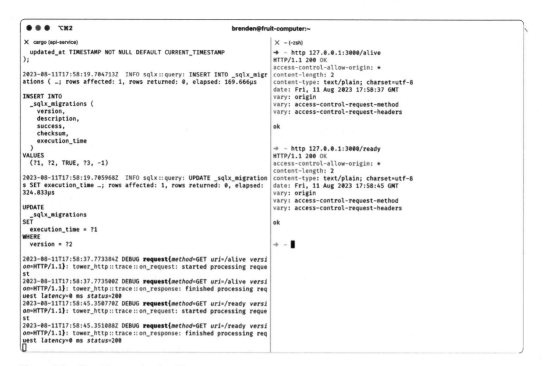

Figure 9.3 Checking service health

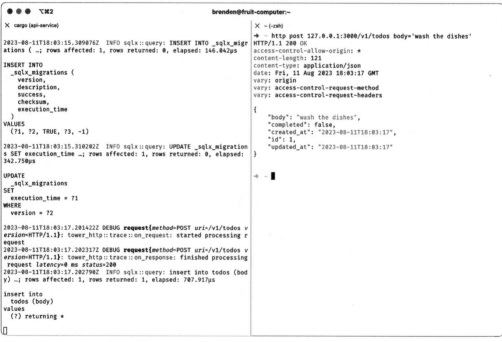

Figure 9.4 Creating a todo with POST

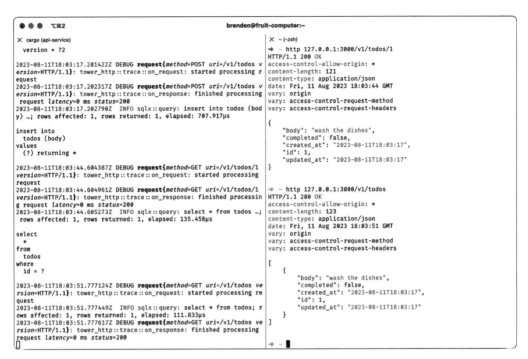

Figure 9.5 Reading todos with GET

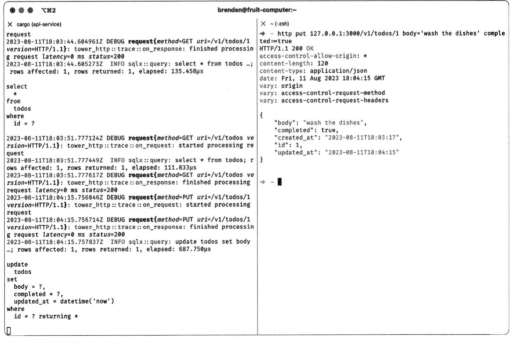

Figure 9.6 Updating todos with PUT

Notice how we need to specify both the `body` and `completed` fields, which is a bit annoying. It would be nice if we gracefully handled only the required fields when updating a record, but I'll leave that as an exercise for the reader. Finally, let's check that we can delete our todo with `http delete 127.0.0.1:3000/v1/todos/1`, as shown in figure 9.7.

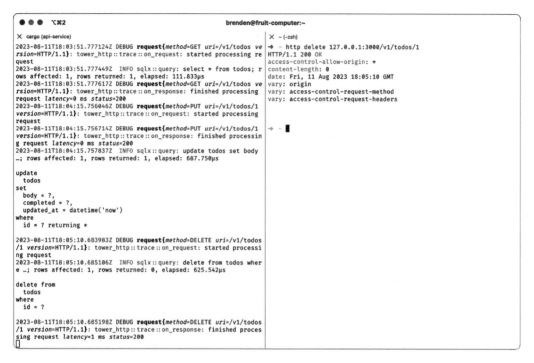

Figure 9.7   Deleting todos with `DELETE`

Success! It looks like everything works. As an exercise for the reader, I suggest running a few more tests and experimenting with some of the following options:

- Adding multiple posts
- Listing multiple posts
- Permitting optional fields (as already suggested)
- Trying a different primary key type (such as a UUID)
- Changing the response for POST to include the resource URL or a 3xx redirect, a pattern sometimes used in RESTful APIs

Summary

- `axum` is a web framework that provides everything needed to build web service APIs in Rust using the Tokio async runtime. Although there are other Rust web frameworks, `axum` provides a type-safe API without the need for macros.

- `axum` can be used together with a number of other crates to provide everything you need in a web framework, but the `axum` crate itself is fairly small and only provides a few key abstractions: the router, extractors, responses, error handling, and integration with the `tower` and `tower-http` crates.

- `axum` supports HTTP/1 and HTTP/2 via the hyper crate, can handle TLS termination with `rustls`, and is built on Tokio's insanely fast async runtime with stable Rust support for the async/await syntax.

- Most of the work in building an API service involves designing a data model, deciding on state management, adding tracing and logging, deciding how to render the client-side data (HTML, JSON, etc.), and choosing an architecture that suits your needs.

- The standard web-tier architecture will fit the needs of a considerable portion of applications, and it's relatively robust, highly scalable, well understood, and backed by well-known standards, like HTTP.

10
Building an
HTTP REST API CLI

This chapter covers

- Deciding which tools and libraries to use
- Designing the CLI
- Declaring the commands
- Implementing the commands
- Implementing requests
- Handling errors gracefully
- Testing our CLI

Continuing the work we did in the previous chapter, we'll write a CLI tool for the API service we wrote. Using a CLI tool, we'll demonstrate another way to interact asynchronously in Rust by making HTTP requests with a separate service (which we also wrote). Our CLI tool will provide a convenient way to interact with our todo app backend (the API service). We'll use Rust's async features to showcase the basics of writing async Rust from the client side of a client–server relationship.

Writing CLI tools is one way to use software to solve problems for us, and building tools is how we avoid repetition, mistakes, and time wasted doing tasks computers are better suited for. Most versions of the Unix philosophy (which has several variations) include the "do one thing and do it well" tenet, which we'll apply to our CLI tool. We'll also make it easy to pipe the output from our CLI into another tool (another point from the Unix philosophy), making it possible to string commands together.

10.1 Deciding which tools and libraries to use

We'll continue working with the Tokio runtime, and for making HTTP requests, we'll once again use the hyper library, which provides an implementation of HTTP (for both servers and clients). I will also introduce a new crate, called *clap* (https://crates.io/crates/clap), which provides structured and type-safe command-line parsing.

It should be noted there is a higher-level HTTP client library called `reqwest` (https://crates.io/crates/reqwest), which is similar to the Python Requests library, but for Rust. However, we'll stick with hyper because it's lower level; therefore, we can learn a bit more about how things work by using it directly, as opposed to using `reqwest`, which wraps the hyper library. In practice, you'd probably be better off using `reqwest` (which provides a more convenient and user-friendly API). Table 10.1 shows the API service dependencies.

Table 10.1 API service dependencies

Name	Features	Description
Clap	`derive`	Command-line framework
colored_json	Default	Pretty-print JSON data
Hyper	`client,http1,tcp,stream`	HTTP client/server API
serde	Default	Serialization/deserialization library
serde_json	Default	JSON serialization/deserialization for the `serde` crate
tokio	`macros,rt-multi-thread, io-util,io-std`	Async runtime, used with hyper
yansi	Default	ANSI color output

For your convenience, you can install everything from table 10.1 in a one-shot, copy-pastable command as follows:

```
cargo add clap --features derive
cargo add colored_json
cargo add hyper --features client,http1,tcp,stream
cargo add serde
cargo add serde_json
cargo add tokio --features macros,rt-multi-thread,io-util,io-std
cargo add yansi
```

After running these commands, your Cargo.toml will look like the following listing.

Listing 10.1   API client Cargo.toml

```
[package]
name = "api-client"
version = "0.1.0"
edition = "2021"

# See more keys and their definitions at https://doc.rust-lang.org/cargo/
➡ reference/manifest.html

[dependencies]
clap = { version = "4.3.10", features = ["derive"] }
colored_json = "3.2.0"
hyper = { version = "0.14.27", features = ["client", "http1", "tcp",
➡ "stream"] }
serde = "1.0.166"
serde_json = "1.0.100"
tokio = { version = "1.29.1", features = ["macros", "rt-multi-thread",
➡ "io-util", "io-std"] }
yansi = "0.5.1"
```

Now that we've specified our dependencies, we'll discuss the design of our command-line interface (CLI).

10.2   Designing the CLI

Our CLI will be very straightforward; we're going to map our five CRUD plus list commands to CLI commands, which will do exactly what you expect, as shown in table 10.2.

Table 10.2   CLI commands

Command	Action	Method	Path
create	Creates a todo	POST	/v1/todos
read	Reads a todo by ID	GET	/v1/todos/:id
update	Updates a todo by ID	PUT	/v1/todos/:id
delete	Deletes a todo by ID	DELETE	/v1/todos/:id
list	Lists all todos	GET	/v1/todos

We'll return the response directly from the API by printing to the standard output, and for JSON responses, we'll pretty-print them for readability. This will enable piping the command to another tool (such as jq), while also making the output human readable.

The clap library lets us build command-based CLIs, with either positional arguments or optional parameters. Clap will automatically generate help output (which we can obtain with the `help` command), and we can have parameters that apply to either the top-level command or one of the subcommands. Clap will take care of parsing arguments and handling errors in the case of incorrect or invalid arguments, provided we define the types correctly. Once clap's parsing is complete, we're left with a struct (which we define) that contains all the values parsed from the command-line arguments. Let's go ahead and dive into the code by looking at how we define the interface using clap.

10.3 Declaring the commands

Clap's API uses the `derive` macro in addition to some procedural macros to declare an interface. We want to use the command-based interface, which we can enable with clap using the `#[command]` macro, as shown in the following listing, where we define our CLI.

Listing 10.2 Top-level CLI definition for clap from src/main.rs

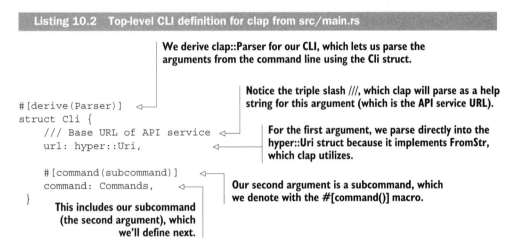

We derive clap::Parser for our CLI, which lets us parse the arguments from the command line using the Cli struct.

Notice the triple slash ///, which clap will parse as a help string for this argument (which is the API service URL).

```
#[derive(Parser)]
struct Cli {
    /// Base URL of API service
    url: hyper::Uri,

    #[command(subcommand)]
    command: Commands,
}
```

For the first argument, we parse directly into the hyper::Uri struct because it implements FromStr, which clap utilizes.

Our second argument is a subcommand, which we denote with the #[command()] macro.

This includes our subcommand (the second argument), which we'll define next.

For the top-level CLI, we've defined two positional arguments: the base URL for our API service and the subcommand (one of create, read, update, delete, or list). We haven't defined the commands yet, so we'll do that in the following listing.

Listing 10.3 CLI subcommands definition from src/main.rs

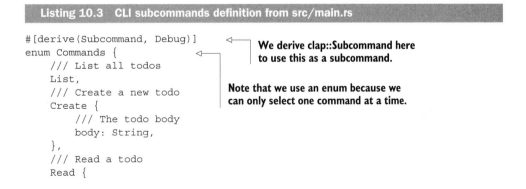

```
#[derive(Subcommand, Debug)]
enum Commands {
    /// List all todos
    List,
    /// Create a new todo
    Create {
        /// The todo body
        body: String,
    },
    /// Read a todo
    Read {
```

We derive clap::Subcommand here to use this as a subcommand.

Note that we use an enum because we can only select one command at a time.

```
        /// The todo ID
        id: i64,
    },

    /// Update a todo
    Update {
        /// The todo ID
        id: i64,
        /// The todo body
        body: String,
        /// Mark todo as completed
        #[arg(short, long)]
        completed: bool,
    },
    /// Delete a todo
    Delete {
        /// The todo ID
        id: i64,
    },
}
```

For this Boolean argument, we'll make it optional using an argument switch instead of a positional argument.

Notice how we've introduced arguments for our commands, but the preceding List variant does not require any arguments. After we implement main() in the next section, we can run our CLI with cargo run --help, which will print out a help message like this (note that the arguments need to come after the double-dash "--" when using cargo run):

```
Usage: api-client <URL> <COMMAND>

Commands:
  list     List all todos
  create   Create a new todo
  read     Read a todo
  update   Update a todo
  delete   Delete a todo
  help     Print this message or the help of the given subcommand(s)

Arguments:
  <URL>  Base URL of API service

Options:
  -h, --help  Print help
```

Each subcommand will also print its own help, for example, with cargo run --help create or cargo run --create --help:

```
Create a new todo

Usage: api-client <URL> create <BODY>

Arguments:
```

```
<BODY>  The todo body

Options:
  -h, --help  Print help
```

Nice! We can move on to implementing the commands now.

10.4 Implementing the commands

The type-safe API provided by clap makes it incredibly easy to handle each command and its arguments. We can match each variant in our Commands enum and process the command accordingly. Before we handle each command, there's some boilerplate to parse the CLI arguments and the base URL.

> **Listing 10.4 CLI argument-parsing boilerplate from src/main.rs**

```
#[tokio::main]

async fn main() -> Result<(), Box<dyn std::error::Error + Send + Sync>> {
    let cli = Cli::parse();

    let mut uri_builder = Uri::builder();
    if let Some(scheme) = cli.url.scheme() {
        uri_builder = uri_builder.scheme(scheme.clone());
    }
    if let Some(authority) = cli.url.authority() {
        uri_builder = uri_builder.authority(authority.clone());
    }
}
```

Call Cli::parse() to parse the CLI arguments in main() into our Cli struct.

Extract the base URL scheme (i.e., http or https).

Parse the base URL into its parts, and we'll add them into a new hyper::Uri builder.

Extract the base URL authority (i.e., localhost or 127.0.0.1).

In the preceding code, we break the base URL into its parts, although, notably, we choose to ignore the path of the base URL. You might want to allow specifying a prefix base and append each request URL to the prefix, but for this example, we ignore the path.

Now, let's look at the code to handle each command.

> **Listing 10.5 CLI command handling from src/main.rs**

```
match cli.command {
    Commands::List => {
        request(
            uri_builder.path_and_query("/v1/todos").build()?,
            Method::GET,
            None,
        )
        .await
    }
    Commands::Delete { id } => {
        request(
            uri_builder
                .path_and_query(format!("/v1/todos/{}", id))
                .build()?,
            Method::DELETE,
```

```
                    None,
                )
                .await
        }
        Commands::Read { id } => {
            request(
                uri_builder
                    .path_and_query(format!("/v1/todos/{}", id))
                    .build()?,
                Method::GET,
                None,
            )
            .await
        }
        Commands::Create { body } => {
            request(
                uri_builder.path_and_query("/v1/todos").build()?,
                Method::POST,
                Some(json!({ "body": body }).to_string()),
            )
            .await
        }
        Commands::Update {
            id,
            body,
            completed,
        } => {
            request(
                uri_builder
                    .path_and_query(format!("/v1/todos/{}", id))
                    .build()?,
                Method::PUT,
                Some(json!({"body":body,"completed":completed}).to_string()),
            )
            .await
        }
    }
}
```

For each command, we call the request() function (which we haven't defined yet),
where we pass the request URI, the HTTP method, and an optional JSON request
body. We use the uri_builder defined in listing 10.4 to build the URI.

Because Rust is strict about always handling each variant from the enum, we can
confidently assert that we've dealt with every command case and their parameters
(provided we correctly defined them all in the Commands enum). Now, we can go ahead
and implement the HTTP requests.

10.5 *Implementing requests*

We put a lot of thought into defining the commands and arguments, so now, executing
the actual requests against the API is very easy. We have all the pieces we need (the URI,
HTTP method, and an optional request body), so all we need to do is execute the actual
request. We can do this in one single function, shown in the following listing.

Listing 10.6   CLI request execution from src/main.rs

```
async fn request(
    url: hyper::Uri,
    method: Method,
    body: Option<String>,
) -> Result<(), Box<dyn std::error::Error + Send + Sync>> {
    let client = Client::new();

    let mut res = client
        .request(
            Request::builder()
                .uri(url)
                .method(method)
                .header("Content-Type", "application/json")
                .body(body.map(|s| Body::from(s))
                .unwrap_or_else(|| Body::empty()))?,
        )
        .await?;

    let mut buf = Vec::new();
    while let Some(next) = res.data().await {
        let chunk = next?;
        buf.extend_from_slice(&chunk);
    }
    let s = String::from_utf8(buf)?;

    eprintln!("Status: {}", Paint::green
    ➡ (res.status()));
    if res.headers().contains_key(CONTENT_TYPE) {
        let content_type = res.headers()[CONTENT_TYPE].to_str()?;
        eprintln!("Content-Type: {}", Paint::green
        ➡ (content_type));
        if content_type.starts_with("application/json") {
            println!("{}", &s.to_colored_json_auto()?);
        } else {
            println!("{}", &s);
        }
    } else {
        println!("{}", &s);
    }

    Ok(())
}
```

Assume the request body is always JSON if present.

If a request body was provided, we include it. Otherwise, we send an empty request.

We read one chunk of the response at a time, appending each to our buffer.

We'll use a Vec as a buffer to handle the incoming chunked response.

Each time a new chunk comes in, the chunk is appended to the buffer.

Once all of the response has been read, we create a UTF-8 string from the buf, consuming it without requiring a copy.

We print the response status to standard error and use the yansi crate to print with ANSI colors.

If we have a Content-Type header in the response, we'll print that to standard output.

If the content type is JSON, then we use the colored_json crate to pretty-print the JSON to the standard output.

If the content type is not JSON, print the output as a plain string to the standard output.

If there's no Content-Type header in the response, print the output as a plain string to the standard output.

If we reach this point, the request succeeded, so we return unit.

Note how our request always prints the response body to standard output, but we print the request status and content type header to standard error. Separating the response body and metadata allows us to pipe the output of our command into another tool.

10.6   Handling errors gracefully

In listing 10.6, we return a Result and make heavy use of the ? operator. Additionally, we're relying on trait objects by using Box<dyn std::error::Error + Send + Sync> as the error return type. This is a convenient but somewhat lazy way of handling errors. For this particular case, it makes sense to keep it simple (i.e., the KISS principle), but if we were to find ourselves in a situation where we want more complex error-handling logic or want to customize our error logging or error message handling, we'd probably want to create our own error type and use the `From` trait to transform the errors.

Additionally, our `main()` function, shown in listing 10.4, returns the same `Result<()`, `Box<dyn std::error::Error + Send + Sync>>` type. Therefore, we can make use of the `?` operator through the whole program, and it will correctly surface the errors.

10.7   *Testing our CLI*

Finally, let's test our CLI by running it against our API service from the previous chapter. In the following examples, I'll open a split terminal with the API service on the left-hand side. On the right-hand side, I'll run the CLI we just wrote to demonstrate each command. First, we'll create a new todo with `cargo run --http://localhost:3000 create "finish writing chapter 10"`, shown in figure 10.1.

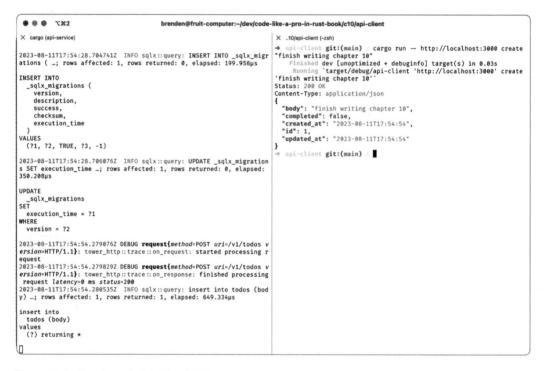

Figure 10.1   Creating a todo with our CLI

Nice! Notice the nicely formatted output with colors (in the e-book). Let's try the other four commands, starting with `cargo run --http://localhost:3000 list`, shown in figure 10.2.

Next, we'll update the todo. We do this by changing the body and marking it as completed with `cargo run - http://localhost:3000 update 1 "finish writing chapter 10" --completed`, shown in figure 10.3.

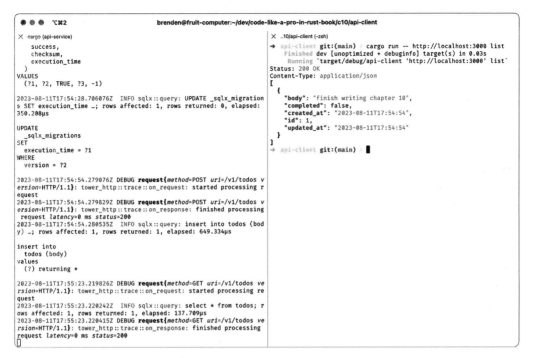

Figure 10.2 Listing todos with our CLI

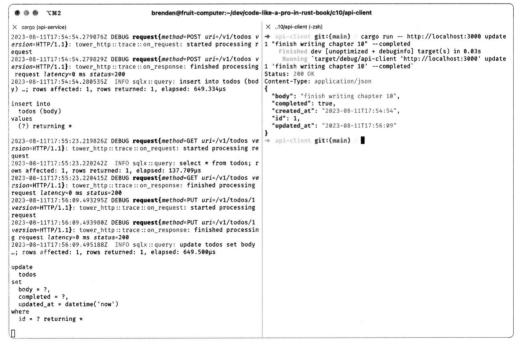

Figure 10.3 Updating a todo with our CLI

Let's read back our updated todo. We'll use `cargo run --http://localhost:3000 read 1`, shown in figure 10.4.

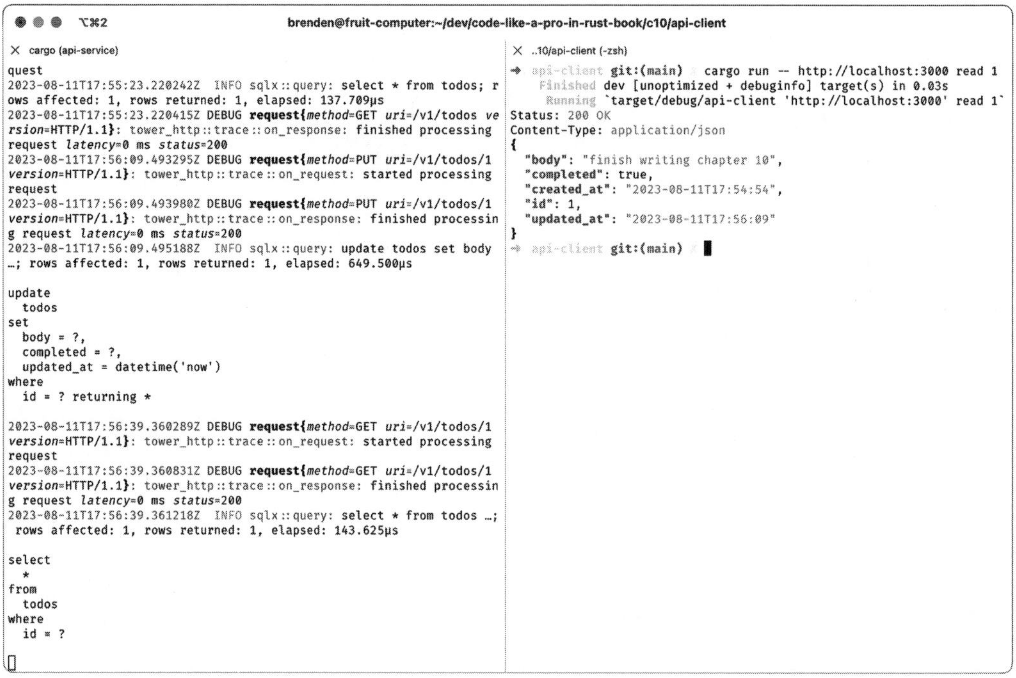

Figure 10.4   Reading a todo with our CLI

We can also test piping our CLI output into another command, such as `jq`, using the command `cargo run --http://localhost:3000 read 1 | jq '.body'`. This will select the `body` field from our JSON output, shown in figure 10.5.

Note how Cargo conveniently prints its output to standard error (instead of standard output), so we can still use pipes with `cargo run --…`. Finally, let's delete our todo with `cargo run --http://localhost:3000 delete 1`, shown in figure 10.6.

That wraps up the demonstration of the CLI for our API. You can use this code as a template or starting point for any of your future projects, although as an exercise for the reader, I'd recommend swapping the hyper crate for `reqwest`.

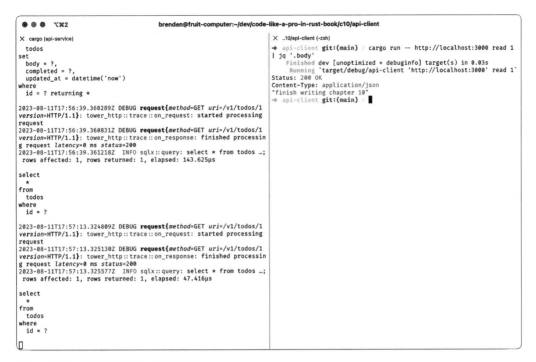

Figure 10.5 Piping our CLI output to `jq`

Figure 10.6 Deleting a todo with our CLI

Summary

- Writing robust CLI tools in Rust is delightfully simple; using type-safe APIs (such as clap) for parsing CLI arguments makes it surprisingly easy to make great tools remarkably fast.

- Thanks to Rust's rich crate ecosystem, we don't have to do much work to add rich features to our CLI, such as well-formatted, human-readable output. We get much of this for free using the `yansi` and `colored_json` crates.

- The hyper HTTP library is a low-level HTTP implementation in Rust that provides both a client and server API; however, in practice, you'd want to use higher-level APIs for HTTP: `axum` for HTTP servers and `reqwest` for HTTP clients.

- If you don't want to worry about handling errors yourself, you can utilize trait objects with `Box<dyn std::error::Error + Send + Sync>` as an error type, which works, provided all error types you encounter implement `std::error::Error`. Several crates also provide this functionality, such as thiserror (https://crates.io/crates/thiserror) and Anyhow (https://crates.io/crates/anyhow).

Part 5

Optimizations

There may come a time when you need to improve the performance of your software beyond what can be accomplished simply through good design, by using the right data structures and applying the correct algorithms. Modern operating systems, CPUs, and compilers are remarkably good at handling most of this job for you, but every once in a while, you'll have to go deeper.

This topic deserves an entire book of its own, but I've distilled the key points down to their essence to provide a good jumping-off point. Rust's safety, concurrency, parallelism, asynchronicity, and SIMD features make it an exceptionally compelling programming language, all packaged as pure, open source software.

Optimizations 11

This chapter covers

- Understanding Rust's zero-cost abstractions
- Using vectors effectively
- Programming with SIMD in Rust
- Parallelization with Rayon
- Using Rust to accelerate other languages

In this final chapter, we'll discuss optimization strategies with Rust. Rust's zero-cost abstractions allow you to confidently write Rust code without thinking too hard about performance. Rust delegates much of its machine code generation to LLVM, which has mature, robust, widely deployed, and well-tested code optimization. Code written in Rust will be fast and well optimized without you spending time hand-tuning code.

There are, however, certain cases in which you may need to dive deeper, which we'll discuss, along with the tools you'll need, in this chapter. We'll also discuss how you can use Rust to accelerate code from other languages, which is a fun way to introduce Rust into codebases without needing to perform a complete rewrite.

11.1   *Zero-cost abstractions*

An important feature of Rust is its *zero-cost abstractions*. In short, Rust's abstractions allow you to write high-level code, which produces optimized machine code with no additional runtime overhead. Rust's compiler takes care of figuring out how to get from high-level Rust to low-level machine code in the optimal way, without the overhead. You can safely use Rust's abstractions without needing to worry about whether they will create a performance trap.

The tradeoff to Rust's promise of zero-cost abstractions is that some features from high-level languages you may have come to expect don't appear in Rust or, at the very least, may not exist in a familiar form. Some of those features include virtual methods, reflection, function overloading, and optional function arguments. Rust provides alternatives to these, or ways to emulate their behavior, but they're not baked into the language. If you want to introduce that overhead, you have to do it yourself (which, of course, makes it much easier to reason about), such as by using trait objects for dynamic dispatch, as with virtual methods.

We can compare Rust's abstractions to those of C++, for example, which *does* have runtime overhead. In the case of C++, the core class abstraction may contain virtual methods, which require runtime lookup tables (called *vtables*). While this overhead is not usually significant, it can become significant in certain cases, such as when calling virtual methods within a tight loop over many elements.

> **NOTE**   Rust's *trait objects* use vtables for method calls. Trait objects are a feature enabled by the `dyn Trait` syntax. For example, you can store a trait object with `Box<dyn MyTrait>`, where the item in the box must implement `MyTrait`, and the methods from `MyTrait` can be called using a vtable lookup.

Reflection is another opaque abstraction used extensively in some languages to dispatch function calls or perform other operations at run time. Reflection is often used in Java, for example, to handle a variety of problems, but it also tends to generate a significant number of difficult-to-debug run-time errors. Reflection offers a bit of convenience for the programmer with the tradeoff of flakier code.

Rust's zero-cost abstractions are based on compile-time optimizations. Within that framework, Rust can optimize out unused code or values, as needed. Rust's abstractions can also be deeply nested, and the compiler can (in most cases) perform optimizations down the abstraction chain. When we talk about *zero-cost abstractions* in Rust, what we really mean is *zero-cost abstractions once all optimizations have been performed*.

When we want to build a production binary or benchmark our code, we must enable compiler optimizations by compiling our code in release mode. We can do this by enabling the `--release` flag with `cargo`, as the default compilation mode is debug. If you forget to enable release mode, you may experience unexpected performance penalties, one of which we'll demonstrate in the next section.

11.2   *Vectors*

Vectors are the core collection abstraction in Rust. As I've mentioned throughout this book, you should use `Vec` in most cases where you require a collection of elements. Because you'll be using `Vec` so often in Rust, it's important to understand a few details about its implementation and how it can affect the performance of your code. Additionally, you should understand when it makes sense to use something other than `Vec`.

The first thing to understand about `Vec` is how memory is allocated. We have discussed this a fair bit already in chapters 4 and 5, but we'll go into a little more detail here. `Vec` allocates memory in contiguous blocks, with a configurable chunk size based on capacity. It allocates memory lazily by delaying allocation until it's necessary and always allocating in contiguous blocks.

11.2.1   *Vector memory allocation*

The first thing you should understand about the way `Vec` allocates memory is how it determines capacity size. By default, an empty `Vec` has a capacity of 0, and thus, no memory is allocated. It's not until data is added that memory allocation occurs. When the capacity limit is reached, `Vec` will double the capacity (i.e., capacity increases exponentially).

We can see how `Vec` adds capacity by running a small test:

```
let mut empty_vec = Vec::<i32>::new();
(0..10).for_each(|v| {
    println!(
        "empty_vec has {} elements with capacity {}",
        empty_vec.len(),
        empty_vec.capacity()
    );
    empty_vec.push(v)
});
```

Note that capacity is measured in number of elements, not number of bytes. The number of bytes required for the vector is the capacity multiplied by the size of each element. When we run the preceding code, it generates the following output:

```
empty_vec has 0 elements with capacity 0
empty_vec has 1 elements with capacity 4      ◁——— Capacity is increased from 0 to 4.
empty_vec has 2 elements with capacity 4
empty_vec has 3 elements with capacity 4
empty_vec has 4 elements with capacity 4
empty_vec has 5 elements with capacity 8      ◁——— Capacity is increased from 4 to 8.
empty_vec has 6 elements with capacity 8
empty_vec has 7 elements with capacity 8
empty_vec has 8 elements with capacity 8
empty_vec has 9 elements with capacity 16     ◁——— Capacity is increased from 8 to 16.
```

We can examine the source code from the Rust standard library to see the algorithm itself, which is part of `RawVec`, the internal data structure used by `Vec`, in the following listing.

Listing 11.1 `Vec::grow_amortized()` from the Rust standard library

```
// This method is usually instantiated many times. So we want it to be as
// small as possible, to improve compile times. But we also want as much of
// its contents to be statically computable as possible, to make the
// generated code run faster. Therefore, this method is carefully written
// so that all of the code that depends on `T` is within it, while as much
// of the code that doesn't depend on `T` as possible is in functions that
// are non-generic over `T`.
fn grow_amortized(&mut self, len: usize, additional: usize) ->
Result<(), TryReserveError> {
    // This is ensured by the calling contexts.
    debug_assert!(additional > 0);

    if mem::size_of::<T>() == 0 {
        // Since we return a capacity of `usize::MAX` when `elem_size` is
        // 0, getting to here necessarily means the `RawVec` is overfull.
        return Err(CapacityOverflow.into());
    }

    // Nothing we can really do about these checks, sadly.
    let required_cap = len.checked_add(additional).ok_or(CapacityOverflow)?;

    // This guarantees exponential growth. The doubling cannot overflow
    // because `cap <= isize::MAX` and the type of `cap` is `usize`.
    let cap = cmp::max(self.cap * 2, required_cap);
    let cap = cmp::max(Self::MIN_NON_ZERO_CAP, cap);

    let new_layout = Layout::array::<T>(cap);

    // `finish_grow` is non-generic over `T`.
    let ptr = finish_grow(new_layout, self.current_memory(),
    ⇒ &mut self.alloc)?;
    self.set_ptr_and_cap(ptr, cap);
    Ok(())
}
```

> Here, the capacity (self.cap) is doubled.

> Self::MIN_NON_ZERO_CAP varies, depending on the size of the elements, but it can be either 8, 4, or I.

What can we do with this information? There are two main takeaways:

- The lazy allocation by `Vec` can be inefficient if you're adding many elements, a few at a time.
- For large vectors, the capacity will be up to twice the number of elements in the array.

The first takeaway (lazy allocation) can be problematic in cases when you are frequently creating new vectors and pushing data into them. Reallocations are costly because they can involve shuffling memory around. Reallocations with a small number of elements aren't as costly because your machine likely has lots of space in memory for small contiguous regions, but as the structure grows, it can become more and more difficult to find available contiguous regions (thus, more memory shuffling is required).

The second problem with large vectors can be mitigated either by using a different structure (e.g., a linked list) or keeping the capacity trimmed with the `Vec::shrink_to_fit()` method. It's also worth noting that vectors can be large in two different dimensions: a large number of small elements or a small number of large elements. For the latter case (a few large elements), a linked list or storing elements within a `Box` will provide relief from memory pressure.

11.2.2 Vector iterators

Another important thing to consider when discussing `Vec` performance is iterating over elements. There are two ways to loop over a `Vec`: either using `iter()` or `into_iter()`. The `iter()` iterator allows us to iterate over elements with references, whereas `into_iter()` consumes `self`. Let's look at the following listing to analyze `Vec` iterators.

Listing 11.2   Demonstrating `Vec` iterator performance

```
let big_vec = vec![0; 10_000_000];
let now = Instant::now();
for i in big_vec {
    if i < 0 {
        println!("this never prints");
    }
}
println!("First loop took {}s", now.elapsed().as_secs_f32());

let big_vec = vec![0; 10_000_000];
let now = Instant::now();
big_vec.iter().for_each(|i| {
    if *i < 0 {
        println!("this never prints");
    }
});
println!("Second loop took {}s", now.elapsed().as_secs_f32());
```

In this listing, we have some large vectors we're going to iterate over with a no-op block of code to prevent the compiler from optimizing it out. We'll test the code with `cargo run --release` because we want to enable all compiler optimizations. Now, if we run this code, it will produce the following output:

```
First loop took 0.007614s
Second loop took 0.00410025s
```

Whoa! What happened there? Why does the `for` loop run nearly twice as slowly?

The answer involves a bit of sugar syntax: the `for` loop expression roughly translates into using the `into_iter()` method to obtain an iterator and looping over the

iterator until hitting the end (the full expression is documented at http://mng.bz/
W1nd). `into_iter()` takes `self` by default, meaning it consumes the original vector
and (in some cases) may even require allocating an entirely new structure.

The `for_loop()` method provided by the core iterator trait in Rust, however, is
highly optimized for this purpose, which gives us a slight performance gain. Additionally, `iter()` takes `&self` and iterates over references to elements in the vector, which
can be further optimized by the compiler.

To verify this, we can update our code to use `into_iter()` instead of `iter()`. Let's try
by adding a third loop:

```
let big_vec = vec![0; 10_000_000];
let now = Instant::now();
big_vec.into_iter().for_each(|i| {
    if i < 0 {
        println!("this never prints");
    }
});
println!("Third loop took {}s", now.elapsed().as_secs_f32());
```

Then, we can run the code again in release mode to produce the following output:

```
First loop took 0.011229166s
Second loop took 0.005076166s
Third loop took 0.008608s
```

That's much closer; however, it seems that using iterators directly instead of `for` loop
expressions is slightly faster. Out of curiosity, what happens if we run the same test in
debug mode? Let's try and see what it produces:

```
First loop took 0.074964s
Second loop took 0.14158678s
Third loop took 0.07878621s
```

Wow, those results are drastically different! What's particularly interesting is that, in
debug mode, `for` loops are slightly faster. This is likely because of the additional overhead imposed by enabling debugging symbols and disabling compiler optimizations.
The lesson here is that benchmarking performance in debug mode will lead to
strange results.

Vectors include quite a few other built-in optimizations, but the ones you'll generally need to concern yourself with are memory allocation and iterators. We can
decrease the amount of memory allocations required by pre-allocating memory with
`Vec::with_capacity()`, and we can avoid confusing performance problems by using
iterators directly rather than `for` loop expressions.

11.2.3 *Fast copies with Vec and slices*

Let's discuss one more optimization with vectors, which has to do with copying memory. Rust has a fast-path optimization for vectors and slices where it can perform a faster copy of everything within a `Vec`, under certain circumstances. The optimization lives inside the `Vec::copy_from_slice()` method, for which the key parts of the implementation are shown in the following listing.

> **Listing 11.3 Partial listing of `copy_from_slice()` from the Rust standard library**

```
pub fn copy_from_slice(&mut self, src: &[T])
    where
        T: Copy,
    {
        // ... snip ...
        unsafe {
            ptr::copy_nonoverlapping(src.as_ptr(), self.as_mut_ptr(),
            ↪ self.len());
        }
    }
```

In this partial listing lifted from the Rust standard library, you'll notice two important things: the trait-bound `Copy` and the unsafe call to `ptr::copy_nonoverlapping`. In other words, if you use a `Vec` and want to copy items between two vectors, provided those items implement `Copy`, you can take the fast track. We can run a quick benchmark to see the difference in the following listing.

> **Listing 11.4 Benchmarking `ptr::copy_nonoverlapping()`**

```
let big_vec_source = vec![0; 10_000_000];
let mut big_vec_target = Vec::<i32>::
↪ with_capacity(10_000_000);          ◁——┐ We initialize the target Vec with pre-
let now = Instant::now();                  allocated memory of the correct size.
big_vec_source
    .into_iter()
    .for_each(|i| big_vec_target.push(i));
println!("Naive copy took {}s", now.elapsed().as_secs_f32());

let big_vec_source = vec![0; 10_000_000];
let mut big_vec_target = vec![0; 10_000_000];
let now = Instant::now();
big_vec_target.copy_from_slice(&big_vec_source);
println!("Fast copy took {}s", now.elapsed().as_secs_f32());
```

Running the preceding code in release mode produces the following result:

```
Naive copy took 0.024926165s
Fast copy took 0.003599458s
```

In other words, using `Vec::copy_from_slice()` gives us about an 8x speedup in copying data directly from one vector to another. This optimization also exists for the slice (`&mut [T]`) and array (`mut [T]`) types.

11.3 *SIMD*

There may come a point in your life as a developer where you need to use *single instruction, multiple data* (SIMD). SIMD is a hardware feature of many modern microprocessors that allows performing operations on sets of data simultaneously with a single instruction. The most common use case for this is either to optimize code for a particular processor or guarantee consistent timing of operations (such as to avoid timing attacks in cryptographic applications).

SIMD is platform dependent: different CPUs have different SIMD features available, but almost all modern CPUs have some SIMD features. The most commonly used SIMD instruction sets are MMX, SSE, and AVX, on Intel devices, and Neon on ARM devices.

In the past, if you needed to use SIMD, you'd need to write inline assembly yourself. Thankfully, modern compilers provide an interface for using SIMD without needing to write assembly directly. These functions standardize some of the shared behavior among the different SIMD implementations in a somewhat portable way. The advantage of using portable SIMD is that we don't need to worry about instruction set details for any particular platform, with the tradeoff that we only have access to the common denominator features. It's still possible to write inline assembly if you choose, but I'm going to focus on portable SIMD. One convenient feature of portable SIMD is that the compiler can automatically generate substitute non-SIMD code for cases in which features are not available at the hardware level.

The Rust standard library provides the `std::simd` module, which is currently a nightly only experimental API. Documentation for the portable SIMD API can be found at https://doc.rust-lang.org/std/simd/struct.Simd.html.

To illustrate, we can write a benchmark to compare the speed of some math operations on 64 element arrays with and without SIMD.

> **Listing 11.5   Multiplying vectors with SIMD versus iterators**

```
#![feature(portable_simd, array_zip)]          ◁──┐  Enables experimental
                                                   │  features for this crate
fn initialize() -> ([u64; 64], [u64; 64]) {
    let mut a = [0u64; 64];
    let mut b = [0u64; 64];
    (0..64).for_each(|n| {
        a[n] = u64::try_from(n).unwrap();
        b[n] = u64::try_from(n + 1).unwrap();
    });
    (a, b)
}
```

```
fn main() {
    use std::simd::Simd;
    use std::time::Instant;
                                        ┌── Initializes our 64
    let (mut a, b) = initialize();  ◁──┘   element arrays

    let now = Instant::now();           ┌── Perform some calculations
    for _ in 0..100_000 {           ◁──┤   using normal math.
        let c = a.zip(b).map(|(l, r)| l * r);
        let d = a.zip(c).map(|(l, r)| l + r);
        let e = c.zip(d).map(|(l, r)| l * r);   ┌── Stores the result
        a = e.zip(d).map(|(l, r)| l ^ r);   ◁──┘   back into a
    }
    println!("Without SIMD took {}s", now.elapsed().as_secs_f32());

    let (a_vec, b_vec) = initialize();  ◁──── Initializes with the same values again

    let mut a_vec = Simd::from(a_vec);  ◁──── Converts our arrays into SIMD vectors
    let b_vec = Simd::from(b_vec);

    let now = Instant::now();  ◁──── Perform the same calculations with SIMD.
    for _ in 0..100_000 {
        let c_vec = a_vec * b_vec;
        let d_vec = a_vec + c_vec;
        let e_vec = c_vec * d_vec;   ┌── Stores the result
        a_vec = e_vec ^ d_vec;   ◁──┘   back into a_vec
    }
    println!("With SIMD took {}s", now.elapsed().as_secs_f32());

    assert_eq!(&a, a_vec.as_array());   ┌── Finally, check that a and
}                                   ◁──┘   a_vec have the same result
```

Running this code will produce the following output:

```
Without SIMD took 0.07886646s
With SIMD took 0.002505291s
```

Wow! We got a nearly 40x speedup by using SIMD. Additionally, the SIMD code provides consistent timing, which is important for applications that are timing dependent, such as cryptography.

11.4 Parallelization with Rayon

For problems where performance can be improved with the use of parallelization (i.e., parallel programming with threads), the Rayon crate is your best place to start. While the Rust language certainly provides threading features as part of its core library, these features are somewhat primitive, and most of the time, it's better to write code based on higher-level APIs.

Rayon provides two ways to interact with data in parallel: a parallel iterator implementation and some helpers for creating lightweight tasks based on threads. We're going to focus mainly on Rayon's iterator because that is the most useful part of the library.

The typical use case for Rayon is one where you have a significant number of tasks, each of which are relatively long running or compute intense. If you have a small number of tasks or your tasks are not very compute intensive, introducing parallelization is likely to actually *decrease* performance. Generally speaking, parallelization has diminishing returns as the number of threads increases, due to synchronization and data starvation problems that can arise when moving data between threads (as shown in figure 11.1).

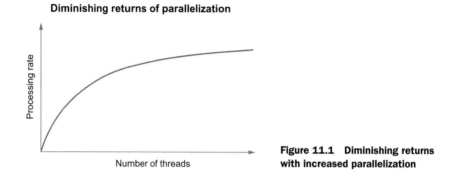

Figure 11.1 Diminishing returns with increased parallelization

One handy feature of Rayon's iterators is that they're mostly compatible with the core `Iterator` trait, which makes it very easy to quickly benchmark code with or without parallelization. Let's demonstrate by creating two different tests: one that will be slower with Rayon and one that will be faster with Rayon.

First, let's write a test that's faster *without* Rayon:

```
let start = Instant::now();
let sum = data
    .iter()
    .map(|n| n.wrapping_mul(*n))
    .reduce(|a: i64, b: i64| a.wrapping_add(b));
let finish = Instant::now() - start;
println!(
    "Summing squares without rayon took {}s",
    finish.as_secs_f64()
);

let start = Instant::now();
let sum = data
    .par_iter()
    .map(|n| n.wrapping_mul(*n))
    .reduce(|| 0, |a: i64, b: i64| a.wrapping_add(b));
let finish = Instant::now() - start;
println!("Summing squares with rayon took {}s", finish.as_secs_f64());
```

We use reduce() instead of sum() because sum() performs addition without handling overflow.

Notice the slight difference in signature of reduce() with Rayon, which requires an identity value that may be inserted to create opportunities for parallelization.

In the preceding code, we've generated an array filled with random integer values. Next, we square each value and then calculate the sum across the whole set. This is a classic map/reduce example. If we run this code, we get the following result:

```
Summing squares without rayon took 0.000028875s
Summing squares with rayon took 0.000688583s
```

This test *with* Rayon takes 23x longer than without! This is clearly not a good candidate for parallelization.

Let's construct another test, which will use a regular expression to scan a long string for a word. We'll randomly generate some very large strings before we run the search. The code looks like this:

```
let re = Regex::new(r"catdog").unwrap();     ◁──┘  Regex is both Send and Sync. We can
                                                   use it in a parallel filter with Rayon.

let start = Instant::now();
let matches: Vec<_> = data.iter().filter(|s| re.is_match(s)).collect();
let finish = Instant::now() - start;
println!("Regex took {}s", finish.as_secs_f64());

let start = Instant::now();
let matches: Vec<_> =
    data.par_iter().filter(|s| re.is_match(s)).collect();
let finish = Instant::now() - start;
println!("Regex with rayon took {}s", finish.as_secs_f64());
```

Running this code, we get the following result:

```
Regex took 0.043573333s
Regex with rayon took 0.006173s
```

In this case, parallelization with Rayon gives us a 7x speedup. Scanning strings is one case where we might see a significant boost in performance across sufficiently large datasets.

Another notable feature of Rayon is its parallel sorting implementation, which allows you to sort slices in parallel. For larger datasets, this can provide a decent performance boost. Rayon's `join()` also provides a work-stealing implementation, which executes tasks in parallel when idle worker threads are available, but you should use parallel iterators instead, when possible. For more details on Rayon, consult the documentation at https://docs.rs/rayon/latest/rayon/index.html.

11.5   *Using Rust to accelerate other languages*

The last thing we'll discuss in this chapter is one of the coolest application of Rust: calling Rust code from other languages to perform operations that are either safety critical or compute intensive. This is a common pattern with C and C++, too: many language runtimes implement performance-critical features in C or C++. With Rust, however, you have the added bonus of its safety features. This, in fact, was one of the major motivating factors behind the adoption of Rust by several organizations, such as Mozilla, with their plans to improve the security and performance of the Firefox browser.

An example of how you might use Rust in this case would be to parse or validate data from external sources, such as a web server receiving untrusted data from the internet. Many security vulnerabilities are discovered by feeding random data into public interfaces and seeing what happens, and often, code contains mistakes (such as reading past the end of a buffer), which aren't possible in Rust.

Most programming languages and runtimes provide some form of foreign function interface (FFI) bindings, which we demonstrated in chapter 4. However, for many popular languages, there are higher-level bindings and tooling available, which can make integrating Rust much easier than dealing with FFI, and some also help with packaging native binaries. Table 11.1 provides a summary of some useful tools for integrating Rust with other popular programming languages.

Table 11.1   Rust bindings and tooling for integrating Rust into other languages

Language	Name	Description	URL	GitHub stars[a]
Python	PyO3	Rust bindings for Python, with tools for making native Python packages with Rust	https://pyo3.rs	10,090
Python	Milksnake	setuptools extension for including binaries in Python packages, including Rust	https://github.com/getsentry/milksnake	783
Ruby	Ruru	Library for building native Ruby extensions with Rust	https://github.com/d-unseductable/ruru	822
Ruby	Rutie	Bindings between Ruby and Rust, which enable integrating Rust with Ruby or Ruby with Rust	https://github.com/danielpclark/rutie	812
Elixir and Erlang	Rustler	Library for creating safe bindings to Rust for Elixir and Erlang	https://github.com/rusterlium/rustler	3,999
JavaScript and TypeScript on Node.js	Neon	Rust bindings for creating native Node.js modules with Rust	https://neon-bindings.com	7,622
Java	`jni-rs`	Native Rust bindings for Java	https://github.com/jni-rs/jni-rs	1,018
Rust	`bindgen`	Generates Rust FFI bindings from native Rust	https://github.com/rust-lang/rust-bindgen	3,843

[a] This is the GitHub star count as of December 30, 2023.

11.6 *Where to go from here*

Congratulations on making it to the end of *Code Like a Pro in Rust*. Let's take a moment to reflect on what we've discussed in this book and, more importantly, where to go from here to learn more.

In chapters 1 through 3, we focused on tooling, project structure, and the basic skills you need to work effectively with Rust. Chapters 4 and 5 covered data structures and Rust's memory model. Chapters 6 and 7 focused on Rust's testing features and how to get the most out of them. Chapters 8, 9, and 10 introduced us to async Rust, and this final chapter focused on optimization opportunities for Rust code.

At this point in the book, you may want to take some time to go back and revisit previous sections, especially if you found the content dense or hard to grok. It's often good to give your brain a rest and then return to problems once you've had time to digest new information. For further reading on Rust, I recommend my follow-up book *Rust Design Patterns* as well as Tim McNamara's *Rust in Action*, both from Manning Publications.

Rust and its ecosystem is forward looking and always evolving. The Rust language, while already quite mature, is actively developed and continuously moving forward. As such, I will close out the final chapter of this book by leaving you with some resources on where to go from here to learn about new Rust features, changes, and proposals, and how to get more involved with the Rust community.

Most of Rust language and tool development is hosted on GitHub, under the rust-lang project at https://github.com/rust-lang. Additionally, the following resources are a great place to dive deeper on the Rust language:

- *Release notes for each Rust version*—https://github.com/rust-lang/rust/blob/master/RELEASES.md
- *Rust request for comments (RFCs), proposed Rust features, and these features' current statuses*—https://rust-lang.github.io/rfcs
- *The official Rust language reference*—https://doc.rust-lang.org/reference
- *The official Rust language users forum, where you can discuss Rust with other like-minded people*—https://users.rust-lang.org

Summary

- Rust's zero-cost abstractions allow you to write fast code without needing to worry about overhead, but code must be compiled in release mode to take advantage of these optimizations.
- Vectors, Rust's core sequence data structure, should be pre-allocated with the capacity needed, if you know the required capacity ahead of time.
- When copying data between structures, the `copy_from_slice()` method provides a fast path for moving data between slices.
- Rust's experimental portable SIMD feature allows you to easily build code using SIMD. You don't need to deal directly with assembly code or compiler intrinsics or worry about which instructions are available.

- Code can be easily parallelized using the Rayon crate, which builds on top of Rust's iterator pattern. Building parallelized code in Rust is as easy as using iterators.
- We can introduce Rust into other languages by swapping out individual components for Rust equivalents, offering the benefit of Rust's safety and performance features without needing to completely rewrite our applications.

appendix

This appendix contains instructions for installing the command-line utilities required to compile and run the code samples in this book. These instructions are provided for convenience, but you aren't required to follow these procedures if you already have the tools required, or prefer to install them another way.

Installing tools for this book

To compile and run the code samples provided in this book, you must first install the necessary prerequisite dependencies.

Installing tools on macOS using Homebrew

```
$ brew install git
```

On macOS, you'll need to install the Xcode command line tools:

```
$ sudo xcode-select --install
```

Installing tools on Linux systems

On Debian-based systems:

```
$ apt install git build-essential
```

On Red Hat-based systems:

```
$ yum install git make automake gcc gcc-c++
```

> **TIP** You may want to install `clang` rather than CCC because it tends to have better compile times.

Installing rustup on Linux- or UNIX-based systems

To install `rustup` on Linux- or UNIX-based operating systems, including macOS, run the following:

```
$ curl --proto '=https' --tlsv1.2 -sSf https://sh.rustup.rs | sh
```

Once you've installed `rustup`, it's recommended you make sure both the stable and nightly toolchains are installed:

```
$ rustup toolchain install stable nightly
...
```

Installing tools on Windows

If you're using a Windows-based OS, you'll need to download the latest copy of `rustup` from https://rustup.rs/. Prebuilt Windows binaries for `clang` can be downloaded from https://releases.llvm.org/download.html.

Alternatively, on Windows, you may use Windows Subsystem for Linux (WSL, https://docs.microsoft.com/en-us/windows/wsl/) and follow the earlier instructions for installation on Linux. For many users, this may be the easiest way to work with the code samples.

Managing rustc and other Rust components with rustup

With `rustup` installed, you'll need to install the Rust compiler and related tools. At a minimum, it's recommended that you install the stable and nightly channels of Rust.

Installing rustc and other components

It's recommended you install both `stable` and `nightly` toolchains by default, but generally, you should prefer working with `stable` when possible. Run the following to install both toolchains:

```
                                            Installs stable Rust and makes
$ rustup default stable        <───┘        it the default toolchain
...
$ rustup toolchain install nightly     <──── Installs nightly Rust
```

Additionally, throughout this book, we make use of Clippy and rustfmt. These are both installed using `rustup`:

```
$ rustup component add clippy rustfmt
```

Switching default toolchains with rustup

When working with Rust, you may frequently find yourself switching between `stable` and `nightly` toolchains. `rustup` makes this relatively easy:

```
$ rustup default stable      <──── Switches default to stable toolchain
$ rustup default nightly      <───┐
                                   │ Switches default to nightly toolchain
```

Updating Rust components

`rustup` makes it easy to keep components up to date. To update all the installed toolchains and components, simply run the following:

```
$ rustup update
```

Under normal circumstances, you only need to run `update` when there are major new releases. There may occasionally be problems in `nightly` that require an update, but this tends to be infrequent. If your installation is working, it's recommended you avoid upgrading too frequently (i.e., daily) because you're more likely to run into problems.

> **NOTE** Updating all Rust components causes all toolchains and components to be downloaded and updated, which may take some time on bandwidth-limited systems.

Installing HTTPie

HTTPie is a CLI tool for making HTTP requests and is included in many popular package managers, such as Homebrew, apt, yum, choco, Nixpkgs, and more. If HTTPie is not available in your package management tool, you can fall back to using Python `pip` to install HTTPie:

```
# Install httpie
$ python -m pip install httpie
```

index